Peter Gourevitch had a remarkable set of parents, grandparents, uncles and aunts, and his account of their lives across the 20th century is also a history of those years—and a reflection on the experience of men and women who lived in hard times and made fateful choices. They were revolutionaries in czarist Russia, Menshevik oppositionists in Bolshevik Russia, Jewish socialists in Berlin who fled the Nazis to Paris and then to Toulouse and Nice in Vichy France. Some of them died in Russia, Stalin's victims; some of them died in Auschwitz; some of them escaped to America, with the help of the American Federation of Labor and the Jewish Labor Committee—a largely untold story. Peter has reconstructed their lives from family legends, the archives of brutal regimes, personal letters, official documents, and his own memories. He tells an extraordinarily engaging and moving tale, and concludes with an incisive argument about what we can learn from it about history and politics.

Michael Walzer, Professor Emeritus, Institute for Advanced Study, Princeton

****

"This gem of a book by a distinguished political scientist records the absorbing history of his family. Profoundly uplifting and sad, these stories search for family roots in the escape routes from the revolutionary vengeance of the Bolsheviks, the Holocaust of the Nazis, and Stalin' Gulag. Contingency, context, complexity and causality bring to light different circumstances and choices marked by survival and death, resilience and courage. Peter Gourevitch's curiosity and passion makes a cruel past part of our unsettled present."

Peter Katzenstein, Peter Joachim Katzenstein FBA is a German-American political scientist. He is the Walter S. Carpenter, Jr. Professor of International Studies at Cornell University. Former President of the American Political Science Association.

****

When do we choose to flee from an increasingly precarious fate? How do you know when it's time to go? Through the lens of his fascinating family history, Peter Gourevitch explores how circumstance and happenstance combine to determine how we answer such questions. Some family chose to leave revolutionary Russia for the safety of Germany. Some fled Hitler's Germany for the safety of France. Some took the last train from Paris as the city fell to the Nazis, eventually making it to the United States because they were Socialists rather than because they were Jews. An epic family journey that focuses on the choices that took members down different and sometimes tragic paths.

David A. Lake, Gerri-Ann and Gary E. Jacobs Professor of Social Sciences, Distinguished Professor of Political Science, University of California, San Diego. Webpage: https://quote.ucsd.edu/lake/

****

Peter Gourevitch has written a compelling family tale of identities and political calculation in the harrowing contexts of holocaust, revolution and world war. Why did some escape, while others stayed? The distinguished author of Politics in Hard Times now gives us an account of personal politics in even harder times that shows how epochal events create existential dilemmas for individual lives. Weaving the politics of the day together with the panoramic narrative of a family, this is not only a personal detective story but an illuminating rumination on how human beings make difficult choices under conditions of great uncertainty. Readers will be unable to put it down.

Peter A. Hall, Krupp Foundation Professor of European Studies in the Department of Government at Harvard University, and former Director of the Minda de Gunzburg Center for European Studies.

****

"You are destroying my productivity. I literally could not put this down. Bravo!"

Robert Kuttner, co-Editor *The American Prospect*

****

Peter Gourevitch's book is an intellectual tour de force. By offering a lovingly told, meticulously researched and detailed historical account of his immediate and extended family, Gourevitch dazzles with an encyclopedic knowledge of European political and social developments during the first half of the 20th century. We learn amazing details about the Russian, the German, the French and the American lefts and their inextricable ties with each other that profoundly defined these countries' politics in that period. Through it all, there is the inevitable thread of how the varied -- and often conflicting -- constructions of Jewish identity make this story so complex yet also deeply human.

Andrei Markovits, Arthur F. Thurnau Professor, Karl W. Deutsch Collegiate Professor of Comparative Politics and German Studies, Professor of Political Science, Professor of Germanic Languages and Literatures, Professor of Sociology, The University of Michigan, Ann Arbor

****

It's rare for a family memoir to situate itself in such a rich and dense historical context so that you feel you're reliving the entire history of Russian revolutionary politics, together with the history of European Jewry, culminating in the family's dramatic escape to safety in the United States. It is illuminating at every point, especially on the ways in which the American labor movement acted to save Jewish activists from the Nazi conquest of Europe.

Michael Ignatieff, Rector Emeritus, Professor of History, Central European University, Budapest and Vienna, Former faculty member at Kennedy School Harvard, Univeristy of Toronto, and leader of Canadian Liberal Party.

****

Who Lived, Who Died? is the distinctive story of two grandfathers in a family whose history traversed the worst of the twentieth century. In this moving memoir by an accomplished political scientist, Peter Gourevitch tells the story of his ancestors whose fates diverged out of combination of personal choices and the decisions by the dictators   at critical points in the history of Bolshevism and Nazi Germany. These decisions t made reverberated through the generations of their family and created an awareness, a heightened political sensibility down to the third and fourth generations. This is the rarest of books, a moving personal story retold from the safety of the United States in a United States that now feel less safe, and a deeply political story that shapes the lives of everyone who comes alive in its pages. The strong sense of how politics moulds personal choices again and again in different ways, and the overwhelming sense of contingency in all our lives will stay with you long after you have finished this compelling story of a family caught up in history. Don't miss this very unique and very universal story.

Janice Gross Stein, Belzberg Professor of Conflict Management, University of Toronto, Toronto, Canada

****

A very readable and intelligent account, at once personal, familial, and political. This is a memorable account of Peter's Gourevitch' s life, but also of his parents, grandparents, and great grandparents: his American children and grand-children will be amazed and grateful. But these pages are much more than that. They will also count as an important contribution to the history of tsarist and post-tsarist times, of the Bolshevik and especially of the Menshevik movement before 1917 and after 1918. How to forget Peter's description of a voluble Lenin in Switzerland, suddenly sitting on the bed of Peter's grandmother. Hardly had the expelled Menshevik exiles settled in Berlin in the 1920's (where they were close to Kautsky), that they were forced in 1933 to flee again, to France and then to the United States. Some of them, but not all: some were never made it that far and died in Stalinist prisons; others were imprisoned in Drancy and sent to Auschwitz. This is the history of a memorable family, but it is also a learned contribution to the histories of Russia, Hitler's Berlin, Vichy France, and of the international labor movement.

Patrice Higonnet, Robert Walton Goelet Research Professor Emeritus of French History at Harvard University

****

With extensive and challenging research in many Russian and U.S. archives and family papers, and in straightforward, compelling prose, Peter Gourevitch tells the absorbing story of his four grandparents, two Russian-Jewish political families, buffeted by the storms of politics, totalitarianism, and warfare in the twentieth century. One grandfather left Europe, the other died in Stalin's prisons. Disentangling the facts from the family legends leads Gourevitch and the reader to realize that these divergent fates were determined less by choice than by the collision between individual will and historical contingency.

Eric Van Young, Distinguished Professor of History at University of California, San Diego, is an American historian of Mexico

****

Peter Gourevitch tells the fascinating story of his family's journey through the Europe of Hitler and Stalin. Engagingly written and deeply researched, the author brings to live his protagonists, mostly Jewish democratic Russian socialists. He documents their often twisted paths from the Russia of the Bolshevik revolution through Weimar and Nazi Germany, the cataclysm of the Second World War and the Holocaust, to the eventual escape of some of his family members to the United States. This is a story of courage, of resilience and survival but also of suffering and tragic loss. It provides a deeply personal perspective on some of the key events of the last century. And it raises profound and lasting questions about determinism and agency, about the significance of political commitments, and about the intersection of individual lives with major historical events.

Frank Beiss, Professor of History at the University of California, San Diego , Director of European studies program, UCSD

****

Peter Gourevitch's riveting account of his family's experience with two totalitarian regimes is part detective story, part political thriller, part historical research. All four grandparents were Mcncheviks; two fled the Soviet Union in the early 1920s and made their way to Berlin. Forced to take flight again in 1933, the maternal grandparents sought refuge in France. On the run once more in 1940, they managed to get visas for the United States. The paternal grandfather was killed in the

Purge; the grandmother survived and in the 1960s found their son. As a teenager he had been sent to Berlin. Then, he too, escaped first to Paris and then to the United States. Gourevitch grew up with a Family Legend and now as an older scholar, he has set out to see how that fits with the historical record. He takes the reader along with him on this journey of discovery—a journey made vivid and graphic by his presence in the text.

Judith M. Hughes, Professor Emerita of History, University of California, San Diego

Who Lived, Who Died?

My Family's Struggle with Stalin and Hitler

By

Peter Gourevitch

ISBN 978-1-64504-316-4 (Paperback)

ISBN 978-1-64504-317-1 (Hardback)

ISBN 978-1-64504-318-8 (E-Book)

Library of Congress Control Number:

Printed on acid-free paper

The Gourevitch Family Part I

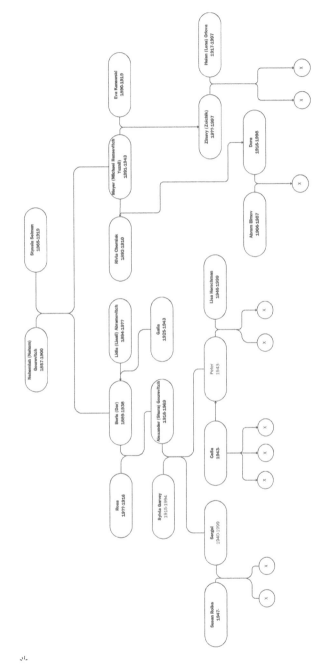

X Children not listed unless mentioned in the book

The Gourevitch Family Part II

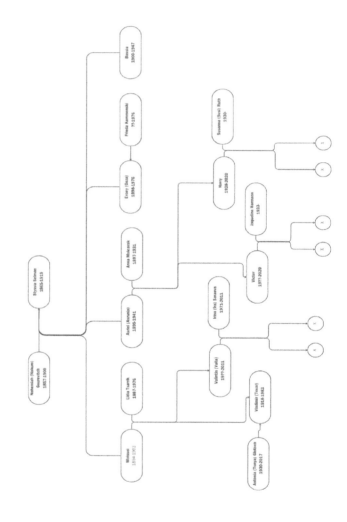

The Garvy-Gourevitch Family Tree

Abbreviated

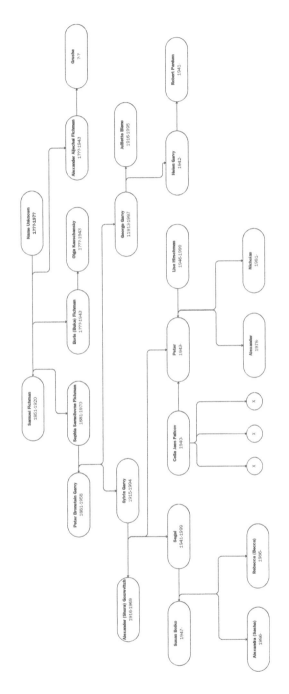

X Children not listed unless mentioned in the book

Table of Contents

Dedication   xiii

Chapter 1   1
How Grandma Lyalya Found Us after 25 Years
    USSR and Syracuse, New York,1937-1962

Chapter 2   21
Who are you? A Socialist, a Jew, or a Russian?
    Russian Empire, 1900-1920

Chapter 3   49
My Grandpas in Jail—Under the Tsars, under the Bolsheviks
    Russian Empire and the USSR, 1900-1923

Chapter 4   57
"Why Him, Not Me?" Who Escaped?
    USSR, 1922-1923

Chapter 5   79
Germany and the Hope of the First Exile
    Berlin, 1923-1933

Chapter 6   99
"This is the Gestapo Calling"
    Berlin, 1933

Chapter 7   123
Third Flight, Second Refuge, and the Long Arm of Stalin
    Paris, 1933-1940

Chapter 8   145
The Miracle of the Visas
    Paris, Marseilles, Lisbon, New York, 1940

Chapter 9   173
The Tragedy of the "Unsung Hero"
    Paris, Nice, Drancy, Auschwitz, 1940-43

Chapter 10   189
The Tragedy of Boris
    Siberia, Vladimir Prison, 1931-1938

Chapter 11   205
"A Knapsack on Their Backs "
    New York, Syracuse, De Witt, 1940-1969

Chapter 12   219
To Stay or Go? To Live or Die? Who Decides?
    Solana Beach, California, 2023

Acknowledgements   245

People in this Manuscript   251

Timeline   259

Dedication

To the Family Members I sadly never knew
Who dedicated themselves to creating a better world
And were prevented from leading productive lives in the service of others:

Boris Ber Gourevitch, Peter Bronstein Garvy, Boris Fichman and Olga
Fichman, Asrail Gourevitch, Galina Gourevitch

And to the children of the above, now deceased, I did know who devoted
themselves to making a meaningful life for their descendants:

Sophia Fichman Garvy, Alexander and Sylvia Garvy Gourevitch, George
and Juliette Garvy, Lydia Abramovich-Gourevitch, Anna Gourevitch,
Victor Gourevitch, Harry Gourevitch

.

Chapter 1

Bonds Broken and Remade

How Grandma Lyalya Found Us After 25 Years

My Father and Mother had not heard from Dad's parents in the USSR for twenty-five years. The last communication was a letter that Boris 'Ber' Gourevitch sent in 1937 from an unknown prison. My parents received that last letter in Paris, where they were living and studying, themselves refugees first from Russia, then from Germany. A quarter of a century later, having reached the US in 1940, my parents were now living in De Witt, a pleasant suburb of Syracuse, New York. In the summer of 1981, aged 18, I came home from work and noticed my mother agitated while she cooked supper. A letter had just arrived that day from the USSR, she told me, from my paternal grandmother, Lydia 'Lyalya' Evseevna Abramovich. To discuss the letter, Mom was waiting for Dad to return from his job as Research Director at Bristol Laboratories, as he did a few minutes later.

Mom's high state of agitation was not all so very unusual for her, a very high-energy, expressive person. Dad, by contrast, was contained and measured in manner. He was very supportive of family members, strong and steadfast in his love and the clear final source of authority to whom my mother turned for finality in case of disputes or problems. He did not talk much about his feelings or his past. We had interaction with some of his relatives in the US, but more with my mother's branch of the family tree. The Cold War raised the barriers to contact with "the other side", which lay in the forbidden USSR, and thus to "exploring the past". Suddenly this letter bursts upon us. I wondered with heightened emotion what impact it would have upon my Dad. What did it say?

The letter confirmed what was long suspected. Grandfather Boris Gourevitch had been killed by Stalin in 1938, a year after the last letter to Paris. It also reported that my father's sister, Galka, had been killed while fighting the German invasion during WW II. Lyalya herself, upon the arrest of Boris in 1937, was sent to Siberia and had, amazingly, survived.

Reading all this indeed shook my Dad. Having his Mother confirm his Dad's death created a painful finality. Galka's death was, in contrast, completely new information. He had a big brother's fondness for her, being about seven years older. Now she too was gone. But all this meant that his Mother was still alive, and thus he could see her!

I don't remember what we had for dinner that evening, but I do recall the high state of emotion in what was normally a fairly calm household. Phone calls and letters followed. Soon plans were afoot to visit the USSR. That was not a simple matter either. My parents were US citizens since the late 1940s, but they and their parents had also been declared enemies of the Soviet state in the 1930s and had been stripped of Soviet citizenship because of their socialist loyalties to anti-Bolshevik Menshevism, for which they had fought in the Revolutionary years of 1917-22. This put the grandparents in constant danger and difficulty with the Bolshevik regime even while living abroad. The assassination of Trotsky in 1940 during his residence in Mexico City is the most famous case, but there were others in the 30s, and the exile community knew of them and felt some anxiety. So would my parents be safe returning for a visit? Did they feel safe? That is getting ahead of the story. Let's get back to Grandma Lyalya and how she found us.

Grandma Lyalya, sister Galka and my father Shura (Alexander) 1925

Grandma Lyalya was released from the Gulag in 1953, when Stalin died, and moved to a tiny town near Kyiv. Initially, she was forced to register with the KGB and report to them weekly. After Khrushchev's denunciation of Stalin in 1956, she was given more freedom to move around. She made her way to Moscow and Leningrad, and in the early 1960s, went to the Russian Political Red Cross Agency (a quasi-political organization, not the relief institution familiar in the West) to seek help in locating my father, Alexander 'Shura' Gourevitch. (Shura is a classic Russian nickname for Alexander; Sasha is the other more well-known one, both used for men and women). Lyalya did not know where her son Shura could be. She knew he had gone to Berlin in 1931.

She surmised that if he were still alive, he must have left continental Europe, so he was in the UK, the US, or Australia. She guessed correctly! My Dad, Shura, had left the USSR in 1931, at age 15, having been born in Imperial Russia in what was then Ekaterinoslav and became Dnipro in today's Ukraine after being Dniepropetrovsk in the Soviet period. Grandpa Boris was an early member of the Russian Social Democratic Workers Party. This group is known in history for one of its branches, the Bolsheviks,

On Left: Galka and Shura, about 1930; On Right, Shura, Galka, Grandma Lyalya and Grandpa Boris, about 1924, likely taken in Tashkent, location of house arrest.

a name it got after a significant split in 1903. The other branch was known as the Mensheviks. The two names mean larger and smaller in Russian. Thus, the Bolshoi Theater in Moscow is the Large Theater. (Many Mensheviks think they were the larger group in 1903, but Lenin showed his political skill by seizing the more imposing name.) The Mensheviks were, in our terms, more Socialist and Social Democratic than the Bolsheviks, who embodied what became the Communist parties of Western Europe. My other grandfather, Garvy, was also a Menshevik, as were both grandmothers.

Before 1917, Boris' political activism got him into trouble with the Tsarist government—prison, banishment to Siberia, and escape to the West, where he studied and met many other exile activists. When the Revolution against the Tsar broke out in February 1917, Boris stayed with the Menshevik position, calling for a constituent assembly of all political forces and a coalition of socialist parties, thus against the Bolshevik Coup of October/November 1917. The Bolsheviks brooked no dissent. Boris was frozen out of power and out of any role to play in constructing the new regime. Civil War broke out over who would govern. Many Mensheviks and other dissidents left the country. Among them were the Garvys, who left with their children, my mother and uncle, ages 8 and 10, in January 1923.

But Grandpa Boris was not allowed to leave. He was repeatedly arrested, released, re-arrested, and re-sentenced. His punishments were banishment to more and more remote cities or towns, colder, more and more isolated. He saw that my father was a bright boy and that the system was punishing children with the wrong family background, be it aristocratic, bourgeois, or political dissident, by blocking his entry to schooling. Seeing he could not place his son in schools, even in the remote countryside, he explored other options. One of these was to have Shura go live with one of Boris' brothers in Moscow and go to school there, which he did in 1930. Then, after much hesitation and deliberation, it was decided in 1931 to take the drastic step that Shura go to Berlin to live with another brother, who had left in the early 1920s. Though the KGB would not let Boris leave the country, it did give Shura permission to do so. Later research revealed that Boris had made such a request in 1928 and received approval but had not sent Shura till November of 1931.

My father's choices as a young émigré helped determine his fate in ways he could not foresee. When he got to Berlin, a major issue arose. Should Shura study the classical educational track by attending a gymnasium (German academically elite high school), which would prepare him for university and to attend training institutions for a profession in science or medicine, or should he go to a technical trade school to become a skilled mechanic or engineer? Though Boris was in the USSR, Shura in Berlin was surrounded by many Menshevik émigrés, all very well educated, each with a strong opinion. Many argued for his going to trade school on the grounds that Shura was poor and needed security and income. Others, including his relatives, such as the Aunt and Uncle with whom he was living, argued for the classical track on the grounds that he was exceptionally smart and this would take him farther.

Shura opted for the gymnasium. He even continued for a year after the Nazis came to power in 1933 to finish the graduation requirements for the "abitur," and then went to Paris in 1934 to rejoin the Menshevik emigres who had already left. Having graduated well, he was able to enter a doctoral program in biochemistry at the Curie Institute. He married my mother in 1938, having met her in the Menshevik youth group association upon arriving in Berlin in '31. Shura was near the end of this doctorate when the French army collapsed in the spring of 1940, and the family had to flee.

The family made it to the US by October 1940. Dad took a job with Allied Chemical, below his educational level, but generating income to support everyone, which included the maternal grandparents, my older brother, born five months after their arrival in the US in a welfare ward in New York City, and me, born in June 1943. My mother, who had also been studying chemistry for an advanced degree, contributed to the family income by sophisticated manual labor —hand-knitting fancy sweaters at which she excelled despite having lost a finger to blood poisoning while a teenager in Berlin. In 1948, Dad got a fellowship at Syracuse University to finish the Ph.D. in biochemistry, which he did in 1952. After a year on the faculty, he went to work for Bristol Laboratories, a subsidiary of Bristol Meyers, now Bristol Myers Squibb, at which he rose to become Director of Research.

Dad was prodigious. He invented, or, it being a lab, helped to develop many important medications: tetracycline, synthetic penicillin, and forms of antibiotics that were targeted to specific diseases and which provided alternatives to people with allergies against the standard medicines. Those achievements got him into the *Who's Who of Medicine and Science* or something like it. So, in 1961, Grandma Lyalya told the Russian Red Cross that if her son were alive, thus having escaped the Nazis, he must be living in the US, the UK, or elsewhere in the English-speaking world. They found his name and address in the relevant reference volumes.

They say that education matters, and here we have one spectacular case where it did. Dad left Russia to have a better education, and in Berlin, he chose the gymnasium track to university, did well there and in Paris, so the Americans let him into a program with a scholarship, permitting him to finish the Ph.D., go on to invent medicines and wind up in a Who's Who, without which Lyalya probably would never have found him.

Soon after receiving Lyalya's letter in upstate New York, we went to visit her in Moscow at the height of the Cold War, the early 1960s. Meeting Lyalya was just unforgettable. It was not only the emotion of seeing her, with Dad, in that cinematic moment of reconnection for them. Nor was it just about my own first time meeting my grandmother. It was the life force from her, mixed with great warmth and devotion, despite all she had endured. I recall her complaining when the taxis did not pick people up. How dare they, was her attitude. Despite enduring years of harsh treatment, she was not beaten down to accept whatever happened. She teased me when I wanted to buy a peasant-style shirt—why would I want a piece of shlock sentimentality like that? She got a policeman to force the taxis to pick people up and then was stuck without a car for herself. My Dad and I took her back to our dorm room, snuck her past the security guard, and gave her my bed while I slept on the floor. I was 23 and could handle it! She radiated love and devotion to my Dad and Grandmotherly warmth to me. She gave us some objects, including an embroidery she made in the *Gulag*, my most precious possession, which hangs in our entrance hall, and which I used to design the cover of this book.

This fragment of the family memory leads to so many questions. If some things became clear—like how Lyalya found my father after 24 years—others were opaque. How did my Dad make it out of the USSR? I knew the date, 1931, but not the explanation. Why was he let out when his own parents were denied exit? And how really did my parents and Garvy grandparents make it to the US, which was hard to do in 1940, and why had they known so quickly they had to get out of Berlin when the Nazis came to power in January of 1933, and by extension, France, in the summer of 1940.

I heard pieces of this story when I was growing up. Among the most dramatic was the flight from Paris in 1940 as the German army blitzed its way toward Paris. When the children got together with family friends who had escaped together, we would ask them to repeat the tale, picking up some more details each time. A crucial sequence turned on what we were told was the last train out of Paris before the German army arrived.

It was a hot, early summer. It took them all day to cross the square in front of the train station, filled with growing fear as each train left; there would be none left for them. As they waited desperately at the train quai, someone hitched a clunky ancient engine onto an old beat-up set of train cars, which then did all it could to chug its way out. As the train left Paris, it was bombed during the journey south, part of the famous chaotic flight from that city, much discussed in film, fiction, and history. The German army entered a day or two later, and the family story has it that the Gestapo arrived at the apartment of my grandparents that day or the next, well prepared with their arrest lists.

This part of my parents' story played an unexpected role in mine. In January 1964, as a newly arrived Harvard graduate student in September '63, I saw the film *Casablanca* for the first time at the legendary Brattle Theater in Cambridge, where it was a staple part of the Bogart Festival shown during each final exam period. The film stunned me. It was not just the luminous beauty of Ingrid Bergman nor the magnetic pull of Humphry Bogart and the excitement generated by all the other character actors. The

Shura and Lyalya in 1930.

movie's whole plot seemed to hinge on a piece of my family's history: who would get the exit visas to Lisbon? At a crucial moment, Bogart is waiting for Bergman at the train station quai. The Nazis are about to enter Paris, and the two movie stars are planning to flee on the last train. Instead of Bergman, it is Sam, the piano player, who arrives with a note.

As Bogart reads the words telling him his beloved Ilsa Lund is not coming, torrential rain hits the paper, blurring the ink. Bogart looks sick and can't move. Sam pulls him on the train, which chugs out amidst rain, steam and smoke. As I left the Brattle theater, I did not wait to return to my apartment, but I called my father from a payphone, expensive in those days before cell phones, and asked:

"Dad, Dad, the day you left Paris, was it raining?"

"No," he replied, surprised that I called and confident in his answer.

"Why do you remember with such certainty, Dad? It was twenty-four years ago," I observed.

"Because," Dad replied, "the dry fields contributed to the rapidity of the German advance, which is why they got to Paris faster than expected and thus contributed to the danger we faced."

 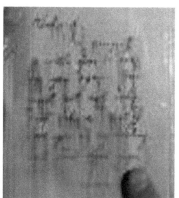

Casablanca— Above: Rick and the piano player.
Above Left: Letter from Ilsa with rain blurring ink.
Below—train at Gare showing rain, steam

I realize that historical accuracy regarding Parisian weather was understandably less important to Hollywood than what made for effective theater. The drama for my family came from the hot, dry weather of real life. To me, the call to my father was an early act in an effort to get the story straight.

Just what were my parents and maternal grandparents doing in France? Why had they waited so long after the French army collapsed to get out of Paris? How did they manage to get entrance visas into the United States? And why did my mother's beloved Uncle Buka (her mother's brother) and his wife Teuta Olya not leave France in time, only to perish in Auschwitz?

Asking those questions led me to ask more. The family came to France from Germany. I knew that Hitler coming to power in January 1933 was the cause of that migration (one of the reasons I went on to study French and German political history). My grandparents were Jewish, Socialists and Russian. Any one of those identities would have been enough to make the Nazi regime dangerous to them. Yet it bears some reflection on why my family got out so quickly, in March of 1933, when many others did not.

Turning the historical dial backward, one more click leads us to the greatest of the family puzzles. Why, in the early 1920s, did Grandpa Peter and Grandma Sonia get out of Bolshevik Russia, whereas Grandpa Boris and Grandma Lyalya did not? The most common answer I got from my parents had to do with ideology: the maternal grandparents were on the right wing of the Menshevik group, saw early on they could not cooperate with the Bolsheviks, and so they left; the paternal grandparents were on the Menshevik left, thought they could cooperate with Bolsheviks, and so they stayed until it was too late. In a very intellectual family that talked about ideas a lot, this made sense, and I did not question it much.

It is only in recent years, as I started to probe the family history that I came to see problems with this story. I found things that indeed did not hang together. As a strong anti-Bolshevik, one might imagine Grandpa Peter would leave soon after the Bolshevik coup of October/November 1917, when many other Menshevik leaders did (1919-20). This is what my parents' "ideological" interpretation led me to expect. But actually, he left rather late, in January 1923.

Then, I discovered more startling information. Left-wing Grandpa Boris had also applied for permission to leave in 1922, at the same time as Grandpa Peter! And not only had they applied at the same time, but they both received permission to leave. One question explodes into three: why had Boris also applied to leave at that time? Why had permission been given to both of them? Why, then, did only one get out?

There had to be more to the story than ideological difference—there was much more to learn. The artistic license of a Hollywood movie is usually easy to notice and to understand, and when you think hard about it, you often find inconsistencies. You don't worry much about it unless you insist that it be high art, like Tolstoy. But the inconsistencies in family history and memory are more troublesome. You want it to make sense. It is real life and is that supposed to hang together. As with good scripts, the process of probing can be rich with meaning.

The decision to write this book and my motives in doing so built up over time. I had been gathering stories about the family over decades without any particular intention. I did not have a professional goal. The family engagement in the Russian Revolution pushed me away from picking it as a specialty for a life's vocation. I did not think I could have enough distance to work as a professional social scientist or historian on the decisions made by each grandparent. Instead, I was attracted to the West European and American experiences of the family and the broader structural forces that shaped our world, and the large forces that pushed some countries toward democracy, and positive social outcomes, while inducing other countries to become authoritarian or grossly unequal. I wrote books about economic and political patterns, trade conflicts, economic depression, trade unions, and regulating powerful corporations.

Now, many years later, I am keenly interested in revisiting what happened in 1917-23. How did the Russian years shape the family destiny? How did they shape my identity? What might they have to teach my grandchildren and the broader public about what seems an increasingly turbulent world? What am I learning about why some in the family survived and others did not, about democracy, its strengths and weaknesses, the dangers of international threats, and the ability of cultures to remake themselves or not? I sought to integrate my focus on the broadly structural with the individually specific. My professional career was inspired in some way by an abstract interest with democracy and its collapse, globalization and economic depression, war and its outcome, with political institutions and their strengths and weaknesses. I had not tried to examine the family story but was inspired by the story to look at those outcomes. Now It was time to put these together. I wanted to understand what happened specifically to the Gourevitchs and the Garvys. The skills I had acquired from these other stories could now prove useful while bearing on the family cases, and perhaps the family story could be of use to the more general ones.

The issues of concern to me involved "agency" and "constraint." By agency, I mean who had the power to cause things, who had the power to decide if my grandpa Boris could leave? Did it lie in his hands or in the hands of someone else? By constraint, I mean what were the limits on decisions and what rules or structures shaped who had the capacity to act or to constrain. As we look at the forces which shaped their lives—the grandparents and the family—what was really up to them, what was in the control of others? The decision to leave or not to leave seemed the most important of these, but there were other choices: where to live, school, job, marriage, and children?

What were the forces, patterns and systems that shaped the environments which constrained them or gave them opportunities? My family lived through some of the most momentous political events of the last century: the Bolshevik coup of 1917 and the Nazi coup of 1933 were the most dramatic. Then world wars and the French defeat in 1940, and the great economic depression of 1929. And there were specific individuals, who granted visas, issued arrest orders, gave permission to leave or not, or to cross a border.

I had worked on these subjects over many years to answer questions that were not personal to me or my family. That provided me with considerable background preparation for this work in understanding big events, bureaucracies, leadership, political systems and the debates that surrounded interpreting historical evidence. More directly, I had considerable personal material to use.

My family experiences rank high among these. I have vivid memories of sitting on the floor at the home of close family friends in Plainfield, New Jersey, or at our house in Syracuse, New York, hearing the parents reminisce. The flight from Paris was among the most vivid stories. We would often ask for the retelling of that one. On my first trip to Paris in 1962, I found the apartment my parents moved to when they got married in 1938. When visiting Moscow with my Dad in 1966, we went to the house where he had lived in 1930 with his uncle,a brother of Boris, before he left the USSR. In Berlin, where I spent a summer in 1972, I looked up my grandparents' apartment from 1923 and found it was still standing!

When I learned the existence of a notebook made in Drancy, the French internment camp for Jews, where they wrote receipts when they confiscated your money, I tracked the book down at a museum in Paris and found a receipt from my great Uncle Boris, just before he was killed in 1943. When I heard of a book that showed people on the train from Drancy to Auschwitz, I looked for his name also and found it. I visited Drancy, and though for many years vowed I never wanted to visit a concentrated camp, I did go to Auschwitz, with the help of other people, my choir.

But even with such evidence in hand, how to interpret it poses significant challenges. When the Washington Holocaust Museum opened in 1993, I went to visit it and was very moved by it as a memorial evoking great loss. I got into a discussion with one of the archivists who was excited to meet the son-in-law of "Beamish," who was among the figures in the important exhibit they had on Varian Frye and the Emergency Rescue Committee, which had saved a number of prominent artists and intellectuals from the Nazis. "Beamish" was the underground name of Albert Hirschman, who had become a famous economist and public intellectual, and also my father-in-law as I had married his younger daughter Lisa in 1976. Hirschman had been an important member of the Fry organization in Marseilles, arranging forged visas and escape routes.

As I summarized my family story, the archivist and I were soon in some disagreement. As I explained the visas that were provided to European labor leaders, among them my family, she thought I was evoking a tiny number of people, whereas a major theme of the Museum's historical account was the anti-Semitism of the State Department Visa Office led by Breckinridge Long in blocking visas to Jews, so that only a few could make it to the US. I agreed with her condemnation of Long and the US government's behavior, but I thought she was underplaying the exceptions to this pattern and the role of Labor organizations in arranging the escape of labor and socialist leaders, many Jewish, many not. The actual history was not nearly as clean as the archivist's account.

This presented an important challenge to me. It was going to take some further reflection and research on my part to grasp how to bring these narratives together: it was not the basic facts over which we disagreed, but on what to emphasize: : she that few Jews were saved; I agreed but insisted that the role of labor in saving a few people was being neglected. Was this an example of competing victimizations, each of us attached to our people, so very familiar to us today? Or was it the inevitable kind of disagreement that comes from different starting points?

These issues remain with us. In 2012, I attended a lecture at UCSD, where I have been teaching since 1979, about the Holocaust given by a German historian, a specialist in that field. During the question period, someone asked why this historian worked on so upsetting a topic. "To ensure we learn lessons, so it does not happen again" was the gist of her answer. Admirable, I thought, such a difficult field to work on; I appreciated the work of anyone willing to undertake it. But, "What are the lessons?" I asked her. "Tolerance," was the reply. Again an admirable sentiment, as intolerance surely enabled the killers to think of their victims as sub-humans in order to slaughter them.

Yet it felt inadequate as an answer, I thought because it does not account for how the Nazis came to power and how they acquired the authority and means to carry out their murderous program. And it does not account for the many kinds of people being killed along with Jews: not only Roma and Slavs, or other ethnics, but labor leaders, socialists, communists, Christian dissidents, liberal opposition leaders, and many individuals who spoke out against the regime and its practices. When I suggested to the historian we might need an account of that process and that destroying the labor movement and the political opposition to the Nazis was part of the story, the historian said the people who thought that way had moved to Soviet-controlled East Germany after WW II—suggesting this was a Communist line of thinking. This comment shocked me, as West Germany remained home to one of the most important Social Democratic Parties of Europe, an organization violently attacked by the Nazis in the 1930s and whose revival was part of the German post-war resurgence of democracy. And I considered myself a strong anti-communist and socialist social democrat all at the same time (and, of course, a strong anti-fascist). The pieces of this story need probing: anti-Semitism, the Nazis and fascism, the destruction of the Weimar Republic, social democracy, socialism and communism, the great economic depression of 1929, World War II, and the Holocaust were all interconnected through a more complex causality than the word "tolerance" could capture or protect us from in the present. Labor and the left were by no means the whole story, but by no means should they be tossed out of the narrative as often seems to happen.

My family's fate shows this. Part of their story belongs in the Holocaust literature in that, as Jews, the family was vulnerable to the Nazi assault. Indeed some of them were killed specifically for being Jews. At the same time being active socialists generated the family its own form of vulnerability and, at the same time, mechanisms of protection. In sequencing the pattern of murder, the Nazis' moved first against their political opponents. They sought to secure power, to make sure they could not be stopped by anyone. The systematic slaughter of Jews started as part of the invasion of the USSR in 1941, following the defeat of France the previous year, eight years after the Nazi's coup in Berlin in 1933. It was in the summer of 1943 that the SS caught in southern France my apolitical Great Uncle Buka and his wife Olga and shipped them east to be killed in Poland.

Another significant part of the family story has to do with the history of Socialism. This movement spread all over Europe and the world. It comprises an important part of the history of factory workers, peasants, farmers, civil servants, teachers, and intellectuals, as socio-economic categories and how we understand the structures of modernized industrial societies. It attracted significant numbers of groups excluded from the established order—among them Jews.

My grandparents were early participants in Socialism's Russian version. The split of the Russian Social Democratic Labor Party into two wings had an immense impact on the world after the Bolshevik coup of 1917 and shaped the lives of these particular individuals. The interaction of the regime's decisions toward the Mensheviks in general and toward Grandpa Boris specifically proved fatal to him. Their socialism was also a reason they and their fellow Mensheviks in exile in Berlin were some of the earliest to be persecuted by the Nazis. I had to find ways of integrating the stories of the two family lines into an analytically coherent whole.

In reflecting on my many questions, it was clear I had to probe the interaction of the element of the family identities, on what was "agentic" and what was "constrained". To what degree could one choose to be Russian, Jewish, or Socialist, thus being the agent of one's identity? One had some control over what kind of Jew and Socialist to be. How about Russian? And then who decided for you? Who put up the constraints? The Russian Empire asked for your nationality and wrote it on your passport. Suppose you did not say "Jew," that line would be empty, unlike the Nazis, who gave you no choice. The Soviets, for a time, did the same as the Tsars.

Even there, some people could emigrate, change their names and disappear. If you stayed, the Russians, Nazi's and Soviets decided for you. By 1940, different parts of my family—the Garvys, the Gourevitchs were all at this point in 1940, stateless, without passports, as the USSR no longer recognized them as citizens. They were ethnically Jewish, secular like many at that time, and they had picked their version of Socialism as anti-Bolshevik. But if they chose to construct their identities in those ways, they did not have a choice as to what their enemies made of them.

Which label put them in the greatest danger— Jewish, labor-socialist, Menshevik anti-Bolshevik, Russian, stateless? The answer changed dramatically by time and place. The more I learned, the more I had to ask. I could unravel more about the politics of each situation. I would have to go back to understand why each person had one or another of these identities and with what consequences.

Did my Grandfathers survive or die because of their own choices or because of choices made by or by large impersonal institutions, like the KGB and the Gestapo, or by individuals within these institutions, or by large social processes like revolution, war and economic depression?

There is also the question of how to interpret the sheer drama of what they experienced. My parents were born during the First World War and lived thru the Russian Revolution, the Russian Civil War and the famine that went with it.

They experienced the Great Depression of 1929 and lived in Germany with the rise of the Nazis and Hitler. Having escaped Nazi Germany, they then in France lived through the tumult of the French

Popular Front, the Spanish Civil War, the Munich Conference and the Czech crisis of 1938, finally facing the stunningly rapid French military collapse in 1940, and barely made it to the US. In the US, arriving with only the contents of a backpack each, they founded a family and led impressive lives. By that time, my family had lived under and, in some cases, escaped two murderous dictators, Stalin and Hitler, guaranteed immortality in history as among the most stupendous killers of all time.

What a string of events! Compared to that, my life has been dull, for which I am grateful, at least that I did not live in danger and fear. I have wondered for most of my life how all this came about and what it was like to experience it.

Converting family stories into a memoir is, in part, an exercise in combining memories with verifiable facts, in "checking up" on the oral tradition. What is made up, and what is real? Suppose we label the oral stories which come down as "Family Legend," and we label real as "verifiable " material, stories that have independent sources? It is pretty easy to check the Paris weather on June 10, 1940. Many family stories are impossible to check. For example, Garvy Family Legend says my grandmother Sophia Fichman knew Lenin when both were in Swiss exile, and they argued while he sat on her bed while visiting in her one-room apartment. I have heard this story several times but have no way to prove it really took place. Another Family Legend has it that before marrying my grandfather Peter, Sophia had an affair in about 1905 with a quite important and shady Bolshevik fellow, Parvus (Alexander Helphand), the fellow who, among other activities, helped persuade the German General Staff to smuggle Lenin in a sealed railroad car from Switzerland to Russia to foment the revolution, and through his successful business dealings funnel a lot of money to the Bolsheviks. The story of the affair has a number of people who knew about and commented on it, so it is verifiable. Do we learn from the stories? Do they matter, even if uncheckable? Some of them are interesting and important, and some are just interesting!

For much of my life, I had heard that my paternal grandfather, Boris, had written letters from deep inside the Soviet Union to his family first in Berlin, then Paris, from 1924-37, while he was in Siberia or internal house arrest, and that many of these letters had survived. My father's Aunt Anya had collected them and given a copy to the family.

In 2018, I had those letters translated and could read them for the first time. The letters brought me closer to one of the relatives I had never met. They told me a lot about the grandfather, his relationship with my father, and the sentiments leading to Shura's departure and his life in isolation.

Reading Boris' letters led me to want desperately to look at the archives of the Russian FSB, the successor of the Soviet era KGB-NKVD, to examine their files on my grandparents, housed in the Annex of the notorious Lubyanka Prison, across from the large store, Detsky Mir, or Children's World, where I had met my grandmother Lyalya in 1966. Could I get permission to look? When I was invited to a conference in Moscow in 2019, I could not refuse, despite the cold January date.

I realized I had to create my own version of events: I had to navigate among Family legends, Public Legends (beliefs about history), documents, memories, histories, and literature to come up with my own judgment.

So off I went looking for more sources. These included the Klarsfeld publications on the French Holocaust, the Labor Archive at New York University, the Holocaust Museum in Washington, the Jewish Documentation Center in Paris, notes from my Uncle George, and discussions with my parents and other relatives. And there is a rich trove of published books providing immense material to find context and supplement the eyewitness accounts, such as the history of Menshevik Refugees by Andre Liebich. Grandpa Peter, my namesake, wrote his own memoirs published in NY a year after he died in 1944.

I come away from all this with a deeper appreciation of the craft of historians, which I now see as the blend of narrative, bordering on a kind of informed fiction, with verification of some facts painfully established and placed into a finely wrought framework.

For my family, there was a lot of turmoil in their lives, danger, threats, expulsion, fighting, new languages to learn, people to meet, friends to make, friends lost, new subway maps, and finding jobs. I long wondered what sustained them through all this, emotionally as well as physically.

Initially, I desired simple answers to these questions of survival and resilience. But the reality is complex and multi-dimensional. What follows is history, narrative, remembrance, interpretation, and lessons.

Turbulence has returned to our lives. When I talk to people about this family story, questions frequently turn to "lessons for the present." So many questions abound about the threats to democracy, the rise of neo-fascist movements in Europe, the revival of interest in socialism, renewed admiration of Stalin in Russia while ever more despised outside, and, deeply disturbing, the turbulence in the American polity – the attack on the US Capitol building and the Voting Certification on 6 January 2021, the challenges to voting, the issues of race and social cohesion—the present seems very unsettled. We seek ideas from the past to understand the present, and the present helps us rediscover the past. Telling my family story may comment on a variety of issues of broader concern.

Indeed, while I was finishing the writing of this project, Russia invaded Ukraine. War now rages in the very territories from which my ancestors came. Laylya came from Kharkiv, my mother from Odesa, my father from Dnipro, one grandfather from Odesa, the other grandfather was born in the Mogliev region of Belarus and moved as a child to Dnipro, the other grandmother was born in what is now Moldova, back then Bessarabia in the Russian Empire.

The frame of Ukrainian and Russian nationalisms has changed quite deeply. What would the various family members make of it? My parents did not think of themselves as Ukrainians, as that culture at the time did not have much place for Jews or Socialists. With the current Russo-Ukranian war, the meaning of each nationality is being reworked by each side, by the processes of war, and by the leadership and population on each side. The Ukrainians seem to be creating a broadly inclusive model of nationality on the West European model. How successful can this be? This compels some reflection by me about my ancestors and their own ideological evolution. How fluid, indeed, are national identities? Do current events lead me to revisit what they thought? Would they think differently today?

Solana Beach, California, 15 March 2023.

Grandpa Peter Garvy in a Tsarist prison camp in Siberia 1903. He is the tall, bearded person at the upper right.

Peter Bronstein Garvy and Sophia Fichman Wedding photo 1910 Odessa

Sylvia Bronstein- Garvy and Alexander (Shura) Gourevitch 1938 at the time of their marriage, Paris.

On left Peter Garvy with his brother in Law, Boris (Buka) Fichman with Sylvia on the left (1year old and George.

On right: Buka Fichman with Sylvia (about 5) and George (about 7 or 8). 1920 Odessa

Chapter 2

Choosing an Identity

Politics, Religion, Nationality

In late 1922, my maternal grandfather, Peter Garvy, was stuck in a Soviet prison in the Ural Mountains. He had been there a year, imprisoned as a Menshevik opponent of the Bolsheviks. His wife, Sophia, my grandmother, was in Moscow, with my mother, Sylvia, 8 years old, and my uncle, George, 11 years old. Suddenly, Grandpa Peter was brought to Moscow and told, "Either leave the country or go into domestic exile with your family." The phrase "domestic exile" meant, at best, highly restricted house arrest, or worse, prison camp. The family quickly packed what little they had and left the country by train. Having made the request to leave, this permission was what they had been waiting for. Years later, when I asked my mother and my uncle for some memories of that trip, I got a few comments about having been met by friends of the grandparents in Latvia, where they had lived for some time years earlier as punishment from the Tsars, a gentle punishment as my grandmother was pregnant with George, and Riga was a gentler place to be while pregnant than many of the alternatives. My uncle expressed some sadness about leaving his friends behind.

Meanwhile, Boris, the other grandfather, is also in prison, having been arrested in the summer of 2022. Boris had received permission to leave the USSR but was still waiting for the Exit Visa. I do not recall my Dad discussing this particular historical moment. I did not understand it myself and never asked him about it. He never brought it up. I do not even know if he knew about it—that the permission had been granted but technically not implemented.

The period of 1921-22 was not the first imprisonment for any of the grandparents. All four of them had been revolutionaries against the Tsarist Autocracy right up to its overthrow in February 1917. Opposing the Tsarist system made them by no means unique. It was broadly unpopular among most elements of Russian society, top to bottom. My grandparents' political difficulties with the Tsars stemmed from their choices on how to express their dislike of the system, and on the way they acted while in the opposition. They were political troublemakers from their early adulthood—activists, dissidents, revolutionaries.[1] They were not bomb-throwers or street brawlers. They advocated change of government and a change of system. Even that was offensive to the Tsar and the police. The grandparents did not make life choices that would have drawn less notice from the forces of repression.

So authoritarian was the Tsarist system, it took little to be critical of it and so to anger the police apparatus. At a minimum, most reformers sought some kind of constitutional government, with an executive accountable to an elective parliament, the rule of law, formal legal equality among citizens, if not social equality, and a more or less neutral judicial system governing a market economy.

By the eve of WWI in 1914, the US, the UK, France, and parts of Scandinavia had evolved constitutional orders with the rule of law and restraint on the monarchy. Even Imperial Germany and the Austro-Hungarian Empire had significant aspects of constitutionalism, with elected national Assemblies, formalized judicial systems, some rule of law, and some legal equality.[2]

By contrast, Russia remained even more directly under the grip of the Romanov royal family, the upper reaches of the aristocracy, the Army, the Church, and a bureaucracy controlled from the top. The identity of the Tsar mattered. The assassination of the liberalizing Tsar Alexander II in 1881, about the time my grandparents were born, led to rule by more reactionary Tsars Alexander III and Nicholas II, both insistent on their right to absolutist rule and preservation of aristocratic hegemony. Some limited reform did occur: Serfdom was abolished in the 1880s, but the essentials of autocracy remained. There was also an intensification of anti-Semitism actively supported by the Tsarist Regime, whose secret police forged the infamous tract, *Protocols of the Elders of Zion*, inventing a Jewish conspiracy.[3]

This leads to one of the many "might-have-beens" or what specialists call "counterfactual" speculations: what if Alexander II had lived a long reign and launched a process of moderate constitutional reform? Would Russia have handled better the shock of WWI? Similar speculation arose with the premature death from cancer of the liberal Kaiser Frederick III of Germany in 1888, which prevented moderate reformism in that country and gave way to the impetuous Kaiser Wilhelm II leading to great power tensions and WWI. These world-level counterfactuals constantly interact in our story with the individual ones concerning actions by the grandparents.

The four grandparents were born in the Russian Empire before 1900, all from the southern part, more or less in what is called the Pale of Settlement, where Jews were allowed to live in what has today become Ukraine, Belarus, Moldova, and Romania, and partly Russia. My maternal grandma, Sophia Samoilevna Fichman, was born in Orgev near Chisinau (then Kishinev), now Moldova, then known as the province of Bessarabia. Her husband, my maternal grandpa, Peter Abramovich Bronstein (Garvy), was born in Odesa in 1881 in what is now Ukraine. My paternal grandpa, Boris Naumovich Gourevitch (Ber), was born in 1889 or 1890 in Orsha, near Mogliev, a small town in what is now Belarus, but his father moved the family when he was young to what is now Dnipro in Ukrainian, in Russian, Dniepropetrovsk, before 1917 Yekaterinoslav, an important city southeast of Kyiv on a major river, the Dnieper, in what is now Ukraine. Grandma Lidiya Evseevna Abramovich came from Kharkiv, an important city also in Ukraine. She was my father's stepmother: his natural mother died in childbirth. From my father's wedding certificate of 1938 in Paris, I see her name listed as Rosalie Sac Chac, but that is all I know about her, or more precisely, all I knew until I started this research and learned a bit more from a Ukrainian researcher I hired and who called me in early fall 2022. My father was very close to his stepmother, referred to among us by her Russian diminutive, which is Lyalya.

All of them identified culturally with Greater Russia, not with the modern national equivalents of the places which contain the cities of their birth. My mother reacted quite strongly when someone, having learned she was born in Odesa, said, "Oh, so you are a Ukrainian." "No," she replied, slamming the table rather hard. "I am not a Ukrainian." The strength of her reaction startled me, as Mother was very anti-nationalist in outlook; on reflection, I understood that she expressed the Greater Russian cultural roots of her parents and their Social Democratic ethos. They dreamt of ending religious and cultural prejudice inside the Russian nation rather than building separate ethnic enclaves for each group. Odesa in those days was a melting pot, a port city, like Chicago, full of people from many places, in this case from the many regions of Russia, but also Turks, Armenians, Jews, Greeks, Azeris, and many others, and relatively few ethnic Ukrainians who at that time lived largely in the countryside. Perhaps she had acquired an unease about Ukraine common to Jews, the same unease felt by many Jews toward Russia and the Tsars. She was proud of the greater Russian culture, as she also became fascinated by the great components of German, French and American culture as she lived and studied in these societies.

As I watch the Russian attack on Ukraine in late February 2022, I cannot help but wonder how my mother and other relatives would react to the "ethnic evaluations" they had made at earlier periods. Given their values, there is no doubt they would support the democratic expression of the Ukrainian government led by Zelensky. They would be horrified by Putin. They would be appalled to watch the Greater Russian apparatus be used to crush Ukraine. Context and situation reverse the framing of judgment. My family would not today self-identify as Ukrainian, but they would certainly defend the values it expresses and oppose the ideology thrust forward by the controllers of Russian power. I can imagine my mother responding differently to being asked, "Are you Ukrainian?" as the meaning of this changes over time. I don't think she would slam the table or not quite so hard.

She would reflect on it, reflect on the Jewish background of President Zelensky, curse the Jewish background of several Putin oligarchs, wonder about the redefinition of nationalism underway, how far it can and will it go, curse also Putin's degradation of the few remaining democratic institutions in Russia, such as independent media and the historical research group, Memorial—in short, she would think and wonder and express sadness at what she was observing. I certainly do.

For my grandparents, as unhappiness toward the Tsarist Regime was very widespread, quite a large range of criticisms and political strategies existed as to what to become, in contemporary terms, what identity to choose. All four picked Socialism. More specifically, they became what we would classify as Social Democrats in the Marxist tradition. Later in the discussion, I will explore what that meant as I try to understand disagreements among them, especially between the two Grandfathers. For now, I am interested in what they did not become: Politically; they did not become Bolsheviks, Bundists, Zionists, Social Revolutionaries, Cadets, or Liberals. One of Grandpa Boris' brothers picked Bolshevism, but neither Boris nor his other brothers did; the Bolshevik brother was also imprisoned and died during Stalin's purges.

Similarly, I don't know why the grandparents did not go into one of the non-political professions: business, medicine, law, teaching. Many people from their social backgrounds did go in these directions. They had plenty of examples in their own families: one great grandfather was a successful grain merchant, and another came from a business family that appears to have lost its fortune. One relative was a noted professor of linguistics, so distinguished as a researcher he acquired a position at St. Petersburg University without renouncing his Jewishness, an unusual achievement in those days. Grandma Sophie's favorite brother Boris became a businessman. Jews were leaving the small towns and ghettos, which confined them for so many generations. And with strong roots in education, many Jews poured into the professions that required training.[4]

Choices existed, and there were forks in the road for the grandparents. The famous writers of this period describe such a range of options and choices. The daughters of Schloem Aleicheim's *Tevye the Dairyman* (the source for *Fiddler on the Roof*) marry some of the many characters in the society around them. I imagine Perchik—the Marxist intellectual who marries Tevye's second daughter and is banished to Siberia—as an example that would fit one of my grandfathers, though the fictional Perchik seems less bourgeois, less well-educated and less well-traveled than my grandfathers.

Many people emigrated in this period. The late 19 century saw huge numbers leaving this part of Russia, some to Western Europe, Berlin, London, and Paris, many more to the US, Canada and Argentina, and some to Australia. Some relatives of my grandparents came to the US. So emigration was another option my grandparents surely knew about.

One hundred and thirty years ago, thus well over a century before I am writing and reflecting on these concerns, my grandparents shaped their respective identities. We used to think these were just given, like nature. You were born this or that; you had little choice. Now we challenge this. People have some choice. They make attachments to values. This shapes who they become.

I can conceptualize their choices and wonder about them. They went down a very challenging road full of hardships and dangers. What led them there? I can brood about these choices, but at the bottom, I have no way of explaining them. I have no references in letters or writings, or comments where they discuss these alternatives head-on. It is a striking fact about all four grandparents that they made the same choice. They made a commitment to a political life; they saw themselves as revolutionaries. The solidarity among them derives from the common political commitment. That likely is an important element of the bond within each couple, but why they made that one rather than another, I can describe, and reflect on the consequences, but not really explain. Socialism was a choice. Political engagement was a specific path, socialism was a conscious location. It got my grandparents dangerous attention first from the far right of the Tsarist police, then from the far left of the Bolshevik police, then in Germany and France, the far right again.

These choices mattered hugely for their lives and, therefore, for their families. Navigating between the two great enmities of the Bolsheviks and the Nazis structured their friendships and foes, their livelihoods, their options and those of their children and grandchildren. The costs of their dedication were very great. It led to a life of flight and imprisonment, poverty and isolation. It put them in grave danger. For some it saved their lives. For others, it killed them. We can wonder about, though not know, what evaluation they made of the trade-offs and risks of these life choices.

Though there are limits to what we can know about the choices, there are some things we can establish. Certain aspects of their lives made these journeys possible: For starters, it took education, a substantial one. All four grandparents achieved high levels of education. Grandma Sophia Garvy went to high school in Kishinev and spent some time at University. Grandpa Peter made it to the University of St Petersburg, an unusual accomplishment for a Jewish boy in those days.

Grandpa Boris and Grandma Lyalya also had some university training, with Grandpa Boris having spent some time studying in Western Europe. Education is where they likely developed their connection to political activism and their affiliations to the growing socialist network. It also took money. While none came from very wealthy families, none came from the impoverished Jewish shtetls so vividly evoked in *Fiddler or the Roof* and the novels of Sholem Aleichem or Isaac Bashevis Singer. I think Grandma Sophia came from the most prosperous background of the four though Grandma Lydia may have had some assets in her family, but I know less about it. My grandparents do not seem to have studied a particular profession. Grandpa Boris seems to have some math and economics, as in later years, he worked for a time in the Soviet planning office.

This educational background enabled their political activity. It helped them engage in the political debates of the era and to occupy various leadership positions at a time when words mattered. But by itself, education did not determine the direction of political engagement.

It is striking that in a period when many Jews joined the Bund, none of my grandparents did, even the children of a Rabbi. Of the great grandfather Rabbi Nahum Gourevitch's six children, five sons and one daughter, it seems none of them were active Bundists as adults. It may be difficult to be too precise on this point, as an important number of political activists belonged to both and moved back and forth. Raphael (Rein) Abramovich, who we meet later in the story, an important Menshevik leader, was a well-known Bundist at the same time as being a Menshevik leader. Formed in the late 1890s, the Bund,[5] shorthand for "General Jewish Labor Bund in Russia and Poland," aimed to unify Jewish workers in the Russian empire into a unified socialist party, and saw itself as a constituent part of the Russian Social Democratic Labor Party (RSDLP), itself formed in 1898. Five years later, when the RSDLP split into Bolsheviks and Mensheviks factions within the same party, Bundists tended to overlap more with Mensheviks. My family members may have been involved with the Bund or influenced by it when young, but it does seem they were not active in it as adults while in the Menshevik grouping.

The RSDLP was a Marxist-inspired party that sought social and political change based on the growing industrial proletariat. Swiftly outlawed in Imperial Russia, the party leaders met outside the country. The Bolsheviks, led by Lenin, advocated a centralized party of committed activists to lead a dictatorship of the proletariat, which would rule in the name of the working class. The Mensheviks, led by Martov, advocated open membership to anyone who accepted the party program and a democratic process of achieving political and social change more gradually through parliamentary democracy. The former became the Communist Party of Russia, and the communist label became generally used around the world for this orientation. The latter group evolved into the SDPs, Social Democratic or Socialist or Labor Parties of Europe, Western Hemisphere, Asia, etc. The split was sharp, but at the time, its consequences were not fully appreciated. There was constant talk of reconciliation. This never occurred.

All four grandparents were members of the RSDLP in the Menshevik faction from the very first days of the split. They do not appear ever to cross back and forth to the Bolsheviks as did numerous people while the boundaries remained fluid, and the barriers to switching much lower as remained the case up until the Bolshevik coup in the fall of 1917, for at this point, individuals had to decide whether to accept the party's leadership under Lenin. All four grandparents refused to do so, then and for the rest of their lives.

While I don't know much about why they made their choices, I know something of their individual stories through which I developed the analysis of this project. I start with my grandmother Sophie Fichman Garvy-Bronstein. She is the only one of the four I knew personally, as she lived through my late teens. Peter Garvy died in New York when I was 8 months old. I met Grandma Lydia only once in 1966, in Moscow, and I never met Grandpa Boris who was killed in 1938 before I was born. Their stories are rich with meaning for our times.

My Revolutionary Grandmother—Sophia Garvy, the extensive Networker

My maternal grandmother, Sophia Samoilovna Fichman Bronstein Garvy, was born in Orgev, a small town near Kishinev in what is now Moldova, then known as the Bessarabia region of the western Russian Empire in the Pale of Settlement. Kishinev was a major city in the region and was infamous for a notorious pogrom against Jews in 1903. Grandma's given name was Sophia, but in my childhood was called

Baba Sonia (the Russian diminutive for Sophia), so I will call her Grandma Sonia. She was sent from the smaller town to a high school for girls in Kishinev. This indicated a high level of educational orientation by her parents, suggesting that they were assimilated, not deeply traditional. For a girl in the 1890s, this would have been unusual but not unheard of. Quite a lot of women from prosperous backgrounds received enough of an education to attend even universities, especially Switzerland, which admitted them to graduate programs, including medical school. A noted example of a woman getting educated is Rosa Luxembourg, a famous Spartacist Revolutionary in Germany, who was killed as a Communist in 1919 in Berlin.[6]

Grandma Sophia –Baba Sonia, as a young woman, the one on left taken in Switzerland. About 1905.

It was surely at the high school in Kishinev that she was exposed to socialist ideas from the teachers. She was "radicalized"—the teachers there made her aware of politics in general, injustices, the ills of the Tsarism system, and most likely, the ideas of socialism.

About the time she was finishing high school, my Great-Grandfather Fichman moved the family to the most important city of southern Russia, Odessa, whose contemporary Ukrainian spelling is Odesa. He was a grain merchant in what was rapidly becoming one of the great entrepôts of the world. Odesa was to Imperial Russia, what Chicago was at the same time in the US and Buenos Aires in Argentina: a metropolis toward which railroads and rivers converged to bring grain and other goods from the famous black earth hinterland of the coun-tryside to this great port for shipment around the world. Production and export were enabled by huge gains in transportation technology, mechanization, refrigeration, and population growth.[7]

This burst of agricultural production and shipment shaped poli-tics and migration around the world. As production expanded, world prices of grain fell starting in 1873. While a boon to the growing mass of city dwellers employed in various urban factories who thus got cheaper food, the agricultural depression was devastating to much of the farming population of Europe, whose small plots of land were inefficient in comparison to the large-scale agricultural production by the new regions of the Great Plains of the United States and Canada, the Pampas in Argentina, the black earth lands of Southern Russia and Ukraine, the fields of Australia and their smaller counterparts around the world. Millions abandoned harsh conditions to migrate across oceans to the Western Hemisphere and Australia and into the rapidly expanding industries and cities. The politics of globalization, the backlash to imports and migrants, as well as the benefits in growth and efficiency, has become quite familiar in our times.

This example of globalization change processes fascinated me. In the early days of my academic career,some of my most im-portant academic work was on these themes: *Politics in Hard Times* and "*International Trade, Domestic Coalitions, and Liberty.*"[8]

 Many years later, when I began to probe into my family history, I was astonished to realize my maternal grandfather was an active partici-pant in the very activities I had spent a good part of my professional life studying.

Grandpa Solomon Fichman was a grain merchant, buying and selling grain futures, initially in Kishinev and then in Odesa. Now I found I was linked, albeit indirectly with a gap of two generations, to what is called in research methodology, "participant observation."

Grandfather Fichman did quite well. The family home in Odesa was on "Greek Street, " a posh address, still a major thoroughfare in that city today.

When my mother's brother George visited Odesa in the 1970s, the house was still there, having survived the Civil War after WWI and the devastation of WWII. He visited the apartment itself and drew out the floor plan in a notebook. It seemed a handsome place, with plenty of rooms, space for servants, a good vehicle for solid bourgeois urban life.

It is likely that Solomon Fichman knew the Ephrussi family, the central players in Edmund de Waal's magnificent book, *The Hare with the Amber Eyes*. This tells the story of what happened to the immensely wealthy and internationally dispersed Ephrussis by tracing the fate of the "netsuke"—a Japanese type of ceramic art—purchased by a French member of the Ephrussi clan (himself featured in Proust novels and Manet paintings) as a wedding gift to his cousin in the Austrian branch of the family. Among the vivid strokes of de Waal's writing are his account of the destruction of the Ephrussi family mansion in Vienna by the Nazis during the Anschluss of 1938 and how nonetheless, the *netsuke* collection survived intact, saved by the family maid. While I had never heard mention in my family of the Ephrussi, I was fascinated to realize that the Fichmans must have known them, as both were prosperous Jewish merchants in the same activity, the grain trade, in the same city at the same time.

Uncle George at about age 1 with Fichman grandparents, 1912

My grandfather's success, not remotely as immense as the Ephrussi, was big enough for an apartment at a fashionable address in a major city of the Russian Empire, and this was significant in the family story. Great-Grandpa's money financed not only my grandmother's education but her radical political activities. Sophia Samoilovna, as my Grandma Sonia would have been called with her patronymic (which I was told I could not pronounce as a child), seemed to have been a feisty, strong young woman and retained features of vitality and engagement her entire life.Grandma had two younger brothers, Alexander, who became a soldier and disappeared from family view after the Revolution, and Boris, the youngest, who remained close to Grandma and the family she formed with my Grandfather Peter Bronstein Garvy, and whose tragic fate as a victim of the Holocaust in Auschwitz is explored in this book.

The family of Grandma : Samuel Fichman and wife, with Alexander, Sophia, and Boris Fichman, their three children. About 1902.

When I got to know her, Grandma Sonia was an elderly woman, well into her 60s and 70s. She had been through a difficult life: banishment to Siberia, or to other parts of the Russian Empire such as Riga, and to Astrachan[9] near the Caspian Sea, where they were when the Revolution of February 1917 broke out. She experienced the turbulence of the Revolution, its civil war, hunger, harsh repression by the Bolsheviks, a husband in prison, fleeing to Berlin in January 1923, only to flee the Nazis, not once but twice, from Berlin in 1933 and from Paris in 1940, to arrive in New York in October of that year. She did not speak much English, so I spoke to her in my childhood Russian which was good enough for cards, Chinese checkers, and other games, or for simple conversations, and even at times, her political and moral interrogation of me.

Like grandmas everywhere, she had some cooking specialties: a kind of pie which mixed cream cheese and cottage cheese. She drank tea from a glass with a piece of sugar in her mouth, an East European custom. I do recall talking politics with her a few times; once, she wanted to make sure I did not believe the ends justify the means and was pleased when I answered her hypotheticals the way she wanted; in the

Sophie Fichman in Paris about 1906.

negative, no, the end does not justify the means. I think I grasped she was re-living quarrels with Bolsheviks. I also recall the shock on my Uncle George's face when I played the old Tsarist anthem on the piano and she enjoyed hearing it; I knew it because it appears in Tchaikovsky's *1812 Overture*, after *the Marseillaise* in order to evoke Napoleon's retreat from Moscow. She enjoyed it not because she was a closet royalist but for its familiarity with her cultural background and that her grandson had learned a bit of Russian culture.

Looking back, she seemed old and tired. I saw only some flashes of the firebrand she must have been. Photos of my grandparents in their 60s in New York show them worn, pale. I wonder if it was the technology of photos or if; indeed, they were worn, ill and saddened by the travail of flight and loss. My grandfather Peter Garvy died in 1944 of a heart attack in an era when they did not yet know how to manage his condition; he would likely have lived much longer in the modern era, as have I after a mild heart crisis in my mid-70s that may have killed him. I have already outlived everyone in my family, but I don't know what their genetic legacy was as they had no medical care for most of their lives. My grandma lived to 80, which was remarkable longevity given her life history.

The image I have of the young firebrand is inferred from her history and the way others talked about her. Way back at the turn of the 19th century, she was active enough to have police arrest her even when quite young. She had a reputation I learned of being stern, resolute, and opinionated in temperament.

My own mother Sylvia was a strong-willed, energetic woman, so I imagine her as resembling her mother in some way. Both my mother and her brother had some friction in their relationship with Baba Sonia, though they certainly took care of her as a widow and, during their difficult years of poverty in Berlin and Paris, helped earn some essential portion of the family's living expenses.

Prudish and strict was the reputation Grandma had, from what I heard. One was not to talk about sex in front of children. In family conversation, the code to change the subject was to say "Pestalozzi" (the name of a famous education theorist), which would signal to everyone the conversation was veering toward dangerous ground with children present. Her own children rebelled in some way. My mother and uncle spent some time at nudist camps in their youthful Berlin years, and while sharing a room for study and sleeping, had little use for clothes—they could not afford a room of one's own.

Despite her reputation as somewhat severe and prudish, she must surely have been more complex, like most of us. I learned just how complex in a startling way. In June 1960, I flew with my mother to Washington, D.C., for the funeral of Wladimir Woytinsky. This was an important figure in world history, by no means as famous as Lenin or Trotsky, but involved in a number of important events. In Russia, he was a leading Menshevik, important enough to be arrested personally by Trotsky. In the early 1920s, Irakli Tsereteli, as Menshevik President of the Georgian Republic, sent him as Ambassador to the Vatican. From there, he never returned to what was now the USSR, as Georgia had been taken over by the Bolsheviks. Woytinsky went to Berlin, became chief economist of the German trade union confederation, and in 1932 wrote the WTB plan, a demand stimulus program to fight the depression. It was rejected by the German Cabinet. When the Nazis seized power in January 1933, he fled to Switzerland and then to the US, where he was the chief technical author of what became the American Social Security retirement system (1936). For my family story, he was an important figure in the Garvy family escape from France in 1940 to which we return in a later chapter. The Woytinskys, Wolik and Emma as I knew them, were close to my grandparents in the Europe years, and we visited them in Washington every year in my childhood. His death was an important event in our family life, and so in 1960, we went to the funeral in Washington.

As my mother and I are sitting in the kitchen of Woytinksy's widow, Emma, a woman enters. She is Ella Wolfe, the wife of Bertram Wolfe. This astonished me as I had only recently read *Three Who Made a Revolution*, Wolfe's monumental study of Lenin, Trotsky and Stalin, and the entire Russian revolutionary episode.[10] Emma seeks to locate for Mrs. Wolfe who my mother was. "Oh, Ella, Sylvia here is the daughter of Sophia and Peter Garvy; you know Sophia, who was mistress of Parvus." At this, my mother's jaw literally dropped open. "What?!" she said. "Yes, of course!" was the reply. The word flabbergasted exists to describe my mother's reaction. Her mother consorting with Parvus seemed most incongruous. With anyone, I suppose, but with Parvus no less! When my father arrived in Washington that evening, he told us his mother-in-law, my Grandma, had told him about it years ago, so why did my mother not know about it? Perhaps it says more about mothers and daughters or that particular mother-daughter relationship, which was not an easy one.

Parvus (Alexander Helfand) was quite a controversial figure in the Russian Revolution. He worked with the Bolsheviks in Russia, co-authored tracts with Trotsky, and funneled money to the revolutionaries, to Bolsheviks as well as Socialists generally. The money came from his success as a businessman, banker, and trader. He also had links to the German military and to the Young Turks in the Ottoman Empire who were preparing its overthrow. And perhaps most famously, it appears it was Parvus who persuaded the German military to smuggle Lenin and some of his associates to Russia in 1917 to help foment revolution in order to knock Russia out of the war. The Bolshevik plan of "peace and land" led to the Brest-Litovsk Treaty of March 1918 between Germany and Russia, which allowed the Germans to send soldiers to the Western Front against the French and British, stopped only by the Americans, now arriving in large numbers. No Parvus, no Lenin in Russia, thus no Bolshevik coup and success in seizing power is one important speculation among historians.

The thought of my Baba Sonia having an affair with Parvus was quite startling to me the more I read up on him and remains so to this day. It certainly rattled the cages of the way she was described by her friends and family in my childhood. At that time it took place (about 1905), the affair made a stir in Menshevik circles, as she was on the youngish side (25, is that really so young?), and he was something of a roué and controversial in many dimensions, not just political. Various letters in the Menshevik archives are quite critical of him as a violator of this young person, not so clearly of her for having it. She was sufficiently agitated by the breakup to have asked her beloved brother Buka (Boris) to come to visit her in Europe, where they took a voyage of recovery to Italy, with, I assume, money from Great-Grandpa Fichman's business, or perhaps Buka himself as a successful businessman.

Does Grandma's love life really merit attention in the historical record, even in the family account? Not for itself, but it does convey some information that matters to the larger story. First, it tells us something about her network of connections: the members of this top network of Russian Socialists knew each other well, whatever their location in the Menshevik–Bolshevik divide, well enough to know of major love affairs. Emma Woytinsky locates Grandma to Ella Wolfe through this relationship some sixty years after it happened, in lightning shorthand, a story they would all have known: Ella was an American, not of the old Menshevik group, so she and Emma most likely gossiped to each other about it. It also shows the bond of Boris Fichman to his sister, as he comes all the way from Russia to Switzerland to console her when the relationship breaks up. When we come to the important moment of the Garvy exit from Moscow in January of 1923, reference is made in the OGPU files to Sophie Garvy's "network of contacts".   I wonder if this was a reference to Parvus. There is no mention of his name. It more likely refers to the very large network of people she had come to know in these exile circles, including Lenin. When my mother was quite sick in 1922 with rheumatic fever, Grandma called a well-placed cousin for help getting medicine from the Kremlin pharmacy.

Sonia/Sophia's time in Switzerland in the first decade of the 20th century crisscrossed with that of other Russian Socialists, indeed with many of the future leaders of the Revolution. The Tsarist policy upon arrest and trial was often to give people a choice of exile to Siberia or to transfer their sentence out of the country altogether. Either choice would get them away from the ability to make trouble in the major population centers, especially the capital, which is where decisive action took place.

Many of those sent to Siberia in Tsarist times managed to escape and make their way to Western Europe. There the paths of future revolutionaries crossed. They shared the refugee life, organizing, talking, writing, editing, study circles, planning, and plotting. These were significant experiences, binding, bonding, and also dividing where there were disagreements, as there were many.

Time in Siberia left one kind of mark, time in Switzerland another. People differed in resources and degrees of privation and hardship. The police did watch them, as there were spies and double agents. They generated networks, plans of action for the home front, and coordination with their European counterparts. They argued and debated.

Switzerland was a major meeting place. It was there that Grandma Garvy met Lenin. The Family Legend about that encounter was that Lenin sat on the bed, as there was little space in her bedsitter room. She argued the Menshevik line in favor of constitutional processes; he argued for dictatorship, that revolutions like omelets require that eggs be broken. Was she more bothered by the ideological point or him sitting on her bed? Before I heard the Parvus story, I accepted the family's chuckle of her as fastidious and prudish; afterward, I wondered who was making fun of her and for what reason in spinning that she was a prude. Was it political disagreement or something about her personality (self-righteous?), a spat among exiles in which political disagreement mixed with personal annoyance and frustration?

While in Switzerland, she met Pavel Axelrod, leader of Russian Menshevism, who financially supported his activism by making and marketing kefir, which by happenstance I have come to love and eat daily for breakfast. She met Karl and Luise Kautsky, a famous theoretician of Marxism, with whom she developed a friendship that resumed when she became a refugee in Berlin after 1923.

By the end of the decade, in 1910, Grandma Sophie married Peter Bronstein, another Menshevik activist. She had met him in political activities, part of the network of refugee socialists. Photos of the married couple show them as quite respectably bourgeois, looking like any other prosperous people from the period, far from the image one might have of turn-of-the-century revolutionaries. Their first child, my uncle George, was born in Riga in 1913, to which they had been sent as a political punishment of internal exile. My mother Sylvia was born in Odesa, home of Sophia's parents, in 1915. At the time of the February Revolution in 1917, they were again in political exile, this time in Astrachan, way south near the Caspian Sea. The photos are of the sort that respectable grandparents would surely have wanted to have and savor. Many family

Peter Bronstein Garvy and Sophie Fichman at the time of their wedding about 1910

Sylvia and George, about 1919 in Odesa.

Sonia, Sylvia, George in Odesa about 1919.

photos come from Odesa. Given the conditions of their flight from Europe, it amazes me that my parents have them. These must have been among the precious items jammed into the one suitcase or knapsack able to be taken, though it does appear some items were recovered from friends after the war.

My Social Democratic Namesake, Grandpa Peter Garvy-Bronstein, the anti-Bolshevik allowed to go.

Peter Bronstein, another Menshevik activist, Sophie Fichman's husband, also came from a bourgeois background, albeit a declining one, at least in his father's generation, not as prosperous as the Fichmans.[11]His father (possibly grandfather) came from Grodno in White Russia (now Belarus) and had a business making cigars which seems to have failed; he had a small inheritance that disappeared fast, and the family lived for a time in poverty, nine in a room, eating potatoes and water, and for a time the father became a bookkeeper for a tobacco warehouse. Peter Garvy's passport listed him as a "son of a merchant's son," but it also noted that he was a worker's son, so perhaps this reflects that he was both, depending on the timing of the father's situation. Or it reflected what they thought the regime of the day wanted to hear. Trotsky's last name was also Bronstein. Though

38

So-

I am often asked if we were related, I have never found a connection. Bronstein, like Gourevitch, is a very common Jewish last name in that part of the world.

Garvy's mother came from a well-networked and prosperous bourgeois family: one of her uncles was Abram Yakovlevich Harkavi, a well-known linguist, who became director of the Oriental Languages Division of the Imperial Public Library in Saint Petersburg and refused to convert from Judaism to advance his career but nonetheless attained and retained this position. Grandpa Peter's party name Garvy is likely an adaptation of Harkavi (which in Russian becomes Garkavi). His mother's family seems to have had various cousins, uncles, and aunts in various cities, as over the years, I heard reference to them under a variety of surnames.

Peter Garvy had several sisters and brothers, some of whom appear to have left Russia. My uncle George visited one of them in Switzerland during the 1930s. A brother had emigrated to the US and met the family in New York when they arrived in 1940 but died soon after. On paper, the family network of each Fichman-Garvy grandparent seems large, not unusually so for families of that era, but it did not seem so in my childhood experience. Our family network seemed small, but that may have to do with how few of them made it to the US and kept in contact with each other. My nuclear family had more contact with its refugee colleagues than with its few blood relatives.

Despite their very limited means, the great-grandparents Bronstein instilled a commitment to learning. Overcoming the severe obstacle in Russia of being Jewish, Grandpa Peter managed to get a gymnasium degree in 1899 and eventually managed to use an exam system as an "external student" to get a law degree from Petersburg University in 1911. How he survived economically remains mysterious. It was certainly as a student that he was exposed to the contending ideas that swirled around in those days.

Unable to continue at the University, Garvy read a lot and plunged into political activity right away. In 1900, he encountered the Russian Social Democratic Workers Party, two years after its formation, and joined an illegal branch in Odesa as a party organizer and propagandist. He contributed to a journal called *Yuzhny Rabochii*, or *Southern Workers*, published in Odesa, marking an early involvement with trade unions. This became his defining political identity and most notable element in history, as he is often cited by historians   for his writing on Russian worker associations. Early in his political involvements, Garvy was arrested and sent to prison in Grodno, where he started a hunger strike, which led to a visit by Stolypin, who later became Prime Minister under Czar Nicholas II. Soon after, he was sent to Siberia, taken by train, passing through the famous Moscow prison Butryka, via Samara, and he spent some time in the also famous Alexandrovsky trans-shipment center near Irkutsk (for which we have some photos of him) far beyond the Ural mountains. During a movement of prisoners, he escaped and made his way to Austria and from there to Paris.

In Western Europe, Garvy met the various political emigres who had fled Russia and learned from them about the debates raging among the reformers and activists. He learned of the famous split between Bolsheviks and Mensheviks of 1903 and immediately sided with the Mensheviks. He met Trotsky (whom he disliked), and other important leaders like Vera Zasulic and Leon Deutch, audited some classes, and heard at a meeting Jean Jaures, the very famous French Socialist leader.

Soon he went to Geneva and befriended Pavel Axelrod, the major intellectual leader of Menshevism and Russian socialism. He apparently helped him edit his writings as Axelrod's health was fading. He participated in discussions about the definitions and concepts of socialism, revolution and strategy while these were being formulated and developed. Garvy's reflections[12] on these developments are credited as valuable history --- one author calls it " by far our best sources of information on ….the deliberations and descriptions of the meetings."[13]

In Switzerland, he met up with the party members active there, notably Julius Martov and Theodore Dan, prominent leaders of the Menshevik wing. He also met there Wladmir Woytinsky, who became a lifelong friend, important to political life in Russia, Germany and the US, and vital in the Garvy survival story. Gathered around Axelrod was a circle of people "preparing to return." Among them was Grandma Sophia, so it was possibly there she and Peter first met. Also at those meetings was Trotsky, who was under the strong influence at that time of Parvus. A periodical for workers, *Socialdemocrat*, was started in Geneva and Garvy was put in charge of the press review.

This is the time of Grandma Sophia's participation in a group presided over by Lenin, which sets up the legend of Grandma's unease of Lenin sitting on her bed, and it is the time of her affair with Parvus.

At the end of 1904, Peter returned to Russia using the passport of a German student and using Yuri as a name, taken from an Odesa worker killed in a prisoner's revolt, a name later given to his son George (Yuri in Russian). In Berlin, during his return, he visited the widow of William Liebknecht, one of the founders of the German Social Democratic Party. He went to Kyiv, where he was co-opted by the RSDLP party committee, where Sophia was already a member. He went to a nearby farm to recover his health (having been diagnosed with tuberculosis). He was soon arrested, ordered to Siberia, and permitted somehow to visit Sophia in prison prior to her leaving for a place of exile in the Siberian north.

Garvy again somehow escaped from Siberia. He went to St. Petersburg and Moscow, where he was assigned to the main workers' district (Presnya-Chamovniki) and simultaneously to an organization working among soldiers (at the height of the Russo-Japanese War of 1905) and delegated to attend meetings of the city "duma" (city council). Russia's defeat in that war, the first of a "European power " by an Asian one, produced a major upheaval in Russia. Demonstrators in St. Petersburg approached the Winter Palace, then home of the Tsars and seat of government, today the Hermitage Museum. Seeking to submit protests, they were led by Father Gapon, dressed in flowing church garb. The soldiers obeyed commands to fire. Hundreds were killed.

Peter Garvy, tall fellow with glasses in upper right, in 1903 prison camp probably Alexandrovsky transshipment camp.

This set off demonstrations, strikes and riots across the whole of the Russian Empire. This in turn produced pressure for reforms, and the Tsar authorized some—such as the calling of a Duma, a parliamentary assembly. Nonetheless, the army and police structures held firm, and so it became a "failed revolution." The reforms drifted off; the autocratic system remained.

The revolutionaries studied this failure carefully, seeking to learn from it to make better use of the next occasion. Peter Garvy wrote quite a lot about this period of agitation, especially the role of trade unions, and this writing contributes to the corpus of his renown in the histories of Russia and Russian socialism.[14] He engaged in the political turmoil of that year. Garvy was directed by party leaders to go to Ekaterinoslav (now Dnipro) and was arrested there. Pretending to be his brother (Alexander), who had emigrated to the USA and identified as such at the prison by his mother and sister Nastja, he was freed after three months.

At the London Congress of the RSDLP (May 1907), Garvy was elected by the Mensheviks to the All-Party Central Committee. In December of that year, a general strike broke out in Moscow. The Government repressed it, and Garvy was nearly caught in the round-up. He managed to escape to Odesa. For the next 10 years, he was in and out of prison and exile.

In 1910, he married Sophia Fichman, and they had two children.

George was born in Riga in 1913. Latvia was considered a milder exile granted because of Sophia's pregnancy. My mother was born in Odesa two years later, in 1915, where her parents had moved to be nearer the Fichman family.

Peter Garvy with his brother-in-law Boris (Buka) Fichman, and George and Sylvia Garvy as children; and Buka with the children, about 1918.

When WWI began, Garvy was in Petrograd. Garvy acted as advisor and staff for the Menshevik group in the Duma. He is credited by one source as helping draft the resolution opposing the war effort, which was supported by the Socialist Party as a whole, Bolsheviks and Mensheviks, both despite their divisions.[15] He was aligned as well with what was called "liquidators", those who were in favor of engaging in political activity in existing institutional structures. Working for the War Industries Committee was a logical extension of that activity. At the same time, his criticism of the regime got him again arrested in 1916 and exiled to Cherny Yar, on the lower Volga, near Saratov and Astrachan, which is where he was with his wife and two small children when the Revolution happened in February 1917.

At this moment, we encounter an interesting Family Legend. The Garvys are in remote provincial exile, cut off from news, when a telegram arrives from Buka, Grandma Sophie's brother, in February 1917: "Peter, do not abandon Sophia." They are startled by this. What can it mean? Why would Buka ever imagine Peter would think of abandoning his family? It must mean some great event has happened, and Buka worries Peter will rush off. And/or Buka is speaking indirectly as a signal to avoid words that would draw unwanted attention from local police. The Garvys go to the telegraph operator, who, after much badgering, informs them that, indeed, something important has happened!: the Tsar has been overthrown! They do indeed rush off, but all together as a family. Now desperate to return to the capitol, the Garvys seek to save time by getting a train but to do that, they have to cross the frozen Volga River, which is at risk of starting its seasonal melt. They take the risk and arrange a sleigh carriage to take them across!

The family goes to St. Petersburg, where Garvy plunges into party activities. He was for a time member of the party Central Committee, editor of Rabochaia Gazeta " Workers Newspaper," and on the Presidium of All Russian Central Council of Trade Unions, and on the Petrograd Soviet.

Then in the fall of 1917 comes the Bolshevik seizure of power. Deep disagreements arise over what to do: preserve unity among all socialist factions or fight it out with the Bolsheviks. Garvy is referred to by Boris Nikolaevsky as "a fanatic for organizational unity," prepared to make concessions to critics of the "Revolutionary Defensists" position (fight against Germany so long as the Provisional government protects the democratic gains in the domestic political system won since the fall of the Tsar). But at this moment in October/November 1917, a resolution passed the Menshevik Central Committee by a narrow margin in favor of Martov's call for negotiation with the Leninists for a coalition that would include all socialists. Garvy opposed this plan. It went against the Mensheviks' analysis that Russia was not politically prepared for socialism and would be damaged by responsibility for bourgeois reforms, thereby endangering the revolutionary movement, as had happened after 1905. Garvy and several colleagues resigned from the party's Central Committee over this issue, as he had done before, in 1907 and 1910,[16] also over policy disagreement, and the same disagreement—he opposed getting too close to the Bolsheviks in coalition arrangements.[17]

In the Revolutionary situation of 1917-18, Garvy found himself in a minority position inside the Menshevik group. He decided to go to Odesa to be with his wife and small children. As the Civil War spread, he suddenly found himself isolated, as pro-Bolshevik troops took control of the railways and prevented his return to Petrograd. He plunged into local and regional political life. He became editor of the Southern Worker, a Menshevik newspaper that disagreed with the Bolsheviks but did not advocate armed struggle against them. Odesa soon fell into difficult times. The sailors of the ship Almaz declared themselves in charge of a revolutionary committee that decided to put Garvy and his co-editor Tuchapskii on trial before a special revolutionary tribunal. Garvy appealed for help to the substantial Menshevik organization of the city. On the day of the trial, many workers poured out into the streets, moving toward the building where the trial took place. The prosecutors' case was quite weak, and the pair were acquitted. A group of workers helped them escape from a group of sailors lying in wait to attack. A turbulent time indeed.

Garvy remained in Odesa another two years, enduring occupation by the Austrian Army, then by a Ukrainian nationalist group, then by the French interventionists, and finally by the triumphant Bolsheviks. Garvy continued to play a leadership role with the Menshevik group, which attracted a fair amount of support from local factories. As the political situation deteriorated, he was imprisoned, then allowed to live in Moscow, where he worked in the central office of the consumer cooperative. In July 1922, he was arrested again and sent to Cherdyn, Perm, in the Ural mountains. In late '22, he was told he could leave the country or go back to prison, so he took the family to Berlin.

In retrospect, Garvy seems to have been fortunate. He was allowed to leave, whereas my other grandfather Ber was not. And he was fortunate not to have been executed or killed during the astonishing turmoil of war, armies, factions, and occupations. Many in the opposition were executed, such as Social Revolutionaries. There was a notable Menshevik trial in 1922, but for a time, the lives of many Mensheviks were spared. The escape from the Odesa trial seems miraculous. There were many such local situations where people fell victim to local anger. Could Garvy really not have gotten back to Moscow or Petrograd? Perhaps he felt more useful in Odesa. Did that make him more or

Peter Garvy with son George in 1914

less vulnerable in the line of fire when Bolsheviks began to clean up against the opposition? And then why had Garvy not left earlier, say 1920 or 21? Many of the top Menshevik leadership had already gone: the most famous was Martov in 1920, but also Abramovich and others had gone to Berlin. Martov requested permission to attend a conference and was allowed to go and not return. He was especially close to Lenin, so perhaps that explains his special treatment.

When Martov was dying in Berlin in the early 1920s, Lenin, already suffering from the attempted assassination, wanted Stalin to send money for doctors to help Martov; Stalin told him to have someone else do it, as Martov was a class enemy, and Lenin did have to turn elsewhere to help an old comrade.

By the end of 1922, the situation for Mensheviks had deteriorated, and they were in grave danger. At this point, the paths of my two sets of grandparents diverged in fateful ways. In January of 1923, the Garvys were on a train to Berlin, but the Ber-Gourevitches were still in the USSR.

This a dramatic historical moment for me. What happened? I became consumed with curiosity to look at the Russian archives, without actually great hope I would find revealing information. Then, in 2016, I got permission from Moscow to do so, which I did in January of 2017. What I found substantially altered how I understood the story.

Peter and Sophia Garvy with newly born grandson Sergei in 1941, in N.Y.

The Family Legend, as I had grasped it, had it that Garvy applied and Ber had not. I thought "agency" was in their respective hands. But now, decades later, I learned **both** applied to leave at about the same time. And startlingly, the OGPU said **yes** to both of them, then reversed its decision in the case of Ber. Why did this happen? To understand that, I had to probe the stories of Gourevitch and his wife, Lydia Evseevna Abramovich, more deeply. What got them into trouble first with the Tsars, then with the Bolsheviks?

Endnotes

1 Among the vast number of histories of Russia, I have found a few general ones most useful for preparing the framework leading to the Revolution. In particular, I recommend the books by Orlando Figes, among which A People's Tragedy: The Russian Revolution, 1996; Revolutionary Russia 1891-1991, 2014)

2 The study of comparative politics was for many years built around the question of why some systems evolved toward constitutional orders and others did not. A few examples pointing in varying examples: Carter, G.M, J.H. Hertz and J.C Ranney, Major Foreign Powers, 3rd ed. New York, Harcourt Brace, 1957) was the textbook I had at Oberlin College in 1960, a classic comparing the UK, France, Germany. It stressed constitutions in a formal way, showing strengths and weakness of the constitutional orders of the British Parliamentary system in contrast with the parliamentary instability of the 3rd and 4th French Republics, the weaknesses of the Weimar Republic and the efforts of the post-war German constitution to repair those deficiencies. The discussion has evolved massively since then toward placement of institutions in the context of social and economic systems, and patterns of international influences of economic competition, military rivalry and processes of state formation concerning the formation of administrative structures. Barrington Moore's Social Origins of Dictatorship and Democracy (Boston: Beacon Press, 1966) influenced me deeply; he traced varying developmental patterns to a variety of forms of modernity involving the content and timing of social bargains among socio economic groups managing the processes of industrialization and the commercialization of agriculture. Samuel P. Huntington's Political Order in Changing Societies (New Haven, Yale University Press, 1968) appeared at the same time, and was quite influential but in my view quite misguided and not an analytic model to follow: it stressed the dichotomy of order vs. chaos, which gave no way of sorting out the difference among regimes within each of these categories, thus regimes of great order, such as Stalinist Russia and FDR's America, nor the great variance in trajectories as to how patterns, or trajectories, of reaching an end point of degree of order, themselves differed. Among important recent accounts are Perry Anderson's Lineages of the Absolutist State (London: NLB, 1974) and Daron Acemoglou and James A. Robinson's Why Nations Fail, (New York: Crown Books, 2012. I published some early reflections on these issues in "The International System and Regime Formation: A Critical Review of Anderson and Wallerstein," Comparative Politics 10 (April, 1978). Reprinted, (London: Edward Elgar Publishing Ltd., 1993). "The Second Image Reversed: The International Sources of Domestic Politics," International Organization 32 (Autumn 1978): 881-911

3 The prevailing analysis of the Protocols is that they were forged by the Tsarist Secret Police, the Okrana, in the first decade of the 20th century, and disseminated into various languages over the following years.

4 On a superb portrait of the myriad destinies for Jews arriving in the US, see Irving Howe, World of Our Fathers: the Journey of East European Jews to America and the Life they Found and made. (New York: Harcourt Brace, 1976); this described the history of many of my friends, but not that of my family who came after the great wave of Jewish migration to the US before WW1. .

5 Minczeles, Henri. Histoire générale du Bund: un mouvement révolutionnaire juif. Paris: Editions Austral, 1995.   new edition 2022 . Jack Jacobs (ed.), Jewish Politics in Eastern Europe: The Bund at 100. New York: New York University Press, 2001. Gitelman, Zvi Y. (2003). The Emergence of Modern Jewish Politics: Bundism and Zionism in Eastern Europe. University of Pittsburgh Press.

6 Deborah Hertz, professional biographies of Jewish women, How Jews Became Germans, Yale University Press, 2007; Hertz , Love, Money and Career in the Life of Rosa Luxemburg," in Leslie Morris and Jay Geller, eds. "Three Way Street: German Jews andthe Transnational,' Ann Arbor: University of Michigan press, 2016)

7 Cronin, Nature's Metropolis, for a superb study of Chicago which shows the way the profound interaction of city and country on each other, Norton, 1991.

8 Long before I became interested in narrating this family story, an awareness of the events that shaped my family's destiny influenced my life's research work. Examples include Peter Gourevitch, Politics in Hard Times, Cornell University Press, 1986. "Breaking with Orthodoxy: The Politics of Economic Policy Responses to the Depression of the 1930s," International Organization, no. 1, winter, 1984. 95-130. Italian translation: "La rottura con l'ortodossia: un'analisi comparata delle risposte alla Depressione delgli anni '30", Stato e mercato, no. 11, agosto, 1984. Reprinted in The Disintegration of the World Economy between the Wars, ed. Mark Thomas, 1994; "The Second Image Reversed: The International Sources of Domestic Politics," International Organization 32 (Autumn 1978):881-911 (Translated into Spanish:"La segunda imagen invertida: las fuentes internacionales de las politicas domestica", Revista Zona Abierta 1996, 74: 21 - 68. 1996.; (reprinted in Theories of International Relations, David Baldwin,ed. Ashgate 2008. "The International System and Regime Formation: A Critical Review of Anderson and Wallerstein," Comparative Politics 10 (April, 1978). Reprinted, (London: Edward Elgar Publishing Ltd., 1993);"International Trade, Domestic Coalitions and Liberty: Comparative Responses to the Crisis of 1873-1896," Journal of Interdisciplinary History VIII (Autumn

1977). Reprinted as Chapter 5 in International Political Economy, Perspectives on Global Power and Wealth, Second Edition, Jeffry Frieden and David Lake, eds., New York, NY: St. Martin's Press, Inc.

9   By odd coincidence, Astrachan is also the last name of my older son's wife.

10 Bertram Wolfe, Three Who Made A Revolution, Cooper Square Press, 1948.

11 A short biography of Garvy can be found Abraham Ascher in the volume of Garvy's writings . Peter A. Garvi, Zapiski Sotsial Demokrata (1906-1921). (Notes of a Social Democrat). Newtonville, Ma: Oriental Research Partners, 1982. Russian Institute, ,Columbia University, Russian Archival Series, No. 1 Leopold Haimson, ed.

12 Early in his life Peter Bronstein started to write poetry, and a collection was published when he turned 60 as "Gorki Svet," (Bitter Flowers).

13 Ibid, p. vii.

14 Peter Garvy, Memoirs of a Social Democrat (Vospominaniya of a Social Democrat) (New York: Grenich Printing Corp. 1945). For example, he is cited 11 times by Leonard Schapiro, in The Communist Party of the Soviet Union (New York: Random House, 1960) with most references to his Memoirs and the development of party organization and Menshevik ideas about mass organization.

15 Schapiro, loc. Cit, p. 144. This of course got them into more trouble with the Tsarist police.

16 Galili, Ziva , The Menshevik Leaders in the Russian Revolution: Social Realities and Political Strategies, (Princeton: Princeton University Press, 1989), p 409. For valuable information on Garvy and Ber see, Vera Broido's book, herself the daughter of of prominent party activists, and old enough to have shared exile under both the Tsars and the Bolsheviks, Lenin and the Mensheviks: the Persecution of Socialists under Bolshevism, Hunts, England: Gower House, 1987. Vladmir N. Brovkin, The Mensheviks after October: Socialist Opposition and the Rise of the Bolshevik Dictatorship, Ithaca: Cornell University Press, 1987).

17 See the discussion of the Foreign Delegation disputes during the exile period, told in considerable detail by Liebich, op cit.

Chapter 3

Troublemakers

Jailtime—First the Tsars, then the Bolsheviks

Of all the relatives I most wish to have met, it would indeed be Grandfather Boris Nahumovich Ber-Gourevitch. He was, after all, my direct ancestor, my dad's dad. He represented a political alternative within the Socialist movement to my other grandfather, the one who got us to the US. I feel a need to dialog with Boris, though I really feel a need to converse with both of them. Peter Garvy has left many writings and eyewitnesses who went west and wrote about him.

About Boris, I know fewer people who knew him. He was also the leader of the Gourevitch clan of his generation and, generally, a leader of some kind, as I can feel from the way he was talked about and referred to. Perhaps this was from the family loyalty, which seems to be a strong component of Russian culture. This family was broken apart by politics, my father ripped away from his parents, the brothers from each other, and yet there seemed to be a lot of interest in each other. Boris was not allowed to lead his own life, either in Russia-USSR, or in exile along with the others in Western Europe. And there is something about the personality that shines through the letters Boris wrote to my family and my father. As I read these I found myself in dialog with him on family matters, not politics—"Why did you say this, or that, to my father, he's only ten, or a teenager, or a young adult"—reproducing in short my own experiences as a father, dialog across four generations—my children, me, my father and the grandpa I presumably never met. I have a sense of him from reading and hearing about him, but still actually meeting someone is still needed to confirm impressions. But I am running too fast. There will be time to come back to this.

Boris' fate embodies the core themes of this inquiry. Just why did Grandpa Garvy get out but not Grandpa Ber? It is the mystery that tears at me for an explanation. It is that which made my Dad a de facto orphan and deprived me of a band of relatives. A self-regarding concern, for sure, but it tells us something about police states, about threats to freedom, and about how people escape and how they and their families deal with it.

Grandpa Boris was born in what is today Belorusia near the small town of Mogliev in 1889. He was the oldest of six children, born to Nachum Gourevitch, a Rabbi, and his wife, Styssia. Not long after, the Rabbi moved the family to Ekaterinoslav ("Catherine's city"), today Dnipro. As noted earlier, Gourevitch is a common Jewish name in this part of the world. It derives from Horowitz, familiar to middle Europeans, changed because Russian has no "H" and turns it into "G", as in Shakespeare's famous play "Gamlet."

A family photo shows Great Grandfather Nachum with a great white beard, eyes looking downward, and fingers on a large open book. Family Legend has it that during a pogrom, attackers burst in and seeing him like that, suddenly stopped, saying, "Hush, this is a holy man in prayer." Could this story describe a real occurrence? Could the image of a worshipful Jewish man stop a band fevered with the intent of destruction? I don't know, but it is a story I heard told many times in the family. The photo of him in prayer provides a compelling image that gives plausibility to it. There were many pogroms in this part of the world, and he did not get killed. But is this a Family Legend or a real event? The Rabbi's son, my Grandpa Boris, married and had a son, my father, Alexander, who was born on 5 May 1916 in Ekaterinoslav. The mother died in childbirth. Her name was Rosalie Sac Chac, the

Great Grandfather Nahum and Great Grandmother Styssia Gourevitch (left) Great Grandfather Nahum Gourevitch

name that appears on my parents' marriage certificate in Paris, 1938, until the fall of 2022, the only document I have that states this fact. Grandmother Styssia found goats' milk to feed baby Shura, as he was called, and took care of him. Russia was already in the second year of WW I, and the Revolution came soon after, followed by the Civil War. My father remembers hunger from the famine caused by the turbulence of this period; he recalls eating plaster from the wall, so desperate was he for calcium. Years later, Dad had lots of allergies, surely connected to his terrible nutrition at this time; I would think about this when my sons were born and the care we took to watch their exposure to allergens in the diet! No strawberries, nuts, or other "dangerous" things before a certain age. My brother and I grew up without allergies. We once walked in shorts and no socks through a field and were told afterward it was full of poison ivy. Neither of us got it. My children seem to be allergy free as well!

Before the Revolution of 1917, Boris had been active in anti-Tsarist politics. He joined the RSDLP as a Menshevik in 1905 and got arrested in 1906, 1907, and 1912. He spent 26 months in prison and 5.5 years in exile.[1] He was active mostly in southern Russia, today Ukraine.

When WWI started, Grandpa Boris was in Scandinavia and returned to Russia in 1916, crossing the same border at Sweden/Finland that Lenin was to use a bit over a year later to reach the Finland Station and promote the Bolshevik Coup of 1917. After the Revolution began following the overthrow of the Tsar in February/ March of 1917, Boris became a member of the Executive Committee of the Kharkiv Council of Workers and Soldiers and a member of that city's RSDLP. He is noted for participating in various important meetings In the political debates of the time. As the Revolution unfolded, he pushed hard for unity among the Socialists. In April of 1917, while attending a meeting in Petrograd, he became part of the secretariat of a group calling for a party unification congress, criticizing Lenin's position of driving hard for Bolshevik primacy on the grounds that this could prove fatal to the progress of the Russian Revolution.[2] At the same time, Grandpa Boris called for the exploration of association with Leninists on the basis of a social democratic platform. At a May 1917 meeting, he aligned with Martov. He was a delegate to the First All-Russian Congress of Soviets on June 12 and spoke on behalf of a

Menshevik draft resolution "on war." He was elected a member of the All-Russian Central Executive Committee of the Socialist Party and urged his group to leave the coalition government and support a radical program of domestic and foreign policy. He opposed the Bolshevik coup of October. (The dates are confusing as Russia had not yet switched calendars, so we think of the Bolshevik coup as November, but in Soviet Russian culture, it is October). In December 1917, Boris became a member of the Central Committee of the Menshevik group.

In 1918, Ber joined the Central Committee of the Ukraine RSDLP, and in April 1920, a member of the national Central Committee of the Mensheviks. For a time, he was sent to work for the Menshevik-dominated government in Georgia, but after the Bolsheviks took that country over, he then went to work as a statistician for the state administration in the Gosplan. This is the only position I have seen noted from which he may have earned an income!

With respect to the political arguments of the day, he is described at this point as on the extreme left of the Menshevik group.[3] At an August 1920 meeting in Kharkiv, it was noted that Ber wanted "to soften the tone of the struggle against Bolshevism."[4] In this regard, he differed from Garvy, who was a vigorous critic of Bolshevik behavior. How much to cooperate—was it possible, would it produce results— was a critical defining point of ideological cleavage. Most Mensheviks wanted an all-socialist alliance. Many thought it was not possible to do it with the Bolsheviks, given their increasingly harsh prosecution of the opposition to them. Ber kept trying.

Ber's position on the Menshevik left did not, however, protect him from imprisonment. Indeed, his activism may have made him more vulnerable to persecution, as it may have made him more visible and, thereby, more dangerous to the regime. He was arrested in 1920, sent to Georgia, and allowed to return and work in Kharkiv and Moscow. Then an apparently significant arrest was in April 1922 when he was taken in with others who had been delegates at RSDLP meetings. Some were placed in prison, some in concentration camps, some in forced labor. Ber, along with some others, was sent to house arrest in Georgia; he was accused of being a cover for right-wing counter-revolutionary agitation. At about this time, Stalin was active in the harsh treatment of opposition in the South, though I have no evidence if

Stalin was directly involved in anything to do with Ber.

Sometime in about 1920, Grandpa Boris remarried Lydia Ev-seevna Abramovich, an activist in the RSDLP of Kharkiv. She is the stepmother to whom my Dad was very attached, never having known his own birth mother. She is described in a biographical entry as "beloved," which I think translates better as "highly appreciated" or "widely liked" party secretary. Born in Samara to a prosperous Jewish family, she had higher education, including a university in Moscow, though it is not clear she graduated with a specific degree. She worked in the Council of Workers Deputies in Moscow at the time of the October Revolution and from 1918-199 in Kyiv and Kharkov in the Council of Trade Unions. The records note that in June of 1922, she was head of the statistical part in the organizational department of the Central Committee of the All-Russian Union of Educational Work-ers. After her marriage to Ber, her record shows a series of arrests, at times served with Boris, at times not. Her crime was participating in Menshevik activities, as was his.[5]

With the April 1922 arrest, Ber was sent to the Butyrka prison in Moscow, then to Yaroslav prison. In jail, Ber helped form a "colo-ny" of leaders from the Menshevik Central Committee. He argued against participating in forthcoming elections but also against refus-ing to participate in future agreements with the Bolsheviks. On June 27, 1922, he was sentenced to two years in central Asia as punish-ment for anti-Bolshevik activities. On August 3, his apartment was searched. A handwritten article written by Kuchin that was found in the apartment was subsequently published in the *Socialist Bulletin*, the Berlin-based publication of the Menshevik group in exile, and this publication was used in evidence against Ber as proof of his illegal contact with the RSDLP "Foreign Delegation." In October 1922, Ber was listed as a member of the Central Committee of the RSDLP.

Then, in the summer and fall of 1922 come the momentous deci-sions about exile. While Garvy receives his visa to leave, Ber does not. And in May 1923, we find papers in his file that say the decision from the previous fall to allow him to leave was a "mistake."[6] It is not clear Ber himself is ever shown this document. This reversal from yes to no is applied both to Ber, well-known as a left Menshevik, and to B.O. Bogdanov, an important leader on the right of the Menshevik group.

This historiography challenges quite severely the Family Legend as transmitted by oral history from parents to children concerning the Grandpa's Fates. To repeat, "The Family Legend" narrative was that Garvy chose to leave, and Ber chose to stay, at least until it was too late, a difference in the choice made because of ideological differences between them. The "agency" lay at least in part with the grandfathers, according to Legend. According to documents, the agency did not lay with them but with the authorities.

What did happen, and can the legend be integrated with the facts?

So there is tension between the Family Legend and the Archival Data. Could I resolve it? I was very eager to find out. Here, I will take you down the journey of my exploration of the "data," such as I can find it, the facts as they exist, or as I am allowed to see. The process of discovery is part of the story and certainly contributes to our ability to evaluate these facts and to come to some judgment of interpretation. The evidence is not so overwhelming, and the room for differing interpretations is large. Conclusions are shaped by frames that come from various places. Where you were when you started the journey of exploration, where you went, what you saw, whom you talked to, why you wanted to know, and your political context at the time of writing all influence your conclusion. And they are part of the story, so let me share them with you.

Endnotes

1. Details on Boris can be found in A.P. Nenarokov. Источ.: Меньшевики в 1917 году. В 3-х томах, 4-х книгах. Под общей редакцией З.Галили, А.Ненарокова, Л.Хеймсона. М.: 1994- 1997; Меньшевики в большевистской России. 1918-1924 гг. в 4-х томах. Ответ. редакторы З.Галили, А.Ненароков. М.: 1999-2004.(Sources: Mensheviks in 1917. The 3 volumes, 4 books. Edited Z.Galili, A.Nenarokov, L.Heymson. M.: 1994-1997; The Mensheviks in Bolshevik Russia. 1918-1924 pp. 4 vols. Answer. Editors Z.Galili, A.Nenarokov. M.: 1999-2004.). A.P. Nenarokov Pravi Menshevism (Right Menshevism (Moscow, 2011)

2. Nenarokov, loc cit *Mensheviks in 1917, p 389.*

3. Nenarokof, loc cit *Mensheviks in 1919-1920. p. 423, 546;*

4. (ibid. p. 540).

5. Archives of the FSB, Case H-46320 "The case on charges of Abramovich Lydia Yevseyevna, Basia Naumovna Gurevich and Frederika Evseevny (1922)" Basia is sister of Boris, and Frederika is sister of Lydia. F. 580813. Case P-43046 / General Investigation Fund. Applies to several Mensheviks at once Resolution Gurevich-Ber number 31424. Contains reference to letter Ber's mother Styssia writes to Trotsky asking to meet him with a noted "refused".

6. The notes from Memorial, St. Petersburg, specify that on Nov. 18 1922, the NKVD allowed him to go leave the USSR, but that in May 1923 it is denied, http://scherbina.net/ukazatel_b.htm;;   Бер (Бер, Гуревич) Борис Наумович (1889–1939)

Chapter 4

"Why Him, Not Me?"

Archives and Experts, Personal Ties and Party Interests

In the summer of 2016, as I sought to understand the divergent fates of my two grandfathers, my state of knowledge of the "facts" was both wide and limited. I had the oral material on which was based the Family Legend, thus conversation as I remembered it from various family members, primarily my parents, but also from other family and friends. There were secondary sources, such as histories of Russia and the USSR, Germany, France, and the World Wars.

Then there was a precious source of primary materials in the letters written by Boris Ber, from 1924-37 to his family in Berlin and Paris, though these tell little about the events of 1922-23. There are also a number of memoirs written by people who experienced some of these events or by their children. There are archives worked on by profes- sional historians or volunteers in various countries. And, of course, there is literature, art and film, which conveys its own insights. But with the exception of the family oral tradition, none of these sources was specific enough to the events of 1922-23 to tell me just what hap- pened to account for the divergent fates of these two individuals, Peter Bronstein Garvy and Boris Ber Gourevitch.

For that, I needed and wanted to see the Soviet-era archives now in the hands of the government of the Russian Federation. Some of this was available to me by the miracle of the internet and the re- markable work of the Russian group *Memorial*. This institution came into being with the fall of the Communist Dictatorship after 1991 to reconstruct and remember the millions killed in the Soviet- Stalinist period. *Memorial* researchers have gone through the archives of the

OGPU-KGB, constructed biographies of thousands of people and, miraculously, put all of this material online. And this is one of the institutions that Putin dismantled in 2021-2022 in his drive to quash diversity of views and institutional autonomy. It is this very institution which has received the Nobel Peace Prize in 2022. I had known of this resource, and so when I began my work several years ago, I used it to track down material about my grandparents. My Russian is rusty, a polite euphemism, but I could figure some things out. Crucially, I know the Cyrillic alphabet, so the Moscow subway does not intimidate me as I have learned it complicates visits for so many people. I can admire the Metro's sweep and artwork and still find my way around. The challenge in using Memorial materials was to be sure how they listed Ber and Gourevitch as well as Garvy and Bronstein and to be sure I had the right ones. Both Gourevitch and Bronstein are very common Russian names and can be spelled in various ways. Fortunately, I knew the patronymics and dates of birth and so could sort my lot from other similar ones.

Quickly I found entries to both grandparents and the two grandmothers. Using another miracle, "Google Translate," I got rough transcriptions. Needing deeper help, I hired a UCSD graduate student, Olga Lazitskaya, of Russian origin. She learned that *Memorial* is decentralized, so that there is more than one website. The one from St. Petersburg yielded the surprise: an exit of November 1922 says Ber is given permission to "transfer his exile abroad." Then when he actually made efforts to do this, he was delayed and then refused exit in May of 1923.[1]

This is what stunned me. I have already shared this with you, but it was at this moment that I saw the documentation for the first time. Permission given. Permission denied. And, even more amazing, these decisions occurred at about the same time as the Garvy family was allowed to leave, that is, also the fall of 1922. I had never thought much or asked about the precise date of the Garvy departure (January 1923). Now I realized it mattered. The two grandparents were being "processed" at the same historical moment. The timing raised some interesting issues of interpretation: If Garvy was so anti-Bolshevik, why had he not left earlier, as had some of the other Menshevik leaders? And if the files were processed at the same time, why the difference in treatments?

Secondary sources suggest some ideas about answers. Several volumes have been published of papers from this period—letters, articles, tracts. They show Ber to have been quite active in communication with fellow Mensheviks within Russia and with the Foreign Delegation of Mensheviks in Berlin, all this in the period while he was seeking to leave the USSR. So, suggested Olga, my research assistant, this activism surely irritated the OGPU. Perhaps they saw him as a troublemaker they did not wish to lose control of. Garvy had been less disruptive to Bolsheviks. Hence they were less threatened by loosening him amidst the group in Berlin and lost little by no longer having him under close surveillance in the USSR. This seemed very plausible and fit the secondary material Olga was reading.

Now my curiosity intensified greatly. I wanted to know more. Olga's theory was shrewd. What did the archives actually say about it? In Moscow, could I go to the FSB, as the OGPU or KGB is now called, look at the dossiers and find out what happened? Perhaps I could meet specialists at *Memorial* and other historians who knew the history better than I did.

As luck would have it, at about this time, I was invited to a conference in Moscow in January 2017. Not keen especially to be there in winter, I accepted the invitation to give myself the excuse of getting to the archives. But how was I to get access to the FSB-controlled files of the OGPU-KGB?

I made inquiries to colleagues and friends as to how one accessed these files. One writes I was told, for permission to see files for specific relatives. This could even be done by email! It was easy, provided you could prove a relationship to the person whose file you requested. How fluid and modern! Email, no less. Modern communication technology allows you to enter the mouth of the "beast," as I thought of the Soviet secret police, even if the regime technically no longer existed.

Yet for me, a substantial obstacle flared up right away: How could I provide proof of a blood relationship to Boris Ber? The turbulence of my family's experience meant my parents lacked official papers. My own father had no birth certificate. He was born in wartorn and ravaged Ekaterinoslav-Dnipro, from which it would be hard to find documents. (I just discovered in the fall of 2022 via a research assistant in Ukraine that in the Dnipro Jewish Registry, there does exist a birth certificate for my father, but I did not know this at the time). My parents arrived in the US in 1940 with only a backpack of possessions, fleeing the Nazis. They (on both sides) had been stripped of Soviet citizenship in the early 1930s as enemies of the Soviet state. Lacking country-specific documents, they obtained Nansen passports (papers developed to help people like them who had become stateless). I found in my mother's records their wedding license of Paris 1938, which mentioned his father and natural mother and my Dad's date of birth. The emergency entrance visa to the US from 1940 does not show grandparent lineage, nor does the record of naturalization papers some years later. None of these documents would be sufficient for the FSB of 2016/17. How to prove Boris was my grandfather, despite all the letters and photographs I had?

Then, unexpectedly a Russian contact sent a most valuable document which had both a big practical effect on my immediate need and revelatory information about the past. I had been in correspondence with a Russian historian for two years, Alla Morozova.[2] She and another colleague TA Semenova had been working on materials related to my grandfather for a number of years as part of their project on resistance to Soviet authority. They had discovered several documents. One of them was a handwritten certificate dated October 31, 1928, signed by the head of the district administrative department with the following content: (N.B. the birth date of 22 April is related to the old calendar; the new calendar date is 5 May)

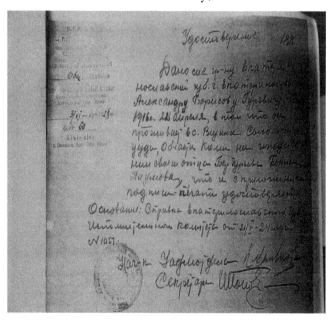

A request dated 1928 by Grandpa Boris to the OGPU asking them to provide my father a passport to go study in Berlin. This request was approved, stamped, dated, showing quite clearly the names and relationships between Alexander, known in the family by his Russian diminutive, Shura, and his father Boris. I had known there was talk of Dad leaving to go study, that eventually he did so in 1931, but I had not realized how early Boris had initiated the steps to effectuate it by obtaining permission in 1928. Did my father know of this when he was 12 years old? I have no memory of him mentioning it, nor was there any reason for him really to know about it.

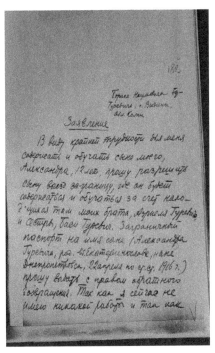 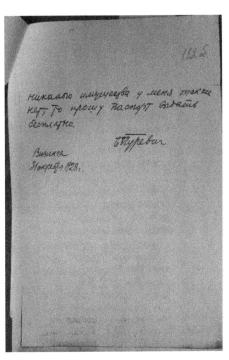

We had often wondered why permission was granted for him to leave in 1931. Now I realize the permission date was already 1928. On the other hand, something given could always be taken away. So "yes" in 1928 could be no in 1931, as "yes" in 1922 for Boris to leave turned into "no" in 1923.

In 2016, a copy of this letter proved sufficient for the FSB as proof that I was properly connected to Boris Ber Gourevitch, and permission to look at the documents about my grandfather came promptly back marked approved. These exchanges happened via email. Again, it astonished me that something as medieval as the "Inquisition"—like the OGPU-KGB-FSB was using such modern communication techniques. I did feel uneasy sending them a scan of my passport as they required. What an invitation for identity theft! But I did all that, filling out the forms with the help of my American and Moscow-based research assistants.

Back came the email approval of my request to look at the archives of Boris Ber Gourevitch, and off I went! As my Russian fluency was not good enough, I hired a colleague who taught in Moscow, an excellent research assistant, a professional historian who worked at Moscow University, Natalia Volodina, a specialist in 19th and 20th century Russia.

Moscow: Lubyanka Prison and Detsky Mir

("Children's World"): 1922, 1966, 2017

Armed with permission to visit the archives, I arranged to meet Volodina on the steps of the main entrance of "Detsky Mir" (Children's World, the Russian equivalent of the once ubiquitous American chain Toys-R-Us), which faces the infamous Lubyanka Prison, where I knew various of my relatives had spent time along with countless others. It is in front of this huge building, originally built to house an insurance company, where stood the statute of the notorious Felix Dzerzhinksy (creator of the Cheka, which became the GPU inside the NKVD), which toppled when the Communist regime fell in 1991. This happened to be the very spot where I had last seen my grandmother Lyalya when we met in 1966 to walk around that part of Moscow. So I felt considerable emotion as we began our task, a mixture of aversion to the police, some trepidation, fond memories of family, a sense of history with this building as a witness to so much political terror, and some excitement of anticipation as to what I might find.

The archives turned out to be in an annex building, not the Lubyanka itself. We entered a small room, with desks, like a library reading room. Volodina spoke with the staff, who were quite friendly, and, as this had been scheduled by appointment, within minutes, five fat binders arrived, and we began looking through them. There was a lot of material. Alas, it soon became clear that within each binder, there were a number of pages stapled shut. It is 100 years after the events in question, but the current rulers still do not want to allow full access. There is information seen as somehow too sensitive for family members to see. Why? The reason, I was told by a seasoned scholar, seems that they wish to protect the descendants of people in the files, that one of their ancestors may have done something that would anger a relative looking at the file. Could it be that it would be publicly embarrassing to the security services even after several generations that it had done something controversial, like ship people to concentration camps? It could be learned that some specific order to do this could be traced to a specific person. This is speculation because one is not told.

Photocopies cannot be made of certain pages, and no photographs can be made of the folders. I wanted a photo of the binders, at least, to show what they looked like, to show family and friends. This was not allowed. So, in short, they consist of big albums, the kind that tie shut, that I had come to associate with European bureaucracies, as I had seen in France in my work there, but not in the US.

Volodina and I opened the binders and started leafing through them.[3] We found the memo which gave permission in November 1922 for Grandpa Boris to leave USSR for two years, then return. It seemed odd to expect a return, but that is how it was written. No one applies to emigrate! Technically they are given permission to transfer the sentence from prison within the country to outside it, to have parole abroad in our terms. The logic is to ban them from political activity in important places within the country, but the presumption is they wish to return to life in the political center! A few pages later in the file, there are passport applications to leave Russia for Boris and Lydia and visa applications for travel to Germany.

Then, we found a most stunning letter. March 1923, hand-written by Grandpa Boris, addressed to OGPU. The letter observes:

"It has been several months now since the permission to leave USSR was given, and still no visa enabling this has been provided. Why,"(he wonders), "is this the case?" (And he notes quite pointedly) "Why is it that I have not received a visa when that permission has been given to Peter Bronstein Garvy who has in fact left."

How amazing to find, combined in one letter, in Grandpa Boris's own handwriting, the statement of his situation and the reference to my OTHER grandfather. I had always known they knew each other as party activists. I had heard, Family Legend, that while taking a Russian-style sauna—after time in the heat, one plunged into snow or cold water—Grandpa Peter observing the hirsute character of Grandpa Boris (a feature common to the Gourevitch side of the family) commented, "Now, I believe Darwin." That Boris refers to Peter in his letter shows how fast news traveled and that the cases mingled in the minds of the applicants. Did it mingle in the minds of the decision-makers? In general terms, certainly yes, as they were dealing with the Menshevik opposition. In specific terms, we cannot be certain as the files do not refer to them together. No answer to Boris's question appears in the archives.

Then there is the matter of the dates, the timing. Until now, I had only vaguely wondered why Garvy had delayed leaving till January 1923. But now that it mattered, it was worth pushing on. If he was so anti-Bolshevik, why did he wait so long to leave? I realized I had accepted the Family Legend and had never interrogated it on this point.

With this letter in the archives, I realized the timing mattered because the two cases crossed in history. This information spurred me to dig deeper. I went back to my Garvy sources. Uncle George notes in a "Memoir" he wrote when in his sixties (thus about 1970), which is now the possession of his daughter Helen.

> "In January of 1923, Peter Garvy is summoned to Moscow from prison or exile in the Urals and told he has 24 hours to get out or go back to prison. So they left." [4]

They were given a few days to get things sorted out, but they left as soon as possible. Grandpa Peter, whatever his politics, did not leave earlier because he could not: he was in prison. Then at the end of 1922, they accepted his request to transfer his sentence out of the country. The archives say this was approved in November, and the actual departure was in January 1923.

Sitting in the archive room in Moscow, I continued to turn pages. A bit farther along in the dossier, I found another document that chilled me. It said, "the decision to let Boris Ber-Gourevitch leave was a mistake." This was a bureaucratic memo, similar in looks to the one which approved the request in November of 1922 to leave. My mediocre Russian skills did make out the Russian word for "mistake," which transliterates as "oshipka." I tugged the sleeve of Volodina. "Does this say what I think it says?" Indeed it did. The author of that memo was an official, different from the person who wrote the first affirmative authorization.

I realized I had erred in not asking for the Garvy file. I had assumed there was less to learn, as we knew his story from a variety of sources: he had published his memoir, and people had written about him in New York when he died in 1944. Now that I saw the two stories were temporally intertwined, and that Ber's letter refers explicitly to Garvy about their fates in 1922/23, I realized I needed to see Garvy's file. As I was soon leaving Moscow, I arranged with Volodina to give her power of attorney so she could request the Garvy files.

In March 2017, Volodina sent me copies of the Garvy materials, which she had examined in Moscow. In July of 1922, he had been sentenced to two years under "select detention in custody" to Cherydn, Perm province, in the Ural mountain region, for anti-Soviet activities. The file discusses the possibility of transferring his sentence to exile out of the country.

The author of a note to the file, Syrtsov, comments that he knew Garvy when they were in Tsarist prison together in 1915.

> "Bronstein {Garvy} is almost blind, and the kidneys require constant medical care. Asks to replace the link in Cherdyn with deportation abroad. The order is made about it. But the exit will be allowed to Moscow only after receiving a visa from Germany. Getting a visa is a long thing, and he, in the condition of his health, can die three times before he leaves Cherdyn and from Russia. Another problem is also complicated by the fact that his wife and a couple of guys want to go with Garvy. They also need to think about visa and travel arrangements. But this can be done only when there is a certainty that they are leaving..."

Through her ministerial German ties, Bronstein's wife can very quickly obtain a German visa. I appeal to you with a request to allow Bronstein's arrival in Moscow so that within two weeks, they, having liquidated their property and received visas, go abroad... I am sure that under the present state of his health and marital status, he will not be up to politics. He could be kept under arrest for two weeks. "

> I request your order about the telegraphic permission to leave Garvy for Mos-
> cow because of the dangerous illness of his daughter ({my mother Sylvia}
> scarlet fever in severe form). With comradely greetings, Syrtsov".[5]

To the author of this note, at least, Garvy was not dangerous to the
regime, so why not let him leave? On the other hand, why do it? Sick
and undesirables are often released from regimes, as Cuba did in the
1990s.

Compared to Ber, one could see Garvy as not a threat and about
to die.

Or is this the rationale provided by a friend, Syrtsov, who had
done jail time with Garvy in the Tsarist period? Is Ber treated differently because he was not fortunate enough to have his file handled
by a former friend? Does the illness really matter in the decision?
Garvy was in his early 40s at this point. He did have eye problems that
plagued him constantly. During their time in Berlin in the 1920s, the
Menshevik group raised money, despite ideological disagreements, to
pay for an operation on Garvy's eyes. Was he really dying in 1922, as
alleged by Syrtsov? He lived until 1944, into his mid-sixties, dying
of a heart attack, which was not unusual for people of his age at that
time. FDR, who received far more medical attention, died at a similar
age. Or was this an excuse used by a friendly manager of his file? We
know that the relationships between Mensheviks and Bolsheviks mattered. There are many allusions to it. At about this time, the governing
leadership circulated a directive criticizing Bolsheviks for being too
friendly to their former Menshevik brethren! Did that message strike
the manager of Ber's file and bounce off the consciousness of Garvy's?

What of the reference to my grandmother Garvy's "connections"
and "the dangerous illness of the daughter?" Did the connections refer
to family, marriage or party? My mother Sylvia was, in fact, quite sick
with scarlet fever. Her mother's connections to the Kremlin pharmacy
were via a cousin, who was married to Portuguès, an important political figure. Grandma was from a more prosperous family than Peter
Garvy, but not a grandly wealthy one, nor were either of them so high
up in party circles. Is this an oblique reference here to Grandma Sophie's relationship with Parvus, or did that not matter so much at this
point, or even a negative, and was it so widely known or even relevant

in lower party ranks? Is it a more general remark that the Garvys knew many people in the Menshevik–Bolshevik circles, including Lenin, or to the tight bonds that formed in a Siberian prison in Tsarist days, or exile in Western Europe, that still operated as a network? Lenin sending money to the ailing Martov in Berlin is a famous example; my grandma getting medicine or visas, in this case, a smaller one.

Or is this not so important? Was it connections that mattered? Perhaps even more important was the historical accidents of who processed the files of the two grandfathers. Perhaps more important still, was it political concerns of the Bolshevik Party toward these two individuals? How dangerous to the Bolshevik project were these two figures, inside the country or outside it?

Boris could not leave because they would not let him, not because of his own will. The Family Legend about grandparental choice has been shaken. More information and reflection are needed.

Digging Deeper to an Expert's Explanation: A Moving Encounter in Moscow.

At this point, I found myself with contending theories on why one Grandfather was allowed to leave and not the other not. Let us review them. At the most individual level, there is the "accident" of who processed the file. Grandpa Peter, this is the friend from Tsarist days whose signature is on the file of his case. In the case of Grandpa Boris, we have no similar indication of a linkage to him, though it may have existed. So a particular person may have been inclined to treat the file one way or another, either for personal or ideological reasons. Change the person who processed the file, and the outcome changes.

Alternatively, the party itself could have been changing. Policy toward the opposition was hardening. By 1922, a number of people had left the USSR. Other people were put on trial, and still others were condemned to prison. Dissent continued to be stamped out as the civil war ended with the Bolsheviks victorious. This explains the rising difficulty of leaving but does not suffice to explain the different treatment of specific individuals. It may account for differences within the police bureaucracy; as the party line hardened, people adopted the new line at different rates, which takes back to the accident of individual interpretation.

Many theories, limited evidence. Unsure what to conclude, I

turned to an expert, a famous historian, a specialist of this period and specifically of this group of people.

Albert Pavlovich Nenarokov

The visit to the archives with Natasha Volodina was on Monday, January 14, 2017. On that Wednesday, January 16, I went to see the leading Russian specialist on the Mensheviks and dissidents of the period: Albert Pavlovich Nenarokov, Senior Researcher at the Institute of History at the Russian Academy of Sciences. We met in his office, and upon entering, I noted a sign on the wall "Boris Nicolaevsky Archive." Nicolaevsky is a famous Menshevik I heard my parents talk about. He was on the same list of people who escaped France in 1940 as my Garvy grandparents and parents and was on the same boat with them from Lisbon to New York in October 1940. He was noted for gathering masses of documents, getting them out of Europe, and creating important research centers, among them one at the Hoover Institute in Stanford, where many years ago I had seen letters from both Grandfathers. It startled me to see this skillful operator had left his name in the research hearts of the two historical antagonists of the 20th century, Moscow and Stanford!

Nenarokov has edited many volumes of papers on the Mensheviks and people of the 1917-1920s period and is thus a well-known authority. Many of these volumes were co-edited with Zivi Galili, an important historian based at Rutgers University in New Jersey. I had written to her in 2014 as I started the process of tracking down more information on the grandfathers, and I wrote to her again about how to access the archives. Now, another amazing coincidence, for it turned out she knew my close childhood friend and distant cousin, Irene Etkin Goldman, daughter of my parents' close friends who did the same migration as they—Russia–Berlin–Paris–New York. At the Spanish border, the Etkins had to hike over the Pyrenees, whereas my family amazingly were able to cross by train—(that escape moment will be examined when we reach that part of the journey). Irene knew Galili from various activities in New Jersey. Fortunately for me, Irene had decided to come with me to Moscow. She had her own network of contacts in the Russian art community, spoke fluent Russian, and was interested in getting information about her Menshevik grandfather, who had died in Berlin when Irene's father was young and about

whom she knew little. Galili and our Memorial contact, Alla Morozova, helped us arrange an appointment with Nenarokov. He requested from me some copies of Grandpa Peter's writings, in particular his
big autobiography, "Memoirs of a Social Democrat, "[6] published in
New York after his death by my grandmother. Irene carried with her
as well a large box of books Galili wished to convey to Nenarokov.[7]

Our encounter was quite emotional. Nenarokov expressed amaze-
ment and pleasure at meeting the grandson of people he had studied.
When I looked around his office, I saw many photos on the wall under
the heading of the Nickolaevsky Collection, and two, in particular,
leaped out to my eyes, as I was familiar with both of them: one was a
photo I knew, of Mensheviks in front of a train in Berlin, preparing
to leave for a socialist congress in 1928; I saw my grandparents Garvy
among the group. Another photo showed a seated elderly couple with
young teenagers behind them, and I knew this photo also: it showed
the famous Russian socialist Pavel Axelrod with his wife, and behind
them, my mother and her brother George Garvy. So I saw how rooted
my family history was in this Russian historian's work.

Our conversation began. Nenarokov was most gracious. We ex-

Photo in Nenarokov's office, is also in the Leibich book and my family albums; Grandma Garvy is third
woman from left in front row; Grandpa Garvy is second from left in second row on steps, with lots of
hair 1928.

The photo with my uncle and mother with Kautsky and another with Axelrod is in the next chapter.

changed warm greetings and then set off to work.

Why, I asked him, did he think the Bolsheviks did not let Ber go but allowed Garvy to leave? Because, Nenarokov answered quickly, Ber was too important. Ber was a member of the Central Committee of the Russian Social Democratic Labor Party. As such, he was a leading Menshevik, among the most important who remained in what was now the USSR. This would make him a nodal point in a network of communications among the Mensheviks, people writing to him, and to whom he wrote, in the USSR and abroad. By keeping him in the USSR, the Bolsheviks would be able to watch through the network of his activities what the dissidents were up to. They could monitor more closely what was happening in the opposition ranks. In the Nenarokov-Galili volumes, there are many letters of Ber's correspondence with various people and the OGPU's concern about this activism. The OGPU could also watch the flow of traffic between Ber and Mensheviks outside the country, as Ber was someone involved in that correspondence as well. I wonder if Garvy's being in prison at this time, and being sick, protected him from activism which would have caused him the kind of trouble which affected Ber.

At the same time, Nenarokov wondered, the Bolsheviks may have been concerned that letting Ber go to Berlin would strengthen the "Foreign Delegation." The Moscow leadership was coming to see that the FD was costly to them, whereas earlier, they had ignored or neglected it. The FD was the most knowledgeable source of information outside the USSR about who the Bolsheviks were, what they thought, what they were like, and how to read their publications. It was as if a piece of what became the Politburo in the Kremlin had broken off—former intimate colleagues of the USSR's leadership. The FD had extensive contact with the Socialist parties of Europe and was a major source of information to them about what was going on. The analysis they gave thus shaped European attitudes toward the USSR. To some degree, this affected the Soviet Regime, and containing the FD became of increasingly greater concern to the Moscow leadership. Note that this interpretation stressing the OGPU's negative attitude toward Ber's leadership role was first raised to me by my research assistant, Olga Lazitsky, when she found Nenarokov's biographical essay on Ber[8], as well as other documents. Now I was hearing this view put forth by its author, orally and forcefully!

Ber was seen as active and energetic, thus dangerous. He had published an article in the FD's journal that demonstrated he maintained contacts and influence.[9] Material was found that showed him with extensive contacts in Russia as well as Berlin. There seemed evidence of some effort to form a new node of activists. Ber did not step back in his activism to have a lower profile while waiting for his visa. Was this provocative? Perhaps one can say it did not maximize prudence.

Garvy, by contrast, was less influential in the Menshevik world. He was well known, had occupied various positions, and wrote extensively. He had been on the Central Committee but had resigned several times in protest of various decisions. Having gone to Odesa late in 1917 made him less central to events. His being on the factional Right may have induced the OGPU to let him out: he would be less important inside Russia among people the Bolsheviks cared about and possibly a dissident in the somewhat more leftist cast of the figures in the Berlin FD. Nenarokov wondered if OGPU thought sending him to Berlin would help sew dissent there, as he would have been to the right of Dan, the leader after Martov died, and of the dominant group in Berlin.

Often, these evaluations are not direct. The reasoning is by inference. A good example can be seen in an evaluation from two officials in the Political Bureau of the Communist Party objecting to the release of a particular person A.A. Yugov.

> "YUGOV's liberation would not prevent him from engaging in political activity. More so, the State Political Administration witnessed how GOUREVITCH-BER and GONIKBERG, released due to their illness, didn't stop their political activity. The disease did not prevent them from conducting even more vibrant political work."[10]

Ber's name is mentioned among other members of the Central Committee of the Russian Social Democratic Labor Party who were subject to arrest. The researchers see a tightening up, with the Party limiting the release of political activists to go abroad. The logic is applied to Ber.

Overall, Nenarokov did not think that the political point of view, Left vs. Right Menshevik tendency, had much to do with the OGPU decisions on whom to release. I asked him directly, to be clear, so important was this issue in our Family Legend of understanding. He rejected it out of hand—flatly and clearly no. He thought of examples on both sides, left and right political orientation; some people released, while others kept. Overall, Nenarokov thought the key decision was made by the authorities on the criteria of whether that person was more or less dangerous to them as an activist, not according to location or ideological position. It was what served their interests, the party, not that of the grandfathers.

This is, of course, conjecture. However, much expertise lies behind it. These are researchers looking at documents many years later, making inferences, and evaluating the risks posed by Ber in the minds of the Party and State Police officials. The reasons are not given in the files specifically pertaining to Ber, at least not in what I was allowed to see. The specialists on file reading do not expect such things would be written down. It is most frustrating that while access is provided, in

Peter Gourevitch, A.P. Nenarakov, Irene Etkin Goldman, in his office January 2017. On the wall it says Boris Ivanovich Nicolaevsky and has some of the photos familiar to me from childhood.

each dossier, pages are stapled shut, so we lack full information.

The meeting with Nenarokov was a deeply moving experience for both of us, me and my cousin Irene Etkin Goldman. She learned some details about her grandfather she had not known. While I was revising this chapter in the early summer of 2021, by happenstance in an apartment owned by my wife in Coyoacan, Mexico City, not far from where Trotsky was killed under Stalin's orders in 1940, I received a letter from Alla Morozova.

Nenarokov died of COVID in 2020. Morozova was contributing to a volume in his memory. This news hit me hard, as Nenarokov knew more about my grandparents than anyone. I had hoped to visit him again to learn more details, discuss interpretation, show him this manuscript, and learn if he had any sense of the personalities of these grandparents. Now, this could not happen. Another door closed. Morozova sent me a copy of her contribution. It focused on our visit to him in 2017, the way in which she and her colleagues had helped solve the visa problem by proving the birth lineage, and how he had helped me understand the fates of my grandparents. She conveyed how moved he was to find me standing in front of him, the grandson of people he studied, interested In his work. She quotes from the letter of thanks I sent him. "

> "Indeed, it is very important to meet someone who appreciates and understands the historical role that our grandparents played in history and has done so much research on their activities. It is thanks to your work that we can find out what they have done and were striving to do for Russia. I spent the whole day looking through the cases of Boris Ber-Gourevitch. But there are limits to what can be understood from such documents. Your interpretation is so precious. Thanks again for spending time with us !!!![11]

Much as I admire Nenarokov and defer to his superior knowledge, I feel compelled as a researcher to reflect on his interpretation and pose some challenges. We can wonder if his view imputes too much shrewd calculation and knowledge on the part of Bolshevik officials. We are dealing with large organizations, rapidly changing situations and much uncertainty. Do they know what Garvy and Ber are likely to do and how they will interact with the FD? Perhaps there is some projection backward from what we know about the future to that moment. We know that Garvy did have difficult relations over time with some leaders of the FD, such as Dan—indeed, he did sow some dissent. Dan blocked him from joining the Central Committee of the Menshevik group in Berlin and in Paris as too much on the party right. Garvy's standing was always as a trade union expert, to which he could make a reasonable claim to belong. Nonetheless, he was left out. In 1940, when they were all refugees yet again, now in New York, Garvy was added to the central committee of the FD, and Dan left it to form his splinter group so that a tiny number of people now split into factions with their own journal, arguing to the end of their lives, when their discussions mattered even less. Did the OGPU know that would be the case? Does that really explain their decision?

Tactical decisions by the OGPU in the short run seem more plausible than a long-run strategic game. Compared to Garvy, Ber was more well-known among the Menshevik circles still in Russia, still active and energetic. The files show Ber to have health problems, as testified by letters from another brother. But he, too, seems to have survived them. The photo of him in the Vladimir Prison file of 1937 (see page 328) shows a vigorous, free-spirited man, despite everything. Garvy was a less significant figure and, at the time, possibly in worse health. That argument seems plausible in the circumstances, but this framing could be influenced by a bias of the evaluators. Ber had health problems as well, so a friendly spirit could have used these to justify letting him go. Garvy's bad health kept him out of politics at a key moment so he could not cause trouble with activism when decisions were being made. Ber was healthy enough to arouse suspicion.

It is impossible not to wonder about the accidents of personnel in the handling of these files. The fact that the person writing about Grandpa Peter notes he remembers him from Tsarist prison days is haunting. We know personal connections matter. Did Boris have the misfortune of the wrong person processing his case, someone not a friend? When Boris requested a visa for Shura to leave Russia in 1928, was it because of a friend processing it that the request was approved—such is the Family Legend, so did it apply in that case in 1928 and Shura's actual departure in 1931, but not concerning departure for Boris in 1922-23? Or that the file made its way up the hierarchy, where personal contact may matter less and policy more? The refusal to allow Boris to leave in May 1923 did not come from the same person who approved it in November 1922. The impact of hierarchy in organizations is indeed to suppress the role of personal relationships. If the policy was getting harsher, that six-month gap could mark the growth of the hierarchical grip as policy changed. Other specialists on this period comment on how much uncertainty and accident there was. So indeed, there are grounds for different interpretations.

Was the Family Legend's focus on contrasting political positions by the two Grandfathers thus simply wrong? With some mental juggling, I can reconcile the Family Legend with the Party's Strategic Interest interpretation. The two Grandfathers did differ in political position. Garvy was isolated because of it in key circles of Russian left politics, thus more marginal. He was also already safely in jail, unable to cause much trouble at this key moment. He was safe to send out of the country. Ber was still engaged in the arguments too closely, too major a rival in the Bolshevik consolidation of power. Perhaps a vigorous man on the left flank of the Mensheviks, a near neighbor, was more threatening than a more distant one, so he needed to be controlled. Being so engaged may have influenced Ber's timing: others were leaving, but he wanted to remain engaged as a coalition member, until it was too late.

Thus the politics of Ber and Garvy does influence what happened, and in that sense, they have some agency. Could different comportment by Ber have altered the outcome? Suppose Ber had fallen silent or become quieter in this period. If you want your jailors to let you out, perhaps it is best to lie low. Ber seems to have both applied to get out and kept up his level of activity, making the police more wary of him. He never did give in on his principles. He never switched sides or stopped complaining. Both grandfathers stuck to their guns to their political positions, and doing that was their choice, their agency. That feature of them, their political principles, turns into the Family Legend of causality. On its own, it seems not irrelevant but insufficient. I think, on balance, the Nenarokov interpretation is persuasive: Ber was too much trouble for them to let him go. The personal intervention variables, such as powerful friendships, were not enough in this case to release him.

By March of 1923, the Garvys are in Berlin.

And it is about this time, winter 1923, that Boris Ber writes his letter of complaint, that they are not honoring the November 1922 promise to let him leave. When does he conclude they never will? There is no clear document declaring that refusal, or none made public. His letters, examined later in the book, explore moments when he wonders to his family if he and they will be allowed to see each other, but this could be rhetorical.

So it is at this point the paths of the two families diverge: the

Garvys are in Berlin, out of one dangerous jaw in the USSR, and 10 years later into the jaws of another one, the Nazis.

How they escape that menace will be the subject of the next chapters; Grandma and Grandpa Garvy, and my parents, escape the Nazis, but Grandma's brother Buka and his wife, Olga, do not. Boris does not escape Stalin, but my father, Shura, does. We have answers to some questions, but we find new ones. Why is Shura allowed to leave? And why is Boris allowed to live for so long without being put on public trial and executed as a number of Mensheviks are? We will come back to these questions in a later chapter of this book.

On learning about these people, I have gotten a greater sense of them. Grandpa Peter was not quite as quiet as some people had described him. He had taken up important missions for his party leadership; in 1914, for example, or later to be a leader in Odesa during WWI and the revolutionary situation. He was able to tangle when he disagreed with his party leadership. He took as a life partner a very lively, opinionated woman in an age when most men preferred quiet and obedient women, an apparent life partner, who shared his commitment to socialism, a relationship perhaps more modern to us today, but this one formed in 1910. Grandpa Boris seems to have had some skills as a leader and organizer; people followed his opinions. He was being watched by members of his own factional side, as well as the Bolshevik police. He was being picked as a leader and seen as one. There is not much information to me about his personality as I did not grow up knowing people familiar with him. We may be able to learn more later on when I turn to the treasure trove of letters Boris is about to start writing to family in the West, while he is confined to stay in the East.

Great grandma Styssia , mother of Boris

Grandfather Boris Nahum Gourevitch, in his early 20s

Endnotes

1 Memorial, St.. Petersburg, ..

2 Morozova, Alla, Material on AP Nenarokov. " Obdorsk Red Cross and Soviet bureaucracy, or History of one study" 2021. Mimeo, for volume in memory of A.P. Nenarokov.

3 Ber-Gourevitch, Boris Nahum Ber -, GARF archives .. Consulted in January 2017.

4 Garvy, George, "Memoir Notes", handwritten by Garvy in 1970s, vested in Hoover Archive at Stanford University.

5 Garvy-Bronstein, Peter Abramovitch, GARF archives, consulted March 2017 via notarized access of Natasha VoOlodina

6 Peter Garvy, Memoirs of a Social Democrat New York. 1946.

7 Liebich, op cit. photographs. From collection of Lia Andler (Abramovich-Rein).

8 Nenarokov, A.P. essay on Ber Gourevitch.

9 In one of the searches of Ber's apartment, books were taken, and a list appears in the archive. Were these "dangerous books" that indicated an unfavorable position. Or unsurprising and common among intellectuals? The files are not clear on the date of the arrest, which would make a difference on how dangerous such names as Trotsky would be. It is interesting a list was made for the files, and I reproduce it here. Martov, Notes of a Social Democrat; Tsederbaum, From the epoch of "The Spark"; Spiridonova, Party of Socialists Revolutionaries (the SRs); Martov, The History of Russian Social Democracy; Trotsky, What Happened in Spain; Milyukov, Essays on the History of Russian Culture; Women of the Epoch of French Revolution; Kropotkin, The Great French Revolution; Voronsky, Zhelyabovm; Tchernov, Through the Fog of the Future; Political Economy Questions, editor Serebryakova; Bukharin, Imperialism; Bukharin, International Bourgeoisie; Bukharin, The Theory of Historical Materialism; Seleznyov, Trotskism; O. Bauer, A fight For Land; Safarov, Marx on the National Colonial Question; Trotsky, Toward Socialism or Toward Capitalism; Bakunin, Statism and Anarchy; Tugan-Baranovsky, Socialism; Simmel, Issues of Philosophy of History.

10 Morozova, Alla, Obdurok, Красный Крест и советская бюрократия,или История одного исследования (Obdurok, Krasnyy Krest i sovetskaya byurokratiya,ili Istoriya odnogo issledovaniya, "the Red Cross and the Soviet bureaucracy,or History of one study", in Let the Candle Burn (Pust gorit svecha): Essays in Memory of Professor A.P. Nenarokov, Shelokhaev, V.V. and Saveliev, P. Yu,, Moscow: Rosspen, 2021., pp 62-66.

11 Letter from winter 2017. Morozova op cit. The article provides extensive reference locations for the materials relevant to Ber that are cited in her article. This collection, as well as in other collections of the "Kremlin Archives" series, is based on documents from the so-called "Thematic Files" of the current office work of the Politburo, previously stored in the AP RF, and some time ago moved to the RGASPI: file 2 "On the Mensheviks": 1919 - VII.1922; d. 3 "On the Mensheviks": VIII.1922 - 1926; d. 4 "On the Mensheviks": 1929 - 12.12.1930; d. 5 "On the Mensheviks": December 17-25, 1930; d. 6 "On the Mensheviks": 27.XII.1930 - I.1931; d. 7 "On the Mensheviks" II-VI.1931; d. 8 "On the Mensheviks" 1932 -"On the Mensheviks": 27.XII.1930 - I.1931; d. 7 "On the Mensheviks" II- VI.1931; d. 8 "On the Mensheviks" 1932 - IV.1937; d. 9 "On the Mensheviks" May 8, 1937 - May 10, 1938; d. 10 "On the Mensheviks - Rozhkov, Rozanov, Martov and others": 1919-1924. The last case by numbering stands out from the general chronological order in which the cases are located; it is devoted to individual characters. Cases 4-7 are almost entirely devoted to the preparation and conduct of the trial over the Union Bureau of Mensheviks in 1931.

Chapter 5

Hope of the First Exile

Welcome by Europe's largest Social Democracy 1923-33

For the Garvys, Berlin was a welcome refuge for ten years. It was a home culturally because of the very large Socialist Party. They could build a life among the refugees and among the socialist colleagues. Then, toward the end of this period, danger, horrific danger in the form of the Nazis, rose up. They had to flee again, this time to France. How did they manage to do that? What made them "early deciders," people who saw the danger and got out fast?

Much of what I know about the Garvy's experiences in the early years of their migration comes from my Uncle George. I knew this uncle well, as we visited New York at least once a year during my childhood. His daughter Helen was my only first cousin, a year older than me, halfway between me and my older brother Sergei. Uncle George did the things a big city uncle could do with his provincial nephews. He took us to visit the gold reserves in the basement of the Federal Reserve where he worked, stacks of gold bars piled on top of each other, and to lunch in Chinatown, which seemed exotic when they counted the number of circles on each plate as a way of totaling the bill; or to meet him in Paris at the elegant small hotel the Bank could pay for, the Hôtel des Saints-Pères, which he chose over the fancy big cold institutional ones, or to dinner in Paris, always a small but super place I could not then afford. But our relationship was not so much warm as factual, cerebral. He asked about my interests and career goals. He disapproved of my interest in political science as it had no solid profession attached to it. George himself became an economist and rose high in the research division of the New York

Federal Reserve after completing his Ph.D. at Columbia with noted economist Arthur Burns as his advisor, of which he was quite proud. He traveled all over the world, spoke Russian, German, French, and added Spanish and Italian. His bibliography includes debates with Milton Friedman over the velocity of money, a key topic in relation to a Nobel prize-winning monetary theorist.

I enjoyed very much that George and I could communicate via some shared common interests: maps, coins, stamps. He took me with him to see his favorite historical map store in Paris (Paul Prouté) and guided me on my first purchases. He explained his interests in stamps and coins, and how they deepened his awareness of history and geography. I was moved when Helen gave me much of his collection of maps, stamps and coins when he died. Some of them now decorate my study, especially the colorful old maps of early modern Russia, which have small portraits of fantasy elephants and camels decorating distorted images of medieval "Kyivian Rus," Tartar-lands, Persia, Latvia, Corelia and other precursors of modern states—though he may have disapproved of my hanging them since collectors believe they should be flat and away from light.

George was also the family librarian and collector. He kept various documents that appear in this account. He wrote some summaries of key events, described apartments, journeys, incidents. His short family history provides essential material of some key moments. And while I describe his interpersonal interactions with me as cool, his daughter Helen has quite strongly positive emotions about him. I found he wrote with very great feeling about his childhood years of turmoil. The passage in his writing where he comments on the impact migration had on him is one of the most expressive of any I have seen in the family:

> I was a child of those who lost the battle but never the faith in the future, and whose whole life was devoted to a cause. My parent's life shaped mine far beyond the age when an average American becomes independent. My parents' peregrinations broke so many times the continuity of my life and made me spend my formative years in four different countries. I followed their footsteps and fought my own battles, which led only to defeat and heartbreak but never to disillusionment. By the time I was 28, it was clear that I had to start all over again after a third emigration…Three times I made friends, then had

to leave them and start again.

> I regret nothing. In spite of all the hardships, I was a happy child, and I think of those years in Russia as the happiest in my life. I am proud that I gave all my enthusiasm all my time to the Socialist Youth Movement from the age of 13 and until the light went out in Germany. Those were rich years.[1]

I think my mother would have subscribed to these words.

Uncle George's love of stamps proved vital to Garvy family life. In the drama of fleeing to Berlin in 1923, it was George, at age 11, who kept the family going. The hyperinflation of early 1920s Germany is notorious. People had to push a wheelbarrow of money to buy a bottle of milk and a loaf of bread. The Garvys arrived with no money and no jobs. Taking advantage of his parents' connection to all sorts of people from many places, George had become an avid stamp collector. He managed to get his collection to Berlin. They were from the Russian Revolutionary period and thus unusual. They proved exotic enough to have value. George seemed to know how to sell. This helped the family when they arrived in March 1923 through the chaos till the mark was stabilized later that year.

We have proof, thanks again as well to George, of their arrival in Berlin. In George's papers, my cousin Helen and I found the police registration card required of immigrant residents, dated March 1923. I don't recall much conversation about the early days in Berlin, though

I do recall stories about their life as they started to get a little older.

Despite the currency turmoil at the beginning, Weimar Germany was a fairly safe refuge for the Bronstein-Garvys.[2] The state functioned, with some approximation to the rule of law, and administered civil liberties. The family lived in relative safety, with much greater freedom compared to the life of the paternal grandparents who remained in the USSR. The German Social Democratic Party (SPD) was the largest, most established of its kind in Europe. It provided cultural, financial and political shelter to the Mensheviks with whom they shared a substantial heritage. The SPD was ideologically aligned with the Mensheviks; both opposed the Communist Party, which split away in alignment with the Bolsheviks. The Russian political refugees found a niche with the SPD, with jobs for some, schools for their children, and social and cultural connections. They tried, with some success, to create a life.

And then, at the end of the decade, a tremendous mortal peril descended upon them. The Depression of 1929 turned economic and political life upside down. The Nazi movement was one of the significant consequences. As it grew, the Menshevik refugees joined the defenders of the Republic early and fought hard. When Hitler came to power in January of 1933, there was little doubt in their minds about the gravity of the threat to their lives. The Garvys were "early deciders" and left for Paris in March of that year. How did that happen?

The Garvys had little money, were without clear professions and had no family wealth. Prosperous Great-grandfather Fichman died in Odesa during the Civil War there, and there was no money left. My grandfather Garvy eked out a living by working for *Vorwärts (Forwords)*, the Social Democratic newspaper, as a journalist, writing on various international topics for very little pay.

In Berlin, the Garvys lived for some time at 80 Wilmersdorferstrasse, the address my mother gave when I planned my first voyage to Berlin in the summer of 1974 to study German. Despite all the bombing and reconstruction so evident in Berlin, this apartment building was still there. When the Bronstein-Garvys resided in it, the building was a modest place along a busy street. Since then, the Berlin Wall shifted the geography of social class around. It was now a more prosperous-looking area than it had been. The building where my mother went to grade school still stands, intact, not far away on Sybelstrasse.

It is a dark, imposing structure of huge stones. In my mother's time, it was Fürsten (Countess) Bismarck Schule; it became Frau Goebbels Schule, and after the war, Sophie-Charlotten Schule after a Hanoverian princess who married Frederick who became the first King of Prussia, and happened to have been the sister of the first George of Hanover to become King of England, from whom the current House of Windsor is descended. The building is still there, now a gymnasium or advanced high school.

Life for my family centered around the Menshevik refugee group and its allies in the Social Democratic Party (SPD) and the trade union movement of Germany, whose most important component was the ADGB (Allgemeine Deutsche Gewerkschaftsbund—General German Trade Union Federation). These were the most significant organizations of their kind in Europe.[3] With Europe's largest economy, the trade unions and labor parties of Germany were also the most well-developed. Germany had been the intellectual leader of socialist thought in Europe, with a series of notable writers debating the application of Marxism to current situations and political strategy. These writers included not only Marx and Engels, of course, but Eduard Bernstein and Rudolf Hilferding, as leading Social Democrats, and radicals, like Rosa Luxembourg and Karl LIebknecht, both killed in 1919, leaders of the left faction that became the Communist Party. Important intellectuals from other countries lived in Berlin during those years: among them Karl Kautsky, the leading Marxist theoretician of the pre-WWI period, and Pavel Axelrod, a leading Russian Socialist, especially important to the Menshevik group. By the time the Garvys arrived in the winter of 1923, many Mensheviks had already come there and formed a structure, "the Foreign Delegation" of the Russian Social Democratic Labor Party (RSDLP). Martov, having died, it was now led by Dan and included Abramovich, Dallin and others. The Garvys interacted with many of these

Karl and Luise Kautsky, with uncle George and my mother Sylvia behind them, picture in Nenarokov's office noted in previous chapter, and in family albums. Photo in late 1920s

figures. Among the family photos is one of my mother as a young teenager with pigtails standing next to her brother George behind a couch with an elderly couple sitting on it. "Who is that?" I recall asking my mother. "Oh, that is Karl Kautsky and his wife Luise (sic). They gave me my first pineapple." "KARL KAUKTSY!!!" I exclaimed. By then, I was old enough to know that Kautsky was one of the most famous theorists of socialism of the time and the author of many books widely read around the world. He was a noted theorist of reform socialism, anti-Bolshevik, critical of Lenin and later of Stalin. My grandmother had met the Kautskys in Switzerland during the Tsarist exile period and retained a friendship that lasted through the flight from Berlin.

Pavel Axelrod with George and Sylvia Garvy in Berlin 1920s.

Another friend of the grandparents was Pavel Axelrod, a noted socialist theorist as well, less famous internationally than Kautsky but a very revered figure among the Russian socialists. He also was anti-Bolshevik. He appears in several family photos, showing a great beard; in this one, with my mother and uncle standing at his side and behind. He is also a major figure in various group photos of the Mensheviks, often outdoors in Berlin's famous parks.

Emma and Wolik (Vladimir) Woytinsky were very present in Berlin life.[4] Childless, they treated with much warmth the Garvy children and, later on in the US, the grandchildren, my brother and me, and my cousin Helen. My mother and Uncle George were executors of their estate when Emma died. We visited them about once a year in their big house on 39th St NW near Military Road, Washington. Wolik looked a bit like Einstein, with a bald head and wispy white hair. The Woytinsky's were famous for huge books, such as *The World in Statistics*. I recall once helping out with their various research projects by using a very large electronic adding machine, slow and cumbersome today but remarkable and powerful back then. As we shall see, the "Woys," as they were called, played an important role in helping the family escape France in 1940.

Emma and Vladimir (Wolik) Woytinsky circa 1910

For a time, Woytinksy had been on the Bolshevik side of the 1903 party split but soon shifted to the Menshevik wing and stayed there. Active in the Revolution, as noted in many histories, he was personally arrested by Trotsky but escaped and went to work for the Menshevik-governed Republic of Georgia, led by Irakli Tsereteli. He was sent as its Ambassador to the Vatican, so when the Bolsheviks took over Georgia in 1921, he was safely out of the country, and the Woytinskys then went to Berlin. There he became an important intellectual, rising to the position of chief economist of the German Federation of Trade Unions.

This put Woytinsky in a strategic location for European debates over how to handle the Great Depression of 1929. At a key moment in the summer of 1932, as the German government considered plans to deal with the severity of the crisis that had 25-30% of the population unemployed, he led the formulation of the WTB plan (after Woytinksy, Tarnow and Baade, authors of the bill, involving representatives of agriculture and labor).[5] This was a Keynesian-style demand stimulus plan to help the economy by deficit spending to stimulate unemployment. It was proposed before Keynes published the famous *General Theory* book in 1936, which provided the theoretical formulation for breaking the liquidity trap through deficit spending. As a practical idea, these ideas were in circulation among the European applied economists of the period. Woytinsky proposed such a plan in the early 1930s as Chief Economist of the labor organization. The Finance Minister of the coalition government, a Social Democrat, Rudolf Hilferding, himself a famous writer and author of the well-known opus, *Finance Capital*,[6] rejected the WTB plan on the grounds that capitalist economies did not work that way. Thus the orthodox Socialist leader believed in orthodox capitalist theories, while the labor movement intellectual had broken with orthodoxy. In Sweden, the opposite outcome happened. The Socialists joined forces with the Agrarians to form a government that supported a deficit spending plan; democracy was stabilized, and the Scandinavian welfare state emerged there. In Denmark, a similar coalition produced a similar result, and in the US, the New Deal can be described politically in similar terms. Alas, in Germany, the coalition and policy moves failed under a progressive democratic coalition. This was a tragic missed opportunity in German politics, as the economy continued to worsen, and the Nazis came into power some months later. The Nazis coopted some of these policies. The WTB plan figured hugely in my research. My most well-known book, *Politics in Hard Times*,[7] explores why countries made different choices when faced with similar international economic pressures.

When I knew Woytinsky in my youth, I did not know these details about his historical importance. The WTB plan has received a lot of attention among specialists in political economy. Less well-known is his role in shaping American Social Security. When the Nazis came to power, Woytinsky left Germany within weeks. His memoirs say they left after the Reichstag fire (February 27, 1933), when the Nazis expanded the roundup of opposition figures (it is at this time the Garvys left as well). As a precaution, his wife Emma had already arranged visas for going to Switzerland. His prominence in Socialist labor circles made him an obvious target of the Nazis, and indeed it was fortunate that he was not seized earlier. In Switzerland, he worked for the International Labor Organization. In 1935, the Woytinskys came to Washington. Quite soon, he was hired by the US government to provide technical advice on how to structure the Social Security system, which had just been approved by Congress. In so doing, he befriended Wilbur Cohen, many years later Secretary of Health, Education, and Welfare, and with whose children my brother and I played in visits to Washington in the 1950s.

The meaning of this tour of the socialist leadership in 1920s Berlin is to emphasize that the Garvy-Bronstein's arrived in Berlin with no money but with lots of social capital comprised of their network among the German socialist community and their many refugee friends from Russia. Things seemed peaceful for a time.

Germany was moderately stable during the 1920s. The hyperinflation of 1923 lives on in modern culture as the driving determinant factor in the Nazi rise to power. Combating inflation lies at the core of contemporary German economic orthodoxy, the central tenet of the Central Bank's view of economic policy, transferred to how to run the EU's policy. But this view gravely distorts history. Financial stabilization was achieved in 1924 with the Dawes plan. Germany entered a period of relative prosperity. The economy grew. In the 1920s, The Nazi vote was tiny.

Then things went bust. Wall Street collapsed in the fall of 1929. American loans to Germany were called back. Trade dropped. Germany slumped very badly; unemployment skyrocketed to 25%, then over 30%. It was then that the Nazi vote rose sharply. It was the hyper-unemployment of 1929 that pushed the Nazi vote way up, not the hyper-inflation of 1923.

So, for the first part of their stay in Germany, the Garvys and the Menshevik community lived in the prosperous period of the Dawes plan. Life became difficult and dangerous after 1929.

Building the Menshevik Network in Berlin—The Bonds that Tie: The Links to German Social Democracy

This large network of people to which my grandparents belonged gave richness to their daily existence and, I think, helped save their lives. Their fates revolved around a community of people with dense ties of connection, shared experience and deep purpose. Berlin was packed with refugees from the turmoil of the Revolution, but this included people of sharply divergent points of view who had trouble talking to each other despite sharing the language. Aristocrats, grand bourgeois, merchants, along with highly religious or ethnic leaders, and then political dissidents of various kinds, many of whom were the sort of people the Socialists had been fighting. These varied groupings despised each other, though they bought the same specialty foods if they could afford them.

The Mensheviks had been together in their resistance to the Tsarist regime, shared exile abroad, often in Switzerland, and imprisonment and internal exile in Siberia. Now shut out of political life in their native country, they considered what to do as individuals: how to earn a living, how to manage as parents, and how to engage politically.

They discussed, debated, and argued about what was going on in Russia, Germany and the world around them. There were intense disagreements, and deep splits, as we can imagine, among any group of highly intelligent and ideologically charged group of people. At the same time, while disagreeing strongly, they were strongly bonded to each other. At one point, my grandfather needed help with his eyes and could not afford the surgery. Money was successfully raised among the Menshevik refugees from the very group that had kept him off the key governing committee.

In Berlin, the Mensheviks quarreled over how to interpret what was happening in the USSR and what public positions to take in dealing with the Bolshevik government. Grandpa Garvy was on the political right, and the leadership under Felix Dan was on the left, with many issues of contention. Garvy condemned the Bolshevik's repression of political parties, destruction of constitutional processes and the imprisonment of the many Socialists still there. The Left Mensheviks were critical of the dictatorship but cautious to defend the USSR as a progressive force, especially in comparison to the militarists or traditional authoritarians it imagined would have taken over otherwise. All of them were anti-Fascists, hostile to Mussolini, who had seized power in Italy in 1922, and fearful of an intensely negative pressure from Hitler when the Nazi movement rose sharply after 1929. All of them were quite aware of the anti-labor side of the Nazi drive to power. All of them were anti-Bolshevik in some way or another; all knew they would be in danger were they to return to the USSR.

The material conditions of life were difficult for many of the Mensheviks. Grandpa Peter earned some limited income working for the Trade Union newspaper, but this could not have been very much. Sylvia and George were still too young to be important wage earners when they first arrived in 1923. Family notes say that George made his first earnings doing a translation from Russian at about age 14 or 15 (about 1927), and Sylvia started giving private school lessons at age 13 (about 1928). Probably Dadia Buka helped, though I don't know much about his business pursuits when he came to Berlin or how much he could have given them. He was married but childless.

For the children of the emigrés, my parents' generation, their politically active parents, thus my grandparents helped define a community of friendship. In the place of blood relatives, most of whom stayed in Russia, these children had each other, bound by common experience, language, danger, adventure and the connection among their parents. The Social Democratic movement framed a special relationship, something like church connections for the religious or, in the US, ethnic associations. The Mensheviks were secular. The Jews

A Menshevik picnic in teh forest, Berlin, 1927. Seated (L to R): F. Dan P. Axelrod, L. Abramovitch, L. Dan, Roza Abramovitch. Standing: B. Rubinstein, D. Dallin, S. Garvi, E. Landysheva, G. Garvi, N. Rubinstein, T. Rubinstein, S. Schwarz, unidentified woman, Raphael Abramovitch (Courtesy of Lia Andler)

among them were mostly not religious. Through the trade unions and SPD, there were schools, summer camps, youth groups, meetings, and political discussion groups. They traveled to international meetings of socialist youth. They all belonged to the Sozialistische Arbeiter-Jugend (SAJ), known colloquially as the "SAJot."

It was its own world. It sounds very much like what I have read about religious networking, like the counterpart Catholic organizations in Germany, or the equivalents among Christian groups in the US, or Socialist ones in Scandinavia.[8] My mother has commented she felt well located and rooted with this network, one that continued when they moved to France in 1933 and the US in 1940. The network diluted as they became adults, spread into different forms of higher education, different careers, and married. In the US, it diffused further when many of them moved away from the New York port of entry. Many years later, in the US, Mother said at times, she felt lonelier here than in childhood as the group split up.

An important example in this network was Janni (Jacob) Et-

Pavel Axelrod, center, with Woytinsky and Boris Sapir. Berlin 1927

kin, whom my mother had known in Russia even before the family's departure. Etkin's father was a Menshevik activist. Janni and my Mother were close friends, like cousins, and remained in contact through all the turmoil of their lives till they died in the US. Their parents left Russia at about the same time. When Janni's father died in 1928, the son was embraced as an orphaned boy by the Menshevik clan, notably by Rafael Abramovich, one of its most important leaders. Janni and Natasha (Natalie Emanuel), his wife, who met in Berlin, and married in Paris in 1936, had four daughters, who were de facto cousins to me and my older brother. Many of the escape stories I heard growing up were around the hearth of one family or the other, in our house in Syracuse, New York, or with the Etkins in Plainfield, New Jersey. For a time in Germany, the Menshevik community dug roots. They learned the language; the children got strong educational foundations; as the parents arrived with strong "cultural capital," they were able to help the children get the best out of the strong German educational system. The families connected to political life as allies of the Social Democrats. They analyzed and debated, and quarreled about what was happening in the USSR. Both the Soviet dictatorship and the German republic seemed to stabilize. Going home faded as a possibility.

The stories I heard of this period were cultural: I was astonished to learn that my mother attended the first run of the "Three Penny Opera" put on by Brecht and Weill with Lotte Lenya and saw at the movies Marlene Dietrich in the famous *Blue Angel*. Mother had enlightened, leftist parents—other people told me their parents would not allow them to go to such things. I heard stories of hiking and camping and friendship with fellow refugees and with young Germans who did not care about their backgrounds, although a few did. Mother reports having lots of German friends, including boyfriends, who were not bothered by her Jewishness. Many years later, I showed Mother Daniel Goldhagen's well-known book *Hitler's Willing Executioners,* where he describes how widespread was complicity in the Holocaust. Mother, who lost her favorite Uncle to this terror, and did not wish to visit Germany when my father was invited to a meeting there, was angry at the book. "It was not ALL Germans. I knew several who wanted to marry me. He has it wrong. SOME or MANY is not the same as ALL," to paraphrase her comments. I agreed with her judgement, and she had first-hand evidence; for me, it was all inference from my readings or conversations with eyewitnesses who had experienced it, like her.

Then the Depression of 1929 hit. Unemployment skyrocketed. And with it rose the Nazi vote and Hitler. The darkness blew in fast. The Menshevik band now faced danger, again, a very great one.

The Arrival of Shura in Berlin, 1931, and the Rise of Hitler

One experience about which Dad talked vividly was his arrival in Berlin in November 1931 at age 15. He was immediately surrounded by the Menshevik elders. They faced him with what we might call today a "debriefing." What did he know about this person or that person, or this situation or that one? Dad was not only the son of an important colleague but the most recent member of the tribe to come out. Of course, its leaders were intensely curious to learn what he could tell them. Dad told them whatever he knew. I have wondered recently what that could be. Dad was not a party leader or activist. The Soviet Union had become a place where the circulation of information was difficult. Did he smuggle anything out? That would seem quite dangerous, and I find it unlikely. Did he memorize information? More probable, but how did he get it? From his parents or other relatives or other close friends, but still, how did he do that? What conversations, where? The sentimental part concerns me more—how did they say goodbye? Did they all know it was forever? I think Dad's parents sensed it was. I don't know about Dad.

It was through this group, the Mensheviks of the Foreign Dele-

gation in Berlin, that my father Shura connected to Berlin, and specifically to his Aunt and Uncle, Asrunin and Anna Gourevitch, with
whom he went to live. In the Soviet Union, he had lived in various
locations, sometimes with his father in the places to which his arrests
confined him, sometimes with other relatives in Moscow. The Foreign
Delegation was very aware that major members of the group were
trapped in the USSR. People were not able to travel freely, but letters
did go out. One set of letters came from Grandpa Boris to the Gourevitchs in Berlin.

Many of these letters have survived. The first is dated from 1924,
Tashkent, where Boris was sent in his internal exile. We have some
family photos showing my father, his sister Galia, his mother and father, Lydia and Boris, and his paternal grandmother, Styssia. The letters do not discuss politics very much, as Boris knew they were being
read by censors. They provide a lot of rich information about Boris' life
and situation, and I will return to them after we complete the story of
what happened to the Garvys and Great Uncle Fichman.

The period of the 1920s marked great uncertainty for the Menshevik group in Berlin. At first, there remained some hope of return,
as the regime in Moscow seemed unstable, vulnerable to collapse. By
1922 the Civil War ended, foreign intervention ceased, the opposition
was crushed, and the Bolsheviks became entrenched. The hope of return faded.

Moscow softened severe control of economic policy with the
NEP—New Economic Policy— allowing the revival of markets and
cooperative farms. This increased the supply of consumer goods and
eased conflict in the city and countryside.[9] Political repression was
strong, but some hope existed of an easing of repression, and debates
on the probable future were intense.

After the death of Lenin in 1924, the exiles watched with interest
the power struggles among the Bolshevik leaders as Stalin, Trotsky,
Bukharin, Kamenev, Kirov, and Dzerzhinsky maneuvered this way
and that. What was the nature of the regime? Could it reform, was it
the best available option for the working class, or was it already hur-
tling down the path of repressive dictatorship by a new elite? Grandpa
Peter tended toward the most critical of these views, putting him in
the minority among the Foreign Delegation. Grandpa Boris was likely on the other side, but his letters do not contain political commen-

tary. We infer his position from his views in the earlier revolutionary period and from what we know of what others said. The FD position seemed mostly to defend the regime as a progressive force representing workers and defending Russia from regressing to reactionary rule, but critical of its repressive method of rule internally.

For most of the 1920s, the members of the Menshevik group in Berlin coped and adjusted, earning a living and raising children. My dad faced the important decision I noted earlier about which educational track to follow, the elite academic Gymnasium in preparation for the university or the more common one of trade school to become a mechanic or possibly an engineer. The distinction was huge, the consequences were for life because once one picked trade school, there was no going back, and there were no side routes through community college to university as happens in the US. Though "technical " schools were like polytechnics or engineering schools and turned out highly qualified people with solid, often very important jobs, it was a huge social gap between high-level blue-collar and the elite of the professions.

Dad picked the academic track, surely his preference. The support of the Aunt and Uncle was likely quite important. Indeed the overall commitment of them to his support conveys a lot about Russian-Jewish family bonds. The family conditions were difficult when my father arrived. They had two small boys and quite limited economic means. The apartment was quite small; Dad slept on the living room couch. The Aunt Anna I knew in New York into my early adulthood spoke often of the stresses this all involved. Her dedication to my father was unmistakable, as was his gratitude and affection for her. And it was she who saved all the letters from my grandfather, her brother-in-law, and had them transcribed into legible form so I was able to use them for this research. I think she felt not only a familial but an ideological commitment to the life's work of that grandfather and his values. She engaged in discussions among the Menshevik refugees, which continued in New York, involved on the Dan side after the split in 1940.

My father thus arrived in Berlin all alone but with a strong, welcoming embrace. In addition to the family members, the teenage crowd of Menshevik children was there for Dad to join. Along with my mother and uncle, Sylvia and George Garvy, were Mark and Lea Rein (whose father was Rafael Abramovich, among the leaders of the group), Sasha Dallin, Janni Etkin, and Lipa Bers. In the early 1930s, they were all in the Socialist youth movement (the SAYOT). They were joined at various points by people, local Germans, some of whom became prominent after the War: Willy Brandt, Richard Lowenthal, Albert Hirschman, and Henry Ehrmann all joined the same youth group. This was a ready-made network of friends for my Dad and for my mother.

The socialist youth group was in conflict with the Communist youth and with the Nazi groups as they arose, as were the parent organizations to which they were affiliated. They had to train for street fights as the stresses of the Weimar democracy intensified. It is, again, hard to imagine my parents' lives in this situation. I don't know how much of the fighting was done by that group of refugee socialists, who were mostly still teenagers, and how much from the older trade unionists, but it was surely a fact in their lives that the streets could be very dangerous.

Politically, this particular group of young Socialists, as I heard about them, believed in reform from the "bottom up." I recall comments of criticism about the "bonzes"—the established party and union bosses, the senior people of the Socialist establishment, who gave orders and expected the mass membership to follow along, and who believed in a top-down statist, bureaucratic economy. This may have been youthful rebelliousness against the party brass, common in organizations, but it also marked a political sensibility that stayed with many of these people for the rest of their lives. They disliked "top-down" ideas about policy and politics, the command from the top approach common among a kind of statist stance toward policy.

This was a major political divide even within the social democratic community, not just the Bolsheviks against Mensheviks. The debate was over what it meant to have public control of the commanding heights of the economy. To some, it meant public ownership and planning the complete abolition of the market. To others, it meant democratization of decision-making, in all domains, in the political system, the factory, the public services, even the army and other classically authoritarian features of traditional society. These debates continued all over the industrial world in many forms, showing up in distinctive versions of socialism, communism and democracy.[10]

The young Mensheviks were not activists in these arguments, being too young, but many acquired these ideas or attitudes toward political choices. Most of the Menshevik children did not become political leaders; having to flee Germany and France before they were old enough to be politically active, and being outsiders, foreigners wherever they lived, made them seem external to a viable political career. Most of them entered professions of various kinds, which required success in the demanding European School system, thus limiting their time for politics.

My Dad, Shura, was indeed a bright boy, a strong reason his father sent him away to study. Not a talkative raconteur, he did not tell many stories from his school days, but some. Shortly after his arrival in Berlin, while in his gymnasium math class, the teacher was writing an equation on the blackboard, and Dad noticed an error. His German still somewhat rough, he walked up to the blackboard, turned a minus sign into a plus and went back to his seat. That seemed bold to me, challenging a teacher in an authoritarian pedagogy culture, but he seems not to have paid a price for it.

When the Nazis took over in January 1933, most of the Menshevik community left. Dad stayed one more year to finish his *abitur*, the high school leaving certificate. His uncle and aunt stayed as well for another year or two. Why, I wonder, was he allowed, as a foreign Jew, to stay in school?

Dad told me another story, even more bold and dangerous: Berlin has round pillars on the sidewalks, which were used like billboards, holding announcements and posters. One day, Dad went up to a Hitler poster and started to draw a beard on the face. Suddenly he felt a hand on his shoulder and turned to find a uniformed policeman. "Young man, what you are doing is not a good idea." Berlin's police were, to a large degree, unionized social democrats, not yet controlled by the Nazis, and many of the police were hostile to their seizure of power. I do not know the precise date of this incident, sometime in 1933/34. My Dad was a gentle person when I knew him; he was strong, soft-spoken, had a lot of quiet authority, the strength people have who speak only when they have something valuable to say, who are sensible and balanced when they do speak and highly respected by colleagues and friends. He was chosen by graduate school classmates to umpire baseball games because he was so fair (and because being enrolled in both biology and chemistry, he had no conflict of interest when they played each other; and as a foreigner, he had to learn the game on the job!). He ran a whole laboratory in the 50s and 60s. Drawing a beard on a Hitler poster at age 17 or 18, which he surely knew was risky, did not fit my image of him when I knew him as the father of the family and Director of Research and Lab Manager. Indeed, he escaped that moment of danger, and in 1934, left for Paris.

Living through troubled political moments in my younger years—the Civil Rights movement in America, the War in Vietnam, the Cuban Missile Crisis, and the Berlin Wall, I would ask my parents what they thought. They were politically very aware and engaged. Nothing in America was as threatening as Nazi propaganda and what they had lived through. They were quite sympathetic to the political activism of my generation: I went with my parents in my late teens to hear Martin Luther King speak in Syracuse. We stood in line afterward to shake his hand. My Dad was very visibly moved by meeting MLK and congratulated him on his work; rarely did I see words and emotion so forceful from him. I think MLK reminded him of the best of the Socialists he had known—someone risking his life to help his people.

My parents did speak of the 1930s as an upsetting time. The rise of Hitler and the SA violence in the streets broke any sense of safety. I recall asking if they felt any anti-Semitic acts at them personally back in Germany. They had not. They felt the tensions among social groups of all kinds and the status hierarchies of where you were from and class position, but not personally. Being refugees from Eastern Europe put them down the status totem pole inside the older established Jewish community as well as in Christian German society, but they had friends from many categories and groups. They left quite early in the Hitler regime before the regulations and separation began in employment and schools. Friends and relatives who stayed later did experience more direct acts of prejudice as the regime's grip intensified rapidly after the seizure of power in January 1933.

My parents and their Menshevik friends did feel the Nazi danger was real and acute. They recalled discussions within their circle that articulated this. There was explicit consideration that they all faced death from this regime. This sense of mortal danger would be with them in 1940 when the German army headed for Paris. I have long tried to imagine, with limited success, how they felt and the impact on them of all these dangers.

They left Berlin quickly.

Endnotes

1 George Garvy, Notes on Life History, Unpublished. 1973. Hoover Institute. Stanford library

2 Again Liebich, From the Other Shore, is the best detailed account of the life and debates among the Mensheviks.

3 Among the many studies of Germany, Gordon Craig, The Politics of the Prussian Army, (New York, Oxford University Press, 1956). Carl E. Schorske, German Social Democracy, 1905–1917: The Development of the Great Schism (Harvard University Press, 1955). Hajo Holborn, A History of Modern Germany, (New York: Knopf, 1959), 3 vols).; on the SPD, Sheri Berman, The Social Democratic Moment: Ideas and Politics in the Making of Interwar Europe (Cambridge; Harvard University Press, 1998).

4 Wladimir Woytinsky, Stormy Passage: A Personal History Through Two Russian Revolutions To Democracy and Freedom: 1905-1960 (New York: Vanguard, 1961). Emma Woytinsky, Two Lives In One (New York: Praeger, 1965); Peter Gourevitch, Politics in Hard Times: Comparative Responses to International Economic Crises (Ithaca: Cornell University Press, 1986. On Woytinsky's role in the effort to put through what became known later as a Keynesian plan, see chapter 4, "Breaking with Orthodoxy: the Formation of the Mixed Economy, 1929-49."

5 There is a rich literature on the WTB plan, how it anticipated Keynes, the role of ideas vs the role of political forces in bringing about these breaks with orthodox policy making. See Michael Scheider, Das Arbeitsbeschaffungsprogramm des ADGB, Friedrich-Ebert-Stiftung, 120 (Bonn, Neu Gesellschaft, 1975). English introduction by my uncle George Garvy. My chapter "Keynesian Politics: The Political Sources of Economic Policy Choices," in The Political Power of Economic Ideas: Keynesianism Across Nations, Peter Hall, ed., pp. 87-106 (Princeton, NJ: Princeton University Press, 1989). I stress the role of political circumstances in bringing about breaks with orthodoxy more than the development of abstract Keynesian economic modeling.

6 Hilferding,Rudolf. Finance Capital (Vienna, 1910; London, Routledge, 1981).

7 Gourevitch, Peter, Politics in Hard Times (Ithaca, Cornell University Press, 1986.)

8 Molly Nolan, Social Democracy and Society: Working-class Radicalism in Düsseldorf, 1890- 1920 (Cambridge and New York: Cambridge University Press, 1981). Nolan was part of a clan of bright assistant professors and graduate students who met in the newly formed Center for European Studies at Harvard-MIT in the early 1970s. Coming from several different disciplines and countries, the group shared a strong interest in labor history, politics, culture and ideas.

9 Orlando Figes, Revolutionary Russia; Figes, A people's tragedy. Sheila Fitzpatrick, The Russian Revolution. 3rd edition.

10 As an example in the 1960s-1970s many intellectuals were fascinated by the Yugoslav experiments at "workers control," of changing relationships in the workplace. One of my UCSD colleagues, Ellen Comisso, made this the subject of her Yale Ph.D. Dissertation with the noted political scientist, Charles Lindblom, leading to her book, Ellen Turkish Comisso, Workers' Control Under Plan and Market: Implications of Yugoslav Self-Management (Yale Studies in Political Science ; 29)| Jan 1, 1980. Comisso also co-edited a volume with noted economic policy advisor Laura Tyson on similar themes. Power, Purpose and Collective Choice: Economic Strategy in Socialist States (Cornell Studies in Political Economy), Ellen Comisso and Laura D'Andrea Tyson | Dec 1, 1986.

Chapter 6

"This is the Gestapo calling."

New Second Danger and Second Flight and Shura Reaches Berlin while Boris Remains Blocked

A story I have heard repeated many times in the family is that one day in early 1933, soon after Hitler took power and the burning of the Reichstag, the phone rang in my Garvy grandparents' Berlin apartment. My grandmother answers:

"Hello."

"Hello. Is Dr. Garvy there? This is the Gestapo calling."

"No, he is not here just now," replies Grandma while looking straight at Grandpa.

"Well, tell him to wait for us. We wish to speak to him."

That afternoon, a few hours later, Grandpa Peter and my Uncle George are on a train headed for Paris. My mother is ill and stays behind a few days more with Grandma.

This is the sort of story I cannot verify in the archives. It lives vividly in the family lore. It is plausible. The Nazis were throwing the opposition in jail, beating them up, and building concentration camps for them. Often they would rough people up for a few days and then release them to spread the word about what was coming. It was not only Jews who received this treatment but the political opposition generally. Communists were being expelled from the Reichstag and locked up. Not just Communists, but Socialists, liberals, church activists, centrists, trade unionists, educators, and anyone who defended the constitutional government, civil liberties and the rule of law, were dragged into jail, beaten and usually released. My grandfather was just the type they were after—active with the Socialist Party and trade unions. Getting him to leave was just what they wanted.

The dangers were evident by mid-1932, as political life in Germany was becoming increasingly conflictual, and the Menshevik refugee group was aware of the rising danger. The Nazis and their paramilitary arm, the SA, were very active in the streets, brawling, attacking individuals, raiding shops owned by Jews, breaking up meetings, in general, causing trouble. The Nazi vote skyrocketed in July of 1932 to 37%, making them the largest party in the Reichstag, and though the vote declined to about 33% in November of that year, they remained the largest party. Along with Communist deputies, they formed a majority of votes in the Parliament so that, in combination, they could block any legislation or oppose the Cabinet. This was a "negative majority" able only to block action, as they were not able to agree on doing anything either. There was near paralysis in the Weimar system, and governing was increasingly by decree.

The left split badly. Already evident before 1914, this division deepened greatly with the Bolshevik Revolution in Russia. The January 1919 Spartacist uprising in Germany sought to emulate Lenin's success in Russia, but this effort was repressed swiftly. The killing of Spartacist leaders Rosa Luxembourg and Karl Liebnicht along the Landwehrkanal in Berlin is, I noted in a 1974 visit, commemorated with a historical marker. The Social Democrats cooperated with this repression of the German far left, seeking to stabilize the newly proclaimed Weimar Republic. This intensified bitterness among the groups on the left. The quarrel between Communists (Bolsheviks in Russian terms) and Socialists (among whom, Mensheviks) operated during the life of Weimar and would come to be a significant obstacle in dealing with the Nazis. The Communist party of Germany took about 10% of the vote, with Social Democrats at 25%, usually the largest party in the Reichstag, until the rise of the Nazis with the onset of the Depression in 1929.[1]

That divide on the left hurt democracy everywhere, but most consequentially in Germany. During the crisis of the 1930s, the Communists did not cooperate with Social Democrats and other democratic elements in fighting the growing Nazi movement. Stalin's policy line was that the Social Democrats were "social fascists", collaborators with the bourgeois regime and thus the enemy. Stalin and the communists saw no distinction within the opposition, so all bourgeois elements were the same, fascists and anti-fascists alike. The split on the left helped Hitler and the Nazis come to power.

Only after German democracy collapsed and both the Socialists and Communists were repressed did Stalin switch strategies. He came to support Popular Front coalitions in defense of constitutional government against the fascists. At that point, the Mensheviks had to decide whether to cooperate in these moves, a complex choice to be discussed in the next section after the group had moved to France.

That most Mensheviks left Germany soon after the Nazis took power is not surprising. They had good reason to see the danger. How were they different from the many people who sadly did not leave? What gave my grandparents the signal to go, and quickly? The phone call from the Gestapo had little ambiguity to it. It told them they were targeted as individuals and surely as a group of foreign leftists.

While many were Jewish, many were not. Being Jewish did not in the winter of 1933 immediately put every Jew in danger of life and freedom. Being in the political opposition did. In 1933, the Socialist party name Garvy was more dangerous to them than the Jewish name Bronstein. The Nazis turned their attention first to repression of the political opponents—anyone who dissented from the dictatorship being established and who belonged to movements that could organize opposition.

The Mensheviks got the message and saw they were in danger. It was not that their political analysis was superior per se. They may have had a heightened political awareness, attentive to political processes because they were heavily involved in politics. But other factors besides analytic ability mattered in shaping their early flight. Not being German nationals, they had no attachment to the "fatherland," as did many German Jews, who were, for example, veterans of WWI. What the Mensheviks had was direct information from examples. They saw people being hauled away. They had been through this before in Russia.

They saw the Soviet Bolshevik behavior of repression being repeated. They had direct evidence of having people in their network targeted and mauled.

In analyzing that phone call, the historian in me wondered if the voice at the other end actually said, "This is the Gestapo "—was that label being used already? But this is the kind of detail that does not matter. The timing was of significance: right after the Reichstag fire, the Nazis used that event as an excuse to enact all sorts of supposed emergency decrees and intensify the repression. Communist deputies were tossed out of the Reichstag and locked up.

Many people left Germany then, such as the Woytinskys, who had arranged to get visas to Switzerland beforehand. I have no evidence the Garvys needed visas to go to Paris by train, but they may indeed have had to get some kind of work permit or residence permit when they got there. Switzerland was likely more restrictive. France, facing unemployment, was soon to turn hostile to foreigners. It seems likely the labor—Menshevik connection helped them with the French Socialist movement.

During these years in Berlin, Boris (Buka) Fichman, the brother of Grandma Sophia, was living in Berlin as well. He left Berlin for Paris, but I don't know exactly on what day. It is likely he did so to be with his sister's family. I also know little of how he earned his living. He was involved in some kind of commerce and trade. He certainly helped my grandparents financially, but I don't know much detail about how he did so. I will return to his story later.

Why were the Garvys "early deciders" about leaving Nazi Germany? They had lived in Germany but were not deeply rooted, unlike many established German Jews. Of Russian origin, stateless (without government protection), Socialist, and Jewish, they had four vulnerabilities toward which the regime's hostility was rather well known. The Menshevik network gave them early information that people were being rounded up, imprisoned, beaten, let go and told to get out. All of these were not subtle signals, cues that, alas, many people did not get.

Of these factors, the role of networking had the most impact. Jews were badly treated from the beginning of the Nazi seizure of power, but most did not realize "bad" would become deadly when the Nazis unleashed the full murderousness of the Holocaust. The first victims of the regime's brutality were the political opposition. The collapse of Weimar and the failure to defend the rule of law cannot be traced solely to antisemitism. The Nazis came to power for a complex of reasons: hyper-nationalism in response to the defeat in WWI and the Versailles Treaty, the hyper-inflation of 1923, the hyper-unemployment of the Great Depression of 1929-33, the desire to repress the labor movement, fear of bolshevism and radical revolution.

As they attacked the regime's opponents, the Nazis pursued them strategically to destroy potential opposition. The famous quote from Martin Neimöller, a Lutheran theologian, who began with some sympathy for the Nazis, then turned against them, for which he was imprisoned, captures it well (though there is a dispute on exactly what he said, especially in the sequence of which victim came first.

> "First, they came for the Communists, and I did not speak out—Because I was not a Communist.
>
> Then they came for the Socialists, and I did not speak out—Because I was not a Socialist.
>
> Then they came for the Trade Unionists, and I did not speak out—Because I was not a Trade Unionist.
>
> Then they came for the Jews, and I did not speak out—Because I was not a Jew.
>
> Then they came for me—and there was no one left to speak for me."[2]

Does the precise order have some political meaning—Trade Unionists, first, or Socialists, or Communists? There are different versions in circulation, and there is debate about what Neimöller wrote, but in a broader sense, the details of the order matter less than the idea that it does not begin with the attack on Jews (or Roma).

Jews were killed because no one stood up earlier when the defenders of the rule of law were being attached. In the end, the Nazis went after all of them. Conservatives sometimes defend fascism by saying it was attacking the Communists from whom the menace was greater. In 1933 it is less clear the menace was any greater, but at any rate, it is no justification. The key point is that Jews were vulnerable because the rule of law was not protected.

My family and the Menshevik brethren left because they were under attack right away. Many Jews did not leave right away because they did not feel the attack so directly or so extensively.

My grandmother and mother followed my grandfather and uncle not long afterward by train to Paris in March of 1933. Dadia Buka and his wife, Teutia Olya, joined them sometime soon after. My parents were not yet married. My father stayed to finish his high school (gymnasium) leaving certification and left for Paris in 1934. His aunt and uncle left for Belgium in 1935. Germany had been a refuge, with a welcoming large Socialist Party and a large trade union movement. Now all that was destroyed. Once again, they were refugees.

Boris' Life in the USSR: the Tunnel Closes Up.

While the Garvy family first settled into a Berlin existence in '23 and then had to flee in '33, Boris Ber Gourevitch was adapting to the life of a political prisoner in the USSR. He was, for most of the period, under some kind of house arrest or internal exile, from one location or another. The trove of letters from my grandfather to his relatives provides me with insights about him and my father, which I realize my children are not likely to have about me, as we don't write letters much but make emails or text messages or phone calls. As his family and friends escape to the West, Boris often writes from his internal exile or prison in the new USSR. Heavily censored, his letters focus mostly on personal reflections, very often on his eldest child, my father, Shura. I learn a lot about Shura, but also Boris and between the

cracks, something about his realization that he will not be allowed to leave and has to confront a constrained life. The record of arrests is a significant indicator of this. He had less and less freedom of movement and political activity. He had been in contact with colleagues in the USSR, but this was now blocked. He did manage to write letters to

Shura with Lyalya in 1930, the last photo of them together before he leaves and their reunion in 1963.

his family. Living in Russia were his parents and some brothers. He wrote to them, but I have no copies of those letters. He wrote to a brother and sister-in-law living in Berlin, and then to his son Shura, and to some other siblings. These are the letters that have survived, translated in 2015. The letters from Boris Ber are quite evocative.

The letters make quite clear the drama surrounding the fate of my own father, Shura—Alexander Borisovich Gourevitch, as he was formally called. Boris and Lyalya sent him out of the USSR in 1931. I know after the fact that Boris never saw him again. But I did not know the context of the decision, how he felt about sending him away, just why he did so, how final he sensed the departure would be. Was this like Kindertransport for Jewish children in Central Europe in 1938-40, with desperate parents hoping they would reunite someday? Or somehow different, as Shura was alone in this departure. Reading Boris' letters gives some insight. Right away, we see from the earliest of letters the depth of Boris's attachment to his oldest child and only son.

My Dad as a Child: letters from Tashkent 1924:

The first letters come from Tashkent, one of the early places to which Boris was sent. It is a relatively large and warm city, currently with over two million people; the capital of today's Uzbekistan, in the 1920s considerably smaller. Over time Boris was sent to more and more remote towns and villages. My father visited him in some of these places and, at times, lived with him, as well as his mother and his sister. At times these were solitary visits.

The very first letter suggests Boris still wondered if the authorities would give him the promised visa. Tashkent, July 19, 1924, "…officially, the term change {of the confinement} will happen in 10 days. In what direction, only God knows. I will then let you guys know what the situation is with the visas just in case we bring up the possibilities of our travels to you. I really want to, but my hope is small; I will tell you everything. For now, the hopes for the future are such that I don't feel like doing anything, not even reading."

This passage appears over a year after the failure to grant the exit visa and the departure of Peter Garvy-Bronstein and his family. Six months later, Boris writes to Berlin, "One of my hopes is for us to be together next year. Either for you guys to come here or for us to travel there." In retrospect, this seems a wistful longing that they might see each other; a hope remains that voyages would be allowed in one direction or another. One difficulty in interpreting the exchanges is "anachronism"— that is, reading into the past the things you know happened later. In hindsight, we know this reunion did not happen. The hope implied here does not reappear in subsequent letters. And does he really expect it could happen? We can't know.

That very same letter provides a vivid portrait of my Dad, Shura, at age eight.

> "Regardless of the bad weather, Shura has gotten really tan: he walks on the street only in pants without a shirt, because of which everyone is looking at him: every person feels the need to turn around and scold him: some people support him, some people decry his action, some people feel bad for the poor boy, who doesn't have necessary things, like a shirt. Anyways, I must tell you sincerely that most people agree he's probably handsome.
>
> In general, he looks like a Black boy, he looks very nice, and everything would be good if only he would complain a bit less and wouldn't be such a crybaby: he's an unbelievable crybaby, cries about every little thing and then always asks: "why do I have to listen to you?" I have to agree that question puts me in a very hard place. I can't refer to the appropriate commandment because he doesn't know anything at all about the commandments.
>
> Actually, his atheistic upbringing sometimes puts him in a bind, in which he doesn't understand things that kids usually understand very well. For example, he's now reading "The Adventures of Tom Sawyer" by Mark Twain. In that book, there are constant references to religion, references to psalms, Bible verses, and the Sermon on the Mount. Or he reads in one of Pushkin's works: "Why do you wander at night, Cain?" How can you explain to him who Cain is?
>
> It's funny listening to his arguments—in the yard with kids—about God: he's the only one who is atheist. In addition to religious concepts, there are other understandings that are hard to explain to him. For example, the other day, it turned out he doesn't know things that would be elementary for us in our childhood, like a general, a minister, a nobleman; even the word "gendarme," "goroldovoy"—we have to explain them to him by comparison. In general, it's very funny."

So many themes here! Walking around without a shirt, getting looks

for being so dark! When my younger son Nick was about the same age of 8, he too often walked around without a shirt or jacket. He grew up in Southern California, which is drier, less hot than Tashkent but mild, and he wore little clothing even when cold.

Then the phrase, "He tans so deeply, he looks like a Black boy." This very Shura, my Dad, told me that when they moved to New York in 1940, and he went with my mother in the subway, he would hear nasty comments; Dad had black wiry hair and dark tanned Mediterranean complexion with dark freckles, a vaguely North African look. Some people in New York took them as a biracial couple and disapproved. In the 1930s, when he was often hungry as a student in Paris, some Egyptian friends took him to Embassy parties where there was food, introducing him as "Monsieur Shura," and he passed easily. When my wife and I visited Morocco in April of 2015 as tourists, many locals said, "You look Moroccan," which I interpreted as "North African Jew" (and I have slightly lighter hair, and paler skin than my Dad, though like him I tan very fast and deep, and for some reason get taken as a local all over the world—I have been asked for directions in Moscow, Stockholm, Berlin, Paris, London, Rome, Madrid, Mexico, as well as all over the US.) Was there racism in Boris' comment, or more likely to me, was it an observation of how dark was Shura's skin, how easily it tanned?

My Dad did point out to me that the father of the Russian language, Pushkin, was himself partly of African origin! And I did also learn how much racism Africans did find in the Soviet Union when they came to study and how much anti-Semitism still exists in the USSR and Russia. My Dad was a biologist: racism repelled him for many reasons; his scientific comment I heard him say often was that there was as much genetic variety within each race as between them.

Back to Grandpa Boris' letter: he complains that Shura is "an unbelievable crybaby" and wails, "Why do I have to listen to you?" These seem classic paternal complaints! What father has not had a reaction like that to a grumpy child, and what child has not wondered why he has to accept parental authority? But how many of us get to hear our grandfather have such an exchange with our own father, as usually, it is we who are at the receiving end in becoming a parent. Right away, I felt these letters would be an amazing moment for intergenerational dialog where none of the participants actually are actually in the same room. I never met my paternal grandfather; my two sons, Alex and Nick, never met their grandpa, Shura, my dad, who died in 1969, long before they were born.

So here was MY Grandpa Boris commenting on MY Dad Shura, expressing the kind of exchanges I recall having with MY own sons, Alex and Nick, which they, now parents themselves, have had with their children, as I have observed. Suddenly we all somehow know each other. I can't say I recall these testy exchanges with my own Dad, Shura, as he was a gentle soul, and I was a relatively mild-mannered child, I think. But it must have happened.

Then there is the fascinating passage about religion. Grandpa Boris complains that Shura lacks religious knowledge, so he does not understand references to the Sermon on the Mount, Cain and Abel, or arguments about God when he is the only one in the schoolyard who is an atheist. In responding to Shura's challenge to his authority, Boris can't invoke the Ten Commandments, as Shura does not know them. Well, why does Shura not know them? Boris has not taught them to Shura or insisted he learn them through religious education. It is Boris, the son of a Rabbi, who chose a secular socialist path for his son, as he had chosen for himself, departing from the rabbinical traditions of his father.

Years later, I wondered the same about my children: bringing them up in my secular traditions, I too was troubled by their lack of cultural education about religion and history, not so much by the implications that had by the lack of deference to me, but more generally about cultural formation. As the father, their lack was my fault, as I could have shaped that education. So, right away, I thought Shura's lack derived from Boris's choices, and there I was in dialog with the Grandfather I had not met.

All this was from Boris' first letter. Right away, I was moved. These words mixed the anguish of his circumstances—the tense political situation of being controlled by the KGB while yearning to leave—with the deeply personal and individual, involving his children and family, evocative observations about his child, as vivid as anything I have on anyone in my family of any generation.

The early letters communicate family matters. Boris talks about Lyalya, her health and her prison sentence: between the two, which of them has to serve the punishment and where with difficulties posed for taking care of their children. He asks about the lives of his brother and sister-in-law in Berlin: their work, their income, their activities, and when children arrive, he asks about them. And he often writes about Shura, what he is good at in school and what not.

In a very long letter from Vizinga (in the direction of the Urals toward Perm and Ekaterinburg) on May 8, 1928, he writes:

> The boy (Shura) is very responsible; he's especially very good in history and math. He likes these subjects a lot. In biology, I think he knows more than me. He has difficulty with languages. And struggles with Russian writing. He really dislikes writing essays, and it's difficult, but he works very hard, and in the end, it turns out ok. He doesn't write letters because he doesn't like to. When he has to write to his grandma, it's torture for him. He's very energetic when he plays with other kids, but in chores, he's very slow.

At one point, Shura is reading Marx _Das Capital_ with his Aunt Bacya, the youngest of Boris' siblings, and has written Boris something to the effect that it is not so hard. Boris writes sternly back that he should not be so arrogant. It is much harder than he might imagine. Was it offensive for Boris to hear Shura think he did not have to work hard to understand what, for Boris, was a fundamental text in his life?

Were these exchanges "typical" father-son, to be understood psycho-dynamically as Freud might, or intergenerationally, as literature does, such as Turgenev's novel, _Fathers and Sons,_ evokes? I read the Turgenev book in my late teens as a son, then again as a father, and now again in writing this manuscript, as I reflect on being a grandfather myself trying to grasp the relationship of my grandfather to my father. Was there something specifically Boris-Shura in it aside from the idiom of a Socialist bringing up his son in what was a politically stressed and stressful period? I wonder how much the letters were influenced by him being a man in exile, isolated, without much regular work, with more time on his hands than most men in this period had. The letters seem acutely observant and articulate, especially about his son and later his daughter.

We see in them the kernel of the growing anxiety Boris had about Shura's fate. He sees Shura's talent, his brightness, and his capacities in science and math. The boy learns these things quickly, and at one point, Boris says Shura knows more than he does. Indeed, Shura was brilliant, a fundamental fact agreed to by all who knew him.   H   e did get his Ph.D., despite the interruptions of three migrations, four different languages, and four countries. We know he became Director of Microbiological Research at Bristol Labs in Syracuse and is one of the inventors of Tetracycline, synthetic penicillin and other antibiotics. His brilliance and his achievements are crucial to the arc of his life, from his father's decision to allow him to leave the USSR, to support his family to how Grandmother Lyalya found him, but I am running ahead of the story. Shura's brightness posed a most dramatic decision for his parents quite early on: should Shura leave his family to get an education? We know the outcome, but these letters help us understand the process: the first evidence they were considering appears in August 1928, in a letter by Boris to his sister Bacya.

Vizinga August 28, 1928

"Lyalya told you about Shura. Regarding Asrunia and Anya's suggestion {*that he move to Berlin with them*}, I'm uncomfortable about one thing: how do they manage their money, especially if they don't have permanent jobs? In all other aspects, I have no other qualms—I think it would be a lifesaver for Shura.

August 29, 1928 (from Lyalya to Bacya)

"Shura didn't get in again {*to the local school*} even though they said they had nine spots—only two people wanted to go, and then all of a sudden, they didn't have a spot for him. It's very sad. He's not affected by it; he doesn't want to go to school, maybe he thinks he won't have friends anyway, and he says he'll get more done at home. ... I think it's too early to let him go; he's only 12 years old, and he'll be very far away from everyone. Boris agrees that he should go, Shura doesn't want to go, but he can be convinced."

Shura is not being admitted to school! The letters don't say why. They suggest a sudden rejection: they were told there were nine places only two wanted to go, and suddenly no space. Is it because of his father's politically undesirable background? Or is it because he is a Jew? Or both? Experts advise me it was most likely politics. Antisemitism was against Bolshevik official policy in those years, though this may not have prevented its practice at the local level. Stalin did engage in antisemitic practices, but did It was policy and practice to work against class enemies of the regime: By 1928, people were being sorted out according to their social and political background, to favor those working class or peasant background, to strike against those of dangerous backgrounds in the bourgeoisie, the intelligentsia, the aristocracy and the political opposition. The child of a political prisoner, himself educated—this was a bad background. Whatever the reason, it was no longer tolerable, as Shura's talents were becoming clearer and to such parents, the lack of education of their children was no doubt unbearable.

What to do? It is in these letters we see the first written reference to the idea of Shura leaving his parents for Berlin. Anya and Asrunia "are asking for him to move in with them." Boris notes Shura's knack for science and math, which continues in Shura's life. But there is doubt about when to do it. Boris worries that Shura is too young, he will not like leaving his family, and that the Berlin family is economically stressed, already has a child and is now expecting another.

Indeed, soon after the school rejection, Boris requests a visa for Shura to leave the USSR for Berlin. I had not known of this request till I discovered it while searching for evidence that Boris was the father of Shura, something I needed to get FSB access to the archives in 2016-17. Did my father know of this request? I never heard it mentioned in family circles, but that does not prove it was unknown, though I suspect they were not aware of it. The KGB approved the request in 1928, which may be crucial to their approval again in 1931. In the family saga, the letter reveals how strongly Grandpa Boris worried about his son.

> You probably know that Asrunia and Anya are waiting for the addition to their family. In regards to this, we think that we probably won't be able to send Shura—although people already know in Moscow (that Shura is going to Germany)—it's too many additional expenses for them, and it's hard as it is. The other day we got a letter from Moisei. He doesn't recommend sending Shura to Asrunia and instead invites Shura to come to live with him. I don't know what's best. On the one hand, I'm losing confidence in my inclination to send Shura anywhere, just thinking about sending him to Moisei. …And it seems to me it would be good for him to live without the family for a while when he needs to be independent. But about sending him to Moscow to Moisei, my thoughts are the same as yours, and Lyalya is firmly against it, the same as she was about sending him to Asrunia."

A letter of September 28, 1928, from sister Bacya discusses her search for visas and what to bring to their mother (Grandmother Styssia). This seems to be a plan to visit USSR from France. And there were trips from Styssia, my father's grandmother, to Berlin, so some travel was possible back and forth.

At this time, Boris and Lyalya turn to another kind of help with their family problems. An agency, the "Political Red Cross" (not to be confused with the non-political relief Red Cross agency), worked in Moscow to help political prisoners of various kinds, from Mensheviks and other political activists, but also religious people. It turns out to be the vehicle through which Rabbi Scheersohn, the Lubovicher leader who became prominent in Brooklyn, came to the US. An important leader of the Red Cross in Moscow was Catherine (Yekaterina) Pavlovna Peshkova, the first wife of Maxim Gorky, a quite famous writer with international standing and influence in the USSR. In the case of Boris and his family, Mme Peshkova's efforts do not seem to have helped in any way we can prove. It shows the dire circumstances of their lives at this time. In a letter of October 10, 1928, from Lyalya, and from Boris on October 31, 1928, focusing on the schooling problem:

> It is difficult to educate our child, age 13, as he has been excluded from school here in Vizinge. The lack of jobs and constant moving makes it difficult. We have a proposal to send Shura to his uncle and aunt in Berlin. But I don't know how to do this without your help.

Note that this is already a request for help in getting permission for him to leave for Berlin. No reference is made here to the visa request of 1928.

Another set of appeals came two years later. Boris writes on February 10, 1931, to release Lyalya from exile assignment because she has to take care of Galka (age 5) and Shura (14). The children have been with Lyalya's sister in Voronezh, but the sister has a baby and cannot take care of them. The sister herself sends an appeal on February 12, 1931, seeking a release because Shura and Galka are living alone; I do not know whether that means literally with no adults, perhaps it means with grandparents or close relatives. And there is an accompanying statement by Shura himself: "Please release the sentencing of our mother, as we are separated from her and our father, who is in Tobolsk." The children were separated from their parents for political

house arrest, needing care, and writing for help. There is even a letter from Grandma Styssia to Trotsky asking for his help, which suggests that they had known each other; she had little way of knowing what Trotsky's position was in the system at this time. There is no evidence these letters to Peshkova had any direct effect in any way we can prove.

The letters from Boris and Lyalya to Berlin are full of references to this situation: the separation of the children from their mother, Boris' issues of health, and what to do to educate Shura. At one point, Boris writes he does not know where Shura is. The lags of communication must have been maddening to everyone, especially Boris, the most isolated. At times, the references are somewhat confusing to me. I am not sure whether the children are with Grandmother Gourevitch in Dnepropetrovsk (Dnipro) or with the other grandmother or grandfather, Lyalya's parents in Leningrad, or with Lyalya's sister, but where? Russian families are legendary for their interconnections and caretaking. It is quite evident here.

Very often, the letters complain about family members not writing. One package sent clothes, and Boris analyzes which of them make good trades for other things he may need more. He thanks them for postcards and worries they spend too much sending packages. What did he do for food and for money? His letters talk a lot about looking for work.

The intensity of these concerns strengthens in the letters of 1931. This one repeats the observations on his talents in physics and chemistry.

> "But it seems to me that Shura has definite talent and inclination towards a scientific job, especially in physics and chemistry, particularly in the latter. I don't think I'm just convincing myself of this because I am his father, but it's possible I am mistaken. He does very well in these subjects, and most importantly, he understands and can visualize all the concepts in these subjects. His head works in this way. ... *for him to be rejected from school given such talent is not easy for me* " (letter from Tobolsk of May 24, 1931).

And the turmoil with Boris and Shura about leaving or staying:

> Tobolsk – (June 15, 1931). But still, I'm leaning more toward a concrete decision. I confess, with a lot, a lot of inner resentment (much bigger than last time). But at the end of the day, what kind of life can he have here, really? Most importantly—how can we know what prospects he will have here—it's

possible the most unexpected could happen. What's especially making me fluctuate on my decision is what Shura wrote: "I know that if I take your advice and go, that it will be for a long time." Maybe for a very long time—and when will we see each other? But we have to decide. This shouldn't stop me…. Shura himself, clearly, is also struggling and doesn't know what to do. Without his agreement, it can't be done, and I wouldn't want him to agree to it just because of me—I don't want him to go against his will.

"Shura has to want to go himself." I had a letter from Shura (from Leningrad); he's very unhappy with his life there; he writes it's very lonely, and his only happiness is Galya … (who's the "only one not thinking about where they're giving away food").

Several of the letters in this period are quite long, and several of them have long passages discussing theoretical issues of philosophy, though not with any specific political direction. Some letters discuss what to do with Boris's mother, Styssia, and her health problems.

Then comes the very powerful letter where it is quite clear Shura is leaving, and it is quite clear to Boris how momentous this is as they may never see each other again.

October 15, 1931. Obdorsk

I got a letter from mom {*this is Styssia, Boris' mother, Shura's Grandma, whom we have seen in the photos of Tashkent*}, in which she said that the decision about Shura will be made in a positive way: it's coming along. …I told him that besides the theoretical preparation, he would get the opportunity to experience life more vividly and holistically, with all its uniqueness and make a decision about his own life. I felt that I had to warn him. And even then, maybe he's going. Who knows when we'll see each other again or if we'll ever see each other again?

The letter is quite long and covers quite a range of topics, from theory and ideas to family and children, birthdays, health, and work.

This is the final letter before Shura's actual departure. The last phrase speaks for itself. He knows, they know, the decision has to be taken with the likely knowledge they will not see each other again. Imagine you are sending your child away in the hope he will have a better life than you could provide him, knowing you are not likely to see each other again. I had always known this basic fact: that my

Dad left, I had always surmised it was because the child of a Menshevik had no future in Bolshevik-controlled Russia. Reading the letters confirms this, though it rarely explicitly says so. The letters speak a lot about education and talent. Boris sees how bright Shura is, especially in the fields of science and math. He does not talk about talents of philosophy, writing, or integrating ideas, which I sense were Boris' talents, or what I surmise political activist revolutionaries have. He judged correctly about Shura's skills, given what happened.

It was in reading the letters I saw how deeply the concern for Shura's education and personal development influenced the discussions Boris and Lyalya had about what to do. Whether to send him away, then once in Berlin, what kind of a degree to follow in Germany, the question of the "abitur" discussed earlier seems so clear here—Boris and the relatives in Berlin all supported the high academic option because they saw how bright he was at an early age.

I understood the logic behind Shura leaving Russia for a better life; that it was no place for the child of Menshevik to be under house arrest and exiled to remote towns, with so much attention paid to your class and political background. The regime wanted to favor the proletariat, but there were not many of these. The Bolsheviks wanted to evaluate who was politically reliable and who was not.   Shura, for sure, was politically unreliable to the regime, given his parents' political activity and his class background. Political vulnerability alone would have given the parents concern. Shura's brightness added to the anxiety. Perhaps it also reassured them that his brains would help him find a way. So, to repeat, the letters show the importance of education as a theme in motivating the departure. Was this a justification to himself, to ease the pain of losing his son? Suppose Shura had been less bright, a good solid kid, not so great in school. It seems likely he would not have been sent away. His brain, imagination and capacity for work pulled him away from his parents and country of origin and led him to a productive life, as an immigrant, with a family, and ultimately to Lyalya's reconnecting to him after 25 years.

Contact Severed: Shura in Berlin (1931-34) Boris in USSR 1931-34

With Shura in Berlin, the letters from Boris are now to a son he senses he will never see again. Their lives diverge. Shura's life broadens, and Boris's life narrows. Shura embarks on a journey of education and migration. He joins the Menshevik group that eventually lands in New York. Boris remains trapped by his confinement, separation from family, the limits on his freedom, and the constraints on his ability to undertake meaningful work. The letters from Boris to his family are all the more evocative about him as a person. The letters suggest a strongly observant father, attentive to detail and interested in the psychology of his children and situations. Boris' comments are acute, expressive, and insightful. With so much time and little intellectual challenge from his situation, he had time and ability to observe, reflect and write. He must surely have become depressed, lonely and cut off. At times, there is desperation in the tone and annoyance that he has not gotten letters. Though the mail seems so very irregular, for weather, ice, and all sorts of reasons, he complains that Shura does not write, which he no doubt did not do often enough. This evokes to me vivid memories of my own parents pouring over the deep meaning of the words on a postcard they had received in the 1960s from my brother while he was driving out West to California when I knew that the card was written in haste, surely not worth such exegesis. These days, cell phone calls, emails, and Skype change the communication game a lot and often mean fewer records for archivists!!!

Dated December 14, 1931, we have the first letter from Boris since Shura's arrival in Berlin the previous month.

> And I want to tell you again how happy I was to receive your letter. It brought an immense amount of joy to me—that you guys are writing together, Anya and Shura, everything you guys are telling me about, and the tone in which the letter is written.

The father, having sent his son away for the good of the son, is feeling the loss acutely. He senses that he and Shura have grown apart. Is this stronger than what most fathers feel about sons, mothers and daughters, parents and children? "Tell me everything" and "Don't keep anything from me"; that kind of phrasing appears often in these letters.

Galya was doubtless too young to grasp that she might not see Shura again but not too young not to miss him. Their lives were intertwined, together and separated at times. Shura did not learn of her death till 1962 when Lyalya wrote him, and he was strongly moved by the loss.

"My dear, beloved and favorite, " Boris writes in one letter. How much he misses him! Boris asks for information but also for sharing for communication. He wants Shura to discuss whatever he can. "I very sharply feel the need… I dream about it." He asks about the "environment" of relationships, "gravitational tendencies, sympathies, of young men and women." "I know, Shura, how hard and difficult that is, and maybe unusual to talk about it simply and directly. But I am sure we able to do it." (from letters of 1932)

I don't know what Shura felt receiving these painful letters. He was young, busy, like teenagers in school. He surely felt some guilt about having left and how lonely his father was, as well as his mother and sister. The transportation system made it hard to know how many letters were not being received and when they arrived in relation to the date mailed. Every so often, a bunch arrives together. I found myself lurching back and forth as I read these in an internal dialogue with my father and grandfather.

> "Dad, why did you not write your father more often? You must have known how lonely he was;
>
> Grandpa, you are so hard on him; he is trying to lead a life; young teenagers have so many preoccupations; cut him some slack!"

And, of course, I moved back and forth from loyalty to my father, then thinking as a parent, then thinking about myself with my children and themselves with their own kids.

> April 23, 1932.
>
> My dear Shura, on May 5th, you'll be 16 years old; you're already a full adult; I wish you a lot, a lot of happiness and success in life, to grow as a healthy and good person! How did you spend that day? Where did you go? Write about everything in detail. —Your letter arrived on my birthday, thank you, my dear, for the congratulations. I haven't been writing to you all infrequently; I don't know what's going on. I'm writing from here for the first time; I got only one single correspondence from you.

The letter describes Galya at some length. It notes that Grandma Styssia may come to visit for the summer, which seems remarkable, as she is not young and how is she able to travel?. I know she went to Berlin as well and visited that branch of her family.

From Lyalya, April 23, 1932.

…What did you guys decide for the future? Where are you going to study, in school or in a technical institute? It's very hard for me, almost impossible, to give advice without being there, especially since I can't take into account all of your conditions. …. Your mom. {Lyalya} Frida (her sister) and Grandpa (her father) always pass on their hellos to you.

This letter raises the discussion we have noted about technical school versus gymnasium, which Boris followed closely.

Obdorsk, June 12, 1932.

You guys (Anna and Asrunia) asked about my opinion about Shura—whether he should stay in school or transfer to a technical school. What can I tell you guys? The question is dependent on distant possibilities. It's not possible for me to decide from such a distance, and it's clearer for you guys on the spot.

… Of course, receiving a higher education would be very good, but obviously, it means leaving too many years as a student without earnings.

Obdorsk, June 13, 1932. Even with ability, talent, and genius, it is very hard to accomplish anything without hard work, not only in the scientific discipline, where you need to acquire enormous amounts of knowledge and study a bunch of facts.

And one more thing, Shura, my dear! I'm writing about this because I'm scared you're taking for granted that this or that subject is easy for you, easy to understand. In a few spots in your letters, it seemed to me that this made sense to note. Maybe you're a little too confident? Here you write about your reading of *Kapital* with Bacya: "I have to admit to you that all of it turned out to be not so difficult as I expected." I think, my dear, that you're making a mistake. … Ok, now maybe you understand the general outlined ideas, but that's not enough. I also thought when I read it the first time that I understood it exactly. But only later, I understood and realized how little I understood in *Kapital* and learned from it. Plekhanov said that every time he reads *Kapital* again, he discovers something new in it. And it's true. It's not uncommon that when people are familiar with economic literature and are seemingly knowledgeable, meaning they've studied Marx, they still don't understand some situations or Marx's whole theory.

Your Dad.

Boris evokes the Russian cultural greats to convey how much perspiration goes into inspiration and that it takes lots of hard work. And chastising him for suggesting reading Marx wasn't so difficult!

In reflecting on Shura's choice of educational program, Boris engages in a broad exploration of the issues of education, of the advanced worker vs. higher education skills. He admires the skilled worker who is active and knowledgeable, fighting for a new life". Boris warns Shura of being overconfident, as in studying Kapital with his aunt Bacya. This seems a classic father's or older person's response to a younger person. Older people do learn each time they reread something, but that is in part because their perspectives change as they go through life.

Then a strong letter from Boris conveying his longing for news and contact with Shura.

> June 24, 1932 …my thoughts are always with you, my dear; I always remember, think about you—and miss you so much. What's going on with you? I'm trying to imagine what you live like, how you are now—it's hard. So much time has passed, life apart in such different environments in these years… I have a thousand questions floating around in my mind, on my tongue. If you would indulge your "old man" and write everything yourself that you can—the way it used to be

On June 25, 1932 (a date which 11 years later became my birthday), Boris replies to Shura's comments in a recent letter about "contradictions" in the historical situation and raises questions of economic and social theory concerning the communal economic system and the contradictions of capitalism. Clearly, he spends a lot of time thinking about theory—Marxism, socialism, communism but the letters avoid comment on the Stalinist regime and policy. One rare exception was a reference to the great rise in the Nazi vote in the German elections of 31 July 1932, " I am very worried about your situation given the recent event," and wonders if they are considering leaving Germany with the Nazis now the largest party in the Reichstag.

Of course, personal details mix in. And Finally in this letter from Cherdyn, January 18, 1933, notes that "Galya, by the way, every time we get a letter from you guys, jumps on me: did I get a separate one from Shura! And she was really upset when two letters ago there was nothing specifically for her, and she was immeasurably ecstatic when last time she did have a separate one." Later in this letter, he writes at some length about political economy and historical materialism, with references to Newton, Darwin as well as Marx.

The reference to both Marx and Darwin was evocative for me, in that according to Family Legend, Boris gave a copy of *Das Kapital* and *Origin of the Species* as a farewell present to Shura when he left Russia! (The volumes did not make the journey to the US, as my parents arrived with only a knapsack, some photos, a bit of jewelry and some monogrammed silverware belonging to the Garvys). The intellectual point made is also interesting to me personally as it expresses well my view of history and theory: it is hard to understand either without the other, be it in politics, humanities or science. Both books are important in the Socialist Tradition of those years across Europe, as they see science and history as based on laws that can be scientifically ascertained.

And finally, in this letter:

(March 27, 1933). There will still be so much more to write about, Shurycya! Anya wrote that you couldn't bring yourself to start studying the English language. Find a group to sign yourself up for. The issue is that the longer you wait to start learning, the harder it will be. And it's imperative to learn English. I'm begging you, Shura!

And also, my dear: I would really like it if you didn't stop studying the Russian language, Russian literature because otherwise, you'll forget that which you already knew.

Your dad

This next is the first letter after Hitler took power on January 30, 1933. The burning of the Reichstag building was on February 27, after which the Nazis stepped up repression. The Garvys left Berlin right after that, along with many others from the Menshevik refugee group. Shura stayed longer, until 1934, to finish his degree courses, and his aunt and uncle a bit longer after that, till 1935. This letter below shows some awareness of this crisis moment and asks about their plans. It congratulates Shura on his gymnasium graduation, after which he left for Paris.

(Cherdyn Verh-Kamsk March 27, 1933)My dears! I just wrote a card to congratulate Shura, and it turned out I still have about 5-10 minutes. I want to write a little more to again congratulate all of you. I'm so immeasurably grateful to all of you for everything you've done. If Shura finished, it's due to what you have done for him.

At this point, we leave Boris and go back to France. We stay there until Shura, and the Garvys leave for the US: until Nazis arrive on the heels of the German army forcing yet another flight and escape, and the astonishing stories of getting to the US. And then some who do not make it: Buka Fichman and his wife, who are trapped and sent to Auschwitz. And then back to Boris Ber-Gourevitch, who is never allowed to leave and then killed by Stalin.

Endnotes

1 Karl Dietrich Bracher. The German Dictatorship; The Origins, Structure, and Effects of National Socialism; New York, Praeger 1970, translated into English by Jean Steinberg (Die deutsche Diktatur: Entstehung, Struktur, Folgen des Nationalsozialismus, 1969, One of the most important among many interpretations.

Explaining the collapse of Weimar remains deeply controversial. While working on my book Politics in Hard Times, I saw a young historian have his career ruined by getting caught in the midst of a big battle mixing interpretation, power, scholarship over the role of big business interests in helping the Nazis come to power. David Abraham, then a junior professor, was accused of sloppy notetaking and improper use of citations and evidence, which are serious errors for historians. But the actual interpretative side of what he said was never carefully challenged, and the evidence he provided remains strong. In my view, he was not properly treated. David Abraham, The Collapse of the Weimar Republic (Princeton: Princeton University Press, 1981) and the conflict with Henry Ashley Turner, Jr. German Big Business and the Rise of Hitler (New York: Oxford University Press, 1985); On the controversy, see James Joll, "Storm over German History: Business as Usual," New York Review of Books, 32, no. 14 (26 September 1985) 5-10). I cite at length from my notes in Politics in Hard Times because the controversy remains vivid and relevant to debate today – see footnote 13 of chapter 4, p. 253. Joll notes that " … in this as in other cases economic differences led to political divisions. The curious thing that emerges from both Turner's and Abraham's books is in fact how little the leaders of the various economic pressure groups understood where their interests lay; and the Nazis were able to profit from this. "

The core of Abraham's argument is the point stressed by Joll—that the conflict over policy contributed to political deadlock, which the Nazis exploited. The core of Turner's argument is that the Nazis were not the first choice of big business among politicians== a point with which Abraham fully agrees. This is an important statement because of decades of belief in the more primitive, reductionist explanations of the Nazi seizure of power. But if business, or some other groups, contributed to the paralysis of Weimar, then surely they play some causal role, which smoking gun epistemology ignores. "

The relevance of this debate to current discussions (the 21st century) lies in the effort to map social preferences or openness to options on societal actors, which then allows the possibility of modeling the terms of trade along which various bargains and alignments can occur.

Abraham left the field of history to become a law professor.

2 Discussion of the J. Neimöller quotation can be found in Wikipedia, which provides several versions, Accessed on 28 July 2021

3 Peshkova file, sent by Morozova

Chapter 7

Paris

Third Flight and Second Refuge (1933-40) City of Light, City of Hope and The Long Arm of Stalin

"Where did you live in Paris?" I asked my parents when planning my first trip there in the summer of 1962, between my junior and senior years of college. I was very excited about going to Europe, especially France. Many of my Oberlin College classmates were doing the same. For me, it had the extra reward of exploring family roots, what I now see among the first steps that led to this book some sixty years ago. My mother was somewhat mystified.

"Why are you so interested? What is the appeal? Life was difficult for us in Paris, as it had been in Berlin," was the gist of my mother's reply. "We were quite poor and had to work very hard to survive. There was lots of schoolwork, and we had to earn money to keep the family alive."

Nonetheless, she gave me the address. The apartment my parents moved into upon their marriage in the summer of 1938 was at 2, rue du Pot de Fer, in the 5th, just before it empties into the rue Mouffetard, and it is still there. The building looked rather tawdry when I first visited, suggestive of the poor immigrant and student neighborhood to which it then belonged. It had a big sag, a potbelly, as if it were about to burst into the street. Mother spoke of shopping at what was then a poor person's street market, at the bottom of the hill, on the rue Mouffetard; she was veryproud of her friendship with a merchant who would give her cookies for free if she guessed its weight correctly. In the early 2000s, the neighborhood appeared stylish as the Latin Quarter burst forward to envelop the area in fashionable chic. The building's dangerous sag is gone, as everything seems appropriately kept up. The street market there is now one of Paris' most appealing to all and sundry. From this apartment, they had to watch the Nazi danger rise across the Rhine, advance toward Paris, and force them into the rapid decision-making that saved their lives.

Arriving in Paris in the winter of 1933, the Garvy family took an apartment in the 15th arrondissement at 7, rue Jobbé Duval. Grandpa Peter found some employment with the trade union and political movements, continuing to work as a journalist for the labor press earning tiny fees. Perhaps they hoped to re-create a stable life in France, as they had in Germany. Perhaps the grandparents were still hoping for enough change in USSR for a return there? I don't know when those hopes were abandoned, though I imagine the collapse was most extensive when they fled to the US in 1940. Or perhaps in 1930s when they would have heard something of Stalin's vast purges and the relentless growth of his grip on power. My parents and the other Menshevik children went to school in a new language, their third. French came in addition to the Greek and Latin they studied in their academic high schools. My mother Sylvia, quite a bright person, got a fellowship to a fancy private school, the Collège Sévigné. The upper-class girls there were nice to her, as my mother told me; they admired her, which some of them told me 25 years later when I met them in Paris. But Mother felt socially remote from their world, lacking their clothes, apartments, country retreats, and diners _en famille_. One of her teachers was none other than Simone de Beauvoir, the famous philosopher and companion of Jean-Paul Sartre. Mother did very well scholastically and went on to university. At some point, she was quite interested in psychology, went to Geneva to work with Piaget, and got a certificate in psychology. Returning to Paris, she then decided on science and began studying chemistry.

My father Shura reached Paris in 1934, a year later than the Garvys, after finishing his _abitur_ in Berlin. He went to university and embarked on studying science right away at the Curie Institute. I have no idea where he lived. His aunt and uncle went to Brussels in 1935, not Paris, so he was now a single young man, aged 19. He, too, must have had odd jobs and gotten some money via his studies. I do recall him saying he was often hungry.

As the one member of my nuclear family who did not seek to study science (my older brother Sergei did physics), I wondered what shaped my Dad's choices. His intelligence was formidable: I recall that he could beat me easily when playing chess without looking at the board. In Russia, he was seen as having potential as a chess prodigy. Only once do I ever recall beating him, and that perhaps happened because he was doing several things at once, such as watching the Sunday football game on TV, for which he had little interest but wanted to be up to speed to talk to the people in his lab, while at the same time sketching out plans for lab schedules during the week to come. He was so startled to lose he asked for a rematch. Dad was not competitive with his sons: the rematch was to calibrate himself and possibly to see whether I had chess talent, though by then he must have known I did not, so it must have been to be sure he was not aging, the way I feel when I can't remember something I know that I know. He won the rematch easily.

The interest in science and the kind of science he did—applied microbiology, development of antibiotics—I interpret as a response to his father's engagement in making the world better. His father sought to change the structure of society. Dad would do it with medicine. He succeeded brilliantly: in his short years as a researcher, he was one of

Shura in about 1938. His slender features were gone by the time I knew him, not just age, but the result of health, of cortisone injections to combat the emphysema he acquired in his youth

the pioneers in developing types of tetracycline and synthetic penicillin. In reading the letters of my grandfather, I note that my father's interest in the sciences was evident quite early on, before even his teen years, as Grandpa Boris notes it quite often.

As a refugee dealing with his fourth language, politics was not really available to my father as a profession. He remembered as a child teaching literacy in Russia, a kind of engagement likely organized by the school rather than personal initiative. He struggled to get educated in the USSR and then again as a refugee in Germany, France, and the US. In France, after studying at the Sorbonne, he enrolled at the Curie Institute to get a doctorate in chemistry. He had a summer job in 1938 working for a cider

125

brewing company near Antrin, at the border between Normandy and Brittany, as he was an expert in fermentation. He had nearly finished his degree by 1940 when the family had to flee the Na-

zis. This left him likely with a strong desire that his sons get their education as soon as possible: I graduated from high school at 16, college at 20, too young an age; something I would not allow my own children to do!

My mother's turn to science may have been influenced by my father. They had met in Berlin when he arrived in 1931 and traveled in the same socialist refugee circles. Over the years, they went on various group outings together, but theromance started in 1938. Years later, my older brother Sergei and I gave some wine glasses to our parents for their wedding anniversary, which we thought was officially July 8. They smiled and gave each other a look. We asked for explanation. "Well, " they observed, "that is the formal date of our wedding, but we really date early June when the romance really started."

Sylvia did turn to science, taking up chemical engineering. She was also on her way to a doctorate when they had to flee in 1940. She never went back

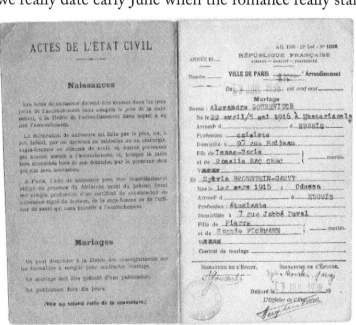

to it, as there was no money for her to do graduate studies when they reached the US. Dad, after a number of years supporting the family as a chemist in industry, commuting from Manhattan to New Jersey to work at Allied Chemical, got a fellowship to Syracuse University to complete his degree, but we will return to that story when we track the family's flight to the US.

It is not clear to me how politically active the Menshevik children were while in France. They were all busy in school and all helping to earn money, as my grandparents earned very little. My mother gave lessons as a tutor. Uncle George got various jobs. Life was hard for her and the whole family. The other refugees saw and noted it: one of them commented that "Sylvia works like a stevedore."[1] As noted, she was a bit puzzled when I was so desperate to go to Europe in my late teens, especially to visit Paris. Europe and Paris were a hardship for her, nothing exotic or exciting about it.

Politics was very much a part of their lives. There were no Nazis to fight in the Paris streets, and France was less dangerously toxic than Germany in the early 30s. But politics was all around them. Headlines charted the rise of German militarism, the harshness of the regime there, the growing persecution of Jews, and the intensifying repression of all the opposition. They followed news from the USSR, more attentive than most to famine in Ukraine and the Stalinist terror as it got underway. And the foreign policy explosions: Hitler's takeover of the Rhineland in 1936, the Italian invasion of Ethiopia in 1935, the Spanish Civil War starting in 1936, the Japanese attack on China first in 1931, then widening in 1937, the Anschluss with Austria of 1938, the Sudetenland crisis of appeasement at Munich, and the dismemberment of Czecheslovakia in the fall of 1938. Within France itself, there was intense political activity. The threat of a coup in 1934 and the Popular Front election of 1936, which brought to power a coalition of Communists, Socialists and the Radical Party (centrist liberals) to protect the Republic, were dramatic moments in French political life that deeply touched the Menshevik group.

As a young adult and college student, when I read extensively about this period, I would ask my parents questions about their reactions to the big events as they were taking place. In the 1950s, the famous journalist Edward R. Murrow put out a record of radio clips taken from 1933-45 called *I Can Hear it Now*. I played it many times and to this day remember passages from it and the voices: famous speeches of FDR and of Churchill, clips from Hitler rantings, the Duke of Windsor abdicating in 1936, the announcer reporting the Hindenburg dirigible bursting into flames in New Jersey in 1937, Joe Louis knocking out Max Schmelling in 1938, the Queen of the Netherlands surrendering in 1940. On the Duke's abdication, Murrow's narration said everywhere people tuned in, "You could hear the world quiet down." Well, I wondered, why did people care? "Did you listen, and if so, why?" I asked my parents. "Yes, indeed. We knew the Duke of Windsor was something of a fascist, so UK politics worried us. His abdication was a plus in resisting Hitler. Indeed, we listened!"[2]

The Long Arm of Stalin via Interventions from the USSR— The Kazan Telegram from Boris and the Disappearance of Mark Rein

While the Menshevik refugees reorganized their lives in Paris, the USSR remained part of their mental universe. Letters from Grandfather Boris continued to arrive to the Gourevitch clan, to Berlin, Brussels, and Paris, as they moved around. Menshevik leaders continued to follow events in the USSR closely: the turn away from the semi-free market of the NEP toward forced collectivization, the famine in the early thirties, though this was poorly covered in the Western press, the political purges in the mid to late thirties, whose spectacular "Show Trials" were covered, but whose mass of deportations and executions were not.

Two smaller events happened which loomed large to my family and the Menshevik group: the arrival of the "Kazan telegram" in 1934, co-signed by Boris concerning discussions in France about creating a Popular Front coalition, and the disappearance in Spain of Mark Rein, son of Raphael Abramovich, at the hands of Stalin's agents in 1936-37, a few years before the internationally famous assassination of Trotsky in Mexico City (1940).[2]

The Kazan Telegram

Prior to Hitler's takeover in January 1933, Stalin had opposed any political cooperation between Communist parties outside of the USSR and any other groups seeking to stop the Nazis or other right-wing extremists. To the Bolsheviks, all non-Communists were enemies, a line which had operational meaning from October 1917 as part of the Bolshevik seizure of power. This included the Socialists, whom the Bolsheviks labeled as "social fascists," no different from all other "bourgeois" parties. In Germany, the Communist line gravely weakened resistance to the Nazis, as it left a "negative" majority in the German Reichstag: the National Socialists (Nazis) and the KPD (Communist Party of Germany) had more votes for a time than all the other parties and so governments could have trouble mobilizing a majority in defense of the parliamentary regime. This unstable situation gave the Nazis the political space to riot and demonstrate, contributing to disorder, and gave a lot of discretion to President Hindenburg and the reactionary advisors around him on how to maneuver. In January of 1933, the German right gambled on inviting Hitler to form a government in the theory that he would provide popular support, but the elite, army, industry, and traditional conservatives could nonetheless control him. This was a colossal blunder. Once in power, the Nazis swiftly destroyed the entire opposition: Communists, Socialists, trade union leaders, liberals, Church activists, and established repressive methods of control. Germany began to militarize quickly, greatly increasing the threat to the USSR.

Stalin finally saw the growing danger and at last switched policy, now concluding that stopping fascism was valuable even if it meant allying with political rivals. This would happen through "Popular Front coalitions"—alliances among Communists, Socialists and pro-constitutionalist bourgeois parties.

Bourgeois democracy was certainly preferable to militaristic fascism. With the destruction of the German Weimar Republic, France was the most important potential partner to the USSR. Among the continental democracies, it had the largest remaining Socialist party and an important Communist one. It also had the largest army on the continent outside Germany and was strategically located to outflank, thus constraining this historic enemy.

The clamor for a Popular Front alliance against the Fascist threat became ever louder. For the Mensheviks, now based in Paris, this posed a dilemma. They had all along insisted that no cooperation with Communist Party was possible until Stalin released the many political prisoners incarcerated in the USSR. Now, in the summer of 1934, a congress of the French Socialist Party was coming up, where the issue of the Popular Front was sure to be an important subject of debate. The Menshevik Foreign Delegation had to decide whether to sustain its continued opposition in light of the catastrophe in Germany.

Suddenly a telegram arrived for the Menshevik group. Sent from the city of Kazan in the USSR on 10 August 1934, printed in *Le Populaire* (the Socialist paper) on 12 August 1934 and in *l'Humanité* (the Communist paper) on 13 August 1934.

"Lets us acclaim with joy the Pact of Unity of Action between the Socialist and Communist Parties who will make of the workers' movement an invincible force that will bar the way to fascism, push aside the dangers of war, accelerate the realization of revolutionary socialist power that represents and reunites the whole of the proletariat and the whole of the working class.

Let us hope that the French example will be followed by the international workers' movement.

Long live the accord of the socialists and communists of the whole world. Long live the unity of action of the Combat.

Long live Socialism:

Signed by: the Socialist militants: Bair-Gourevitch, Zederbaum-Ejow, Zacharova (French spelling of these names)[3]

The Socialist paper goes on to note that all three signatories have been in internal house arrest or prison since 1922 and that Tsederbaum is Martov's brother. It cites the telegram as proof that the Social Democrats in Russia are in complete agreement with their counterparts in France in supporting the French Socialist alliance with the Communists. Next to the telegram is published a strongly approving editorial signed by French Socialist leader Leon Blum, future Prime Minister of the actual Popular Front government that came into being in 1936.

Contrary to the newspaper account, there was not complete agreement among the Social Democrats, or at least among the Menshevik refugees. Given the harsh authoritarian conditions of the Stalinist regime, the telegram can hardly be considered written in free will. The signers were surely selected by the regime and told what to write. At the same time, it may well express something close to their thoughts.

The signatories were coalition-oriented in their politics. Their crit-

icism of the intolerance by the Bolsheviks and Stalin was why they were in prison in the first place. Back in 1917, they had supported a broad alliance among all socialists to replace Kerensky's provisional government and opposed the Bolsheviks' repression of dissent and narrowing of the party base of power. So, if they agreed with the content of the telegram, can we say they were coerced, though they were hardly independent actors? The telegram certainly did express the political views of the French Socialists, as evidenced by the column signed by Blum. The Popular Front coalition did come about but not for another two years, with the election of 1936. This brought in Blum as Premier, who enacted legislation giving paid vacations, a forty-hour work week, and other reforms that signaled what became the "welfare state" all over much of the democratic industrial world after WWII.

Reading about the Kazan telegram jolted me. It integrated some strands of my life, both personal and professional. On the professional side, I have spent much time studying French history and politics. The French Popular Front was an epochal event in this: a moment in the broader European current to find a "third way", a political compromise to stop fascism on one side and the ills of Stalinism on the other. The Spanish Civil War broke out in 1936. The Spanish Republic was defended by a Popular Front, which failed in its fight against Spain's Franco and remains controversial to this day. Stalin sabotaged cooperation among the coalition partners, a fractious group in any case, to advance the Bolshevik hegemony, harking back to the conflicts of October 1917 in Petrograd. Orwell's *Homage to Catalonia*[4] evokes the atmosphere vividly. The anti-Franco alliance was weakened gravely by the refusal of the British and French to provide assistance to the Loyalist government, while Hitler and Mussolini funneled vast amounts of aid to the Franco insurgency. Picasso's *Guernica* represents the horror of German bombs raining down on a Basque region town, so the world of art guarantees the memory of this turbulent period. In my work, I have read a lot about Popular Front efforts in France[5] and elsewhere, why they worked in some places, for example, Scandinavia in the 1930s, but failed in others, as disastrously in Berlin in 1932. Like my grandfathers, I believe coalitions seem essential to advancing progressive ideas.

The Kazan telegram told me a lot about those grandfathers. Stalin reached into the prison camps of the USSR to find people with the highest legitimacy among the Menshevik group meeting in Paris. I knew the importance of Martov to that group, so picking the brother and sister-in-law, I grasped right away. When I began this research, I knew less of what Grandpa Boris meant to the Mensheviks, just what his standing and status were to them. I had some inkling from my Dad's description of what happened when he arrived in Berlin in November 1931, surrounded by all the Menshevik elders seeking information, that they all thought Boris an important figure to them. This event of the Kazan telegram drove the point home. That Stalin picked Grandpa Boris to join Martov's brother in sending this telegram signaled strongly who Boris Ber was, that the Kremlin had picked him for the force his name would convey to the exiled Menshevik community.

Indeed, the telegram did have an impact on the group. Leibich writes that they were all excited by it, some even wondering if the Kazan Telegram meant a sea change in Moscow. He cites Abramovich, a very pragmatic person, as writing that the telegram was the most important event in party life of the past several years but felt some skepticism about Soviet motives and caution on how to interpret it. Fyodor Dan, the major leader of the Foreign Delegation after the death of Martov in the 1920s, seems to have been more forcefully enthusiastic.[6] Many of the exiles comment at length on the telegram, and Liebich devotes several pages of his book to it.

A further dimension of interest for me is that it seems the two grandfathers disagreed about it. Grandpa Garvy wrote strong criticism of the optimistically positive view of the telegram. The signatories were "prisoners of Soviet power, incapable of communicating openly, with their own party, and lacking any guarantees their gesture would not be distorted and exploited."[7] Does he, Grandpa Peter, mean the signatories should not have written it I wonder if they had much choice.Or, more likely, Grandpa Peter was urging caution in overreacting to the meaning of the telegram, not only as to how much freedom the authors had but what it really tells us about Stalin's behaviors and intentions. It was unlikely that the leopard had actually changed his spots, or if so, just the external spots, not the internal ruthlessness. The exiles, Garvy thought, should continue to insist on demanding freedom for the colleagues imprisoned in the USSR and on calling for democracy. Cooperating with the communist parties meant "tacitly sanctioning the Bolshevik experiment as a whole."[8] Allies for the progressive cause should continue to fight for democracy.

By contrast, Grandpa Boris was in favor of the coalition. One of the few open political references in his letters to his family was to express enthusiasm for the Popular Front. This was the spirit of his political thinking in the Revolutionary days when he advocated a broader coalition of progressive parties in disagreement with the Bolshevik drive for exclusive domination.

With the hindsight of history, I find myself on Grandpa Boris's side: against Hitler, opponents of the Nazis should unite, even if this means compromise. Winston Churchill had urged the UK to "strangle" the Bolsheviks at their birthfd in 1917-1920, but in the 1930s, they saw the greater danger and evil from the Nazis and famously led the effort to stop appeasement at Munich and to fight the Germans alone after the French defeat in 1940. When Germany attacked the USSR in 1941, everyone rallied to the Allied Cause; the British and Americans joined forces with "Uncle Joe" Stalin and sent massive amounts of aid to the USSR. The collapse of Weimar had been a disaster. Grandpa Peter detested the Bolsheviks to the point of not cooperating in 1934. Grandpa Peter's position is unyielding in the practical situation. The communist refusal to work with socialists should not be repeated in reverse. I could see how deep these differences were within the Menshevik group and how they expressed themselves.

Sitting in my quiet office as I write, I can pick and choose positions: I see that on some issues, I sympathize with the Menshevik right, more generally preferring compromise and bargains and democratic processes to Jacobin or Bolshevik imposition of a party line. But in other contexts, I see the logic of the left position when fighting the forces of reaction. The contexts and historical experiences of those years were so different compared to my life situations—the huge range of issues the Grandfathers faced about the nature of Russian society, the World Wars and nationalism, how to construct democracy in the midst of chaos, and amidst a massively agrarian society of limited education and weak civil society, how to deal with the Bolsheviks on the far left and the white Russians and Monarchist or military reactionaries on the right, while foreign armies invaded, great hunger and loss of life from the war, the list of challenges goes on.

The Kazan telegram incident taught me important things: that

Grandpa Boris had a very high standing in the eyes of the Mensheviks and among their Bolshevik rivals; that Grandpa Peter was indeed a right-Menshevik, which I had known, but here it was expressed so forcefully on a disagreement between them at a symbolically important moment in the history of this period, one which coincided with my particular expertise on French history and politics.

And it[9] helped remind me of the difficulty of context and 'anachronism"—reading backward into the past what we know about things that happened afterward: When the Germans invaded the USSR on June 22, 1941, the Mensheviks, now all in New York, all agreed on the need to stop Hitler. Allying with the Soviets to stop the German invasion seemed an unquestionable necessity made all the worse by the incredible barbarism of the invading forces, killing millions and millions of people, Jews as is well known, even larger numbers of non-Jews, often less well known, such as Russian prisoners of war, left to starve in open fields, and Slavic civilians of all kinds. The Mensheviks were generally Russian nationalists or Russophiles of some kind, keen to defend their country, internationalists in their political and social outlook, keen to advance their country as a progressive place, opposed to the colonialism of capitalist or fascist kind. Another round of horrors of the Soviet regime developed after 1934, the moment of the Kazan telegram. The mass starvation in Ukraine, known as the Holodomor, was already happening; the great Purges would begin soon after.

In the event of 1934, the Mensheviks did accept the Popular Front coalition, and it did take place after its substantial electoral victory in France in 1936. Was that because of this telegram? Most unlikely, the Mensheviks were not that influential in France. Here as in many events, the Mensheviks could argue about what position they could take on events over which they had, increasingly, less and less influence. The Popular Front did stabilize France for a time and helped introduce an important series of social reforms—France's New Deal, paid vacations, retirement and unemployment insurance, recognition of trade unions, and some contribution to knitting together the social and cultural divides that fractured the country since the French Revolution. For me personally, the Kazan telegram incident helped me locate Boris' political activities, views and place in history. It was, to my knowledge, his last political engagement before his death.

The Kazan telegram seems likely in the short run to have eased the harsh conditions of Boris's life as well as that of his co-signatories. He was allowed not long after that to move to Vladimir. This was not far from Moscow, thus a less harsh winter than northern Siberia. Still, under police supervision, he had greater freedom of movement. He was given permission to go to Moscow to seek employment and, in 1936, to see his mother, who had come back from Germany, where she had been living for a few years. He stayed in Vladimir, hired by the manager of a dairy to handle the books. Then the Stalinist repression intensified again. The purges were launched in full force. Letters from Grandpa Boris stopped in 1937. The hopes among the exiles that the Kazan telegram signaled a change inside the USSR proved illusory. After 1935, large numbers of people were arrested, seized and banished to Siberia or shot or killed in some way or another.

The Disappearance of Mark Rein in Spain

As Hitler clamped down on Germany, Stalin's purges got underway in the mid-30s. The infamous show trials against leading personnel commanded attention worldwide, intensively among the Menshevik emigres. In 1940, Trotsky was murdered in Mexico City, attracting attention worldwide. Much less well-known is that similar things were taking place against less famous people. The refugee community was acutely aware of these incidents, as they were among the prime targets. The Mensheviks had already experienced such a loss in connection with the Spanish Civil War.

Like many people in that era, one of the older members of the Menshevik children's generation, Mark Rein, went off to Spain to fight against Franco's fascists. Rein was the eldest child of Rafael Abramovich, an important leader of the Menshevik group. While in Spain, Mark Rein disappeared, by some accounts, on April 9, 1937, never to be heard from again. Was he killed by Franco's side? Or, as some evidence suggests, and the Mensheviks came to believe, was he nabbed by the Communists, who sought to strike a blow against Abramovich and the Mensheviks? Was he killed in Spain,[10] or sent to the Soviet Union, and killed or imprisoned there, as apparently happened to Swedish diplomat Raoul Wallenberg, seized in Budapest in 1944-45, where he had gone to save Jews, in a much-discussed case?

In the 1990s, while consulting the NYU Labor archive, I saw letters from Abramovich sent in 1937 to many well-known leaders in the European labor and Socialist movements, pleading for help in finding his son.[11] He made the case that the issue was Stalin, a warning to the world and to the left that the Soviet Union had become a dangerous force. This was not an easy argument to make in those days, as in the fight against the fascist menace, there was certainly a tendency to have "no enemies on the left," thus aversion to seeing danger in Stalin and the Communists, all the more so that Stalin had shifted to Popular Front tactics.

Abramovich met a number of US trade union leaders at the time of his visits to the US in the 30s and was a force in warning them about the Communists. His letters to them and other Socialist leaders make for painful reading: a father's plea for help, realizing his son is paying the price for the father's political activism and alliances, that Stalin is punishing him through his son. The Mark Rein story was explored after the Soviet archives opened up in the 1990s, but the case still contains some uncertainties.[12]

The Rein case had a strong emotional impact on the Menshevik group.

Mark was the oldest of the refugee children and a bright, energetic, handsome guy, the de facto leader, the big brother to all. Sylvia, my mother, sounded slightly in love with him when I heard her tell this story, but that may have been as an older cousin or de facto brother. Rein himself had fallen in love with Albert Hirschman's older sister Ursula, and the Family Legend was that he had gone to Spain when she rejected him. Many years later, when I met Lisa Hirschman, we were astonished to discover we had both grown up with the same Family Legend about Mark Rein. It made us feel like distant cousins, with so much common background on top of all the other things for which we felt an attraction, and, well, we got married in 1976. Some years later, we visited Lia Rein (Abramovich) Andler at her country place near Paris. Many of the photos used here and in Liebich's book were in her possession.

The Munich appeasement by Chamberlain of the UK and Daladier of France was seen as catastrophic by my parents. They sensed its danger, having no illusions of Hitler. At the same time, they certainly did not expect the swift catastrophe that happened with the fall of France in May- June 1940.

The Kazan Telegram and the disappearance of Mark Rein vividly expressed the vital connection of the USSR to the lives of its refugees, most of whom were in Paris. Events in the USSR struck them in the heart. They cared deeply about what was going on. They were connected via journalism, letters, a very occasional visitor, and via the ability of the regime in Moscow to strike at its enemies even beyond its borders.

Developments in Germany intensified the anxiety drawing it ever closer.

The refugees closely followed the rise of the Nazis: the occupation of the Rhineland, the remilitarization of Germany, the debates in France and Britain over how fast to remilitarize themselves, the Spanish Civil War, the Italian invasion of Abyssinia, the war in East Asia with Japanese attacks on China, the takeover of Austria, then Munich and the Czech Crisis, these last three in 1938. And indeed, danger struck again in 1939. As I watch the current tensions while writing this book, with Donald Trump and the problems in the Middle East, China, Russia, Korea and terrorism, and while I write and revise passages about the Russian invasion of Ukraine, I wonder what my parents and their generation would have thought in comparison to what they experienced.

Danger Again: War Starts in Sept 1939

When war broke out in September 1939, the Garvy family, like most people, assumed the French army and the Maginot Line would provide at least some protection. The "Phony War"—the many months between the defeat of Poland in late September 1939 and the war in the West starting in April 1940—indeed did keep danger away for almost eight months.

Then things shifted very rapidly. On April 9, the Germans swept over Denmark in a day and invaded Norway, which resisted for two months. On May 10, the German army attacked Holland, Belgium and France. The daring punch through the Ardennes forest astonished everyone, leading to the French encirclement, the irrelevance of the Maginot Line fortifications, the collapse of the Allied forces, and the famous escape of mostly British troops at Dunkirk in early June.

The rapidity of the French defeat stunned the world. It was not that the French lacked arms (they had about as many tanks, if not more than Germany), but they and their British allies had not developed military doctrine over what to do with them. De Gaulle, then an obscure officer down in the ranks, had written a treatise on how to use tanks effectively, in mobile tactics, not as stationery artillery pieces.[13] The French top officers refused to listen, embodying perfectly the famous expression about generals " fighting the last war." Having lost WWI, the Nazis were more open to new ideas and promoted younger, more ambitious military men, somewhat outside the older elite structures.

The "Strange Defeat"[14], as Mark Bloch called it (a book I devoured in graduate school), ascribed several causes. Among them were fascist sympathizers located in strategic places, including the French military establishment. "Better Hitler than Blum" was widely felt. My mother recalled working in the lab of a chemical company owned by a pro-fascist plutocrat: as the German armies approached, he sent materials to the east rather than the west and left the employees working in the highly explosive laboratory during air raid alarms. Mother quit her job in disgust.

The Garvy family had no doubt about the danger they faced. Having lived in Berlin, they were sure of being on lists of people to be apprehended when the Gestapo arrived. The repression in Germany had become ever harsher.

Kristallnacht, on November 9, 1938, displayed plainly the brutality at work, making headlines and photos around the world. The takeover of Prague in March 1939 dispelled any illusions, still widely held by appeasers like Chamberlain, that Hitler sought to unite only German speakers. This was confirmed by the attack on Poland on Sept 1. The Molotov–Ribbentrop pact in August of 1939, shocking the world by making allies of deep enemies, Communist Russia and Nazi Germany, surely surprised everyone, but it fit the family's view of Stalin.[15]

The Garvys were Socialists; they were Jewish; they were stateless, having been stripped of citizenship by the Soviets in 1931. As in Berlin, they were vulnerable, and they knew it. When the Nazis reached Paris, the family learned after the war the Gestapo went straight to Grandpa Garvy's apartment, knowing full well where he lived. Some friends did hide a batch of family letters and photos that were recovered after the war.

As the German armies approached, the family sought to escape. They needed papers, passports, and visas. They had Nansen passports, a document developed in the 1930s for stateless people just like them.[16] French rules required exit visas to leave the country—the very documents Peter Lorre steals in *Casablanca* and gives to Bogart, who decides who gets to use them. In June of 1940, as the German army approached Paris, my family queued French government offices in Paris to obtain these precious permits. Then, Juliette Blanc, the Frenchwoman Uncle George would soon marry, called them from the press office where she worked to say that the news broadcasts were misleading: the German army was quite close, only a day or two away, not four or five as was being broadcast, lying ostensibly so as not to panic the public. The family abandoned the exit-visa line and prepared to leave the next day.

That day, June 10 (German army arrived on June 14), they went to the Gare de Lyon to take the train south. (It is possible they went to the Gare d'Austerlitz, the terminus for trains to Toulouse, where they ended up, but I am quite sure my parents told me Gare de Lyon, terminus for trains to the south, the Midi, such as Lyons or Marseilles, so they may have done that and switched somewhere). They boarded what the Family Legend says was the last train out of the train station.

This is the story I had heard so often as the children—Garvy, Gourevitch and Etkin—asked the parents to describe the events of those years. Then one day, many years later, I, now a parent, was with my younger son Nicholas who had a homework assignment to interview someone about WWII. We were all living in Solana Beach, Ca., and he asked my mother. I decided to tape it. Nick got what he wanted, some memories from a living person, but I thought to continue. For me, it was a moment actually to record one of these stories I had heard so often. Mother was a lively, strong person and had her own opinions on what I should ask. To avoid her interruptions and her opinions on how I was conducting the interview, I decided to switch gears, inspired by having watched Claude Lanzmann's impressive *Shoah* film[17], where he gets lots of information from seemingly tangential or trivial questions.

"What did you have for breakfast that day you left?" I asked. My mother stopped talking for a moment, half closed her eyes, leaned her head back, then poured out words in a torrent, telling me things I had never heard.

> "I had a 'beurre tartine' (bread, butter). We went downstairs from the apartment to pick up my parents; I forgot something and ran back upstairs to get

it. Together we went to the train station by subway. The subway station at the Gare was crowded, and so it took us hours to reach the head of the stairs and all day to cross the square in front of the Gare. It was a hot sunny day (*so much for the rain in Casablanca*). My mother kept fainting, and we had to get water for her.

Finally, in the early evening, we reached the platform only to be told there were no trains left. Desperate, we wondered what to do. Finally, an old broken down engine and beaten-up passenger car arrived, and we climbed on board. The train pulled out, and it was bombed as we went south."

The story came alive to me. I had heard the very last part many times before but not the beginning, from breakfast through the crowded square to the train quai. I knew what the *Gare de Lyon* looked like and the plaza in front of it, having taken trains there many times. I could now mentally conjure up my parents in the scene in its various sites the subway, the stairs, the square in front of the *Gare*, inside the building. And I could sense the tension they must all have been feeling, knowing their lives were at great risk. Another experience with facts and memories intersecting with the *Casablanca* movie reflects on my emerging profession as an expert on French history and politics. Early in the film, Peter Lorre sitting with Bogart at Rick's Café, says, " I have here transit visas signed by "XXX." The audience in the Brattle Theater that January evening in 1964 booed the name they thought they heard: "Charles de Gaulle." But, I thought to myself, Lorre cannot have said Charles de Gaulle. This is Vichy controlled North Africa in the early 1940s. De Gaulle is in London, leading the Free French movement. A visa signed by him would induce Claude Rains, as Captain Reynaud, responsible up the chain of command to the Vichy Government, to put the bearer of the document promptly in jail. The next day I went back to the Brattle Theater, eager to see the movie again to experience its totality and to confirm my suspicion as to who the signer really was. Indeed, I heard Lorre say, not de Gaulle, but "General Weygand," at the time commander of the French Armies under the President of France, Marshall Pétain, commander of French armies in WWI, and now leader of Vichy rump regime, collaborator with the German occupation. When the movie was made in the early 1940s, American audiences would have recognized the name Weygand, arguably better known than de Gaulle at the time, but in 1964, a name unknown to the young who filled the Brattle at exam time. When I became a professor some years later, these questions about the movie became part of "extra credit" quizzes. In our day, many references to the movie print the script as saying de Gaulle, but that is a contemporary projection onto the script, not what the movie makers wrote.

The Garvy-Gourevitch family made its way to Toulouse, where my father's aunt, Bacia Gourevitch, was living. That city was in the safer zone, part of what was to become the Vichy Regime, outside the area of formal German rule, where the Gestapo and SS did not yet operate directly. Family members coordinated to meet there. Uncle George was in the French army. When the front collapsed, and the army disintegrated, an odd coincidence took place, at least in Family Legend. George and his mates see a train car on a railway siding. They looked inside, discover a mail bag addressed to their regiment, and there George found a letter from his family saying they were in Toulouse. George sent a telegram, which survives, as again, Uncle George famously did not throw things away:

"Je suis sain et sauf: Viendrai chez vous après la paix. Baisiers Georges." " (I am safe and sound. I am coming to you after the Peace. Kisses, George)" The Etkin family left Paris in a car about the same day as my parents, with Natasha driving, accompanied by her mother and two friends, to go south. (Janni, the father, was a soldier off at war). The extreme congestion of the roads of France at that moment of military collapse was legendary and was seen as impeding the Allied military movements. At one point, the Etkins took a side road to have lunch and, in coming back to the main route, found bombs had destroyed cars where they had been. The family continued safely, eventually meeting up with Janni in the south near Marseilles and joining the Menshevik group in Toulouse.

The chaos of the departure from Paris has been much discussed. The recently discovered novel by Irene Nemirovksy, *Suite Francaise*, evokes it vividly; there are some shots in the opening of *Casablanca* to convey the mass flight of refugees. The chaos and crowding were used to justify, for military security reasons, the vast public works program during the Eisenhower years of building the US interstate highway system. Another famous version of the flight and congestion can be found at the beginning of the French film *Jeux Interdits*.

France surrendered to Germany on June 22, 1940. The surrender document was signed in the same railroad car in the forest of Compiègne, northeast of Paris, where Germany had surrendered in 1918. Hitler sat in the chair Marshal Foch had used to face the defeated German representatives, and to humiliate the French further, he left after the reading of the preamble. Today, a reconstructed copy of the car, destroyed in 1945 during the fighting, has been turned into a museum in a green and peaceful park, the Clarière de l'Armistice, where it is hard to reconcile the quiet calm of the setting with the catastrophic events connected with both World Wars. I visited there in 1971-72 when I was living in France, drawn by the symbolism of the spot.

Back in 1940, the family had a bit of breathing space in Toulouse but had now to figure out what to do. How long would Vichy remain a relatively safe location were they to remain in France? We have to imagine their state of mind in 1940 without knowing what follows: that the Nazis start the Holocaust along with their invasion of the USSR, that Vichy cooperates by rounding people up and turning them over to the Nazis as in the infamous incident of the "Vél d'hiv" roundup,[18] and after 1943, the direct rule by Germany and the SS over Vichy region when even more people are shipped to their deaths. In that summer of 1940, they knew the Nazis were dangerous to them, but not the breadth of what would happen.

The family wanted to leave but to do that, they needed not only exit visas from France but also entrance visas to someplace else. Getting such visas was famously quite difficult to do: most countries had shut tight their doors of entry, including the United States. The voyage of the passenger liner the St. Louis, vividly conveys the point: the ship left Germany in 1939, bound for Cuba with 908 Jewish refugees. Despite initial assurances of safe passage when the ship left, almost all were denied entry when the ship arrived in Havana harbor and also turned down when it tried to go to Canada and the US. The ship returned to Europe, where various countries took groups of them. About a quarter of the passengers died in Nazi camps. Books, films and even an opera have been written about this, *Voyage of the Damned*, for the book and movie, and it figures importantly in the novel by Leon Padura, *Herejes*[19] (2013).

The memoir *Hotel Bolivia*[20] by Leo Spitzer describes a number of Jews fleeing Austria to   Bolivia, which seemed somewhat more permissive than other coiuntries. When asked what might be an acceptable number of Jews to enter Canada, an official said,"None is too many."[21] So the difficulty of getting out of the Nazi juggernaut and the refusal of counties to admit the vulnerable, especially Jews, is one of the central catastrophes and controversies of the period. My family knew well the difficulty of getting entrance visas anywhere. And they thought it dangerous to stay: a collaborationist fascist Vichy regime could not be safe for leftist and stateless socialists. While I have no records from my primary family about their thoughts at this time, there are plenty of materials in the various accounts written by others among the Mensheviks: everyone in that group knew they faced mortal peril and sought to leave France. But how to get out?

Endnotes

1 Liebich book, From a Distant Shore.
2 On the Trotsky killing, I recommend the remarkable novel by Leon Padura, The Man Who Loved Dogs. Farrar, Straus and Giroux. 2014 trans Anna Kushner. (Tusquets Editors, Spain, 2009). Padura grew up in Castro's Cuba dominated by Soviet ideology that Trotsky was an evil enemy of the Revolution. After the Berlin Wall falls in 1989, Padura learns more about other views, and the novel explores varying interpretations of doctrine, history, and interpretation as it applies to the narrator, Cuba, society, and the various persons of the book, and how each of these deal with the downfall of an ideology.
3 Telegrammes printed in Le Populaire and L'Humanité, 1934, translated by Peter Gourevitch.
4 Orwell, George, Homage to Catalonia. (London: Seckler and Warburg, 1938).
5 On French politics generally, the historical treatments on which I relied were Gordon Wright, France in Modern Times, New York: Norton, 1960). Stanley Hoffmann, et al., In Search of France (Cambridge, MA: Harvard University Press, 1963.)
6 Liebich, op cit., p 254.
7 Ibid., p. 255.
8 Liebich's words, page 255 .
9 Labor archive at NYU, vol xiv. Tamiment and Robert Wagner Labor Archive at New York University.
10 This is what the grandsons of Rafael Abramovich believe, Daniel and Martin Andler, sons of Lia, thus the nephews of Mark Rein. Martin Andler did substantial research on the fate of his uncle, including examination of very thick folders of the German Communist Party for the period of 1937-38. Despite all the archival research in Russia, Germany, the US, and Spain, there remains some doubt as to what happened. Communication to the author Martin Andler, 31 July 2021.
11 Abramovich, Rafael, Tamiment Library and Wagner Labor Archives, NYU.
12 'The Case of Mark Rein.' Socialist Appeal Vol. I No. 11 Saturday October 23, 1937. Orlov claims to have arranged the kidnapping to assist in the show trials I Moscow. Orlov, A.M., The Secret History of Stalin's Crimes. New York, 1953.
13 De Gaulle, Charles, Le Fil de lÉpée. 1923 Translated Gerard Hopkins, NH Criterion Books, The Edge of the Sword,
14 Bloch, Marc, Strange Defeat: a statement of evidence written in 1940. New York: Norton, 1999. I first read this book while taking Stanley Hoffmann's famous course on French Politics and Society my first year in graduate school, the same school year I saw the Casablanca movie to which I refer at the beginning of this book. Lawrence Wylie, professor of French Civilization at the time, and author of the widely read Village in the Vaulcuse, ran a series of French movies at the same time which showed some classics. Recently French Television produced a fine series on the years of the German Occupation, called Un Village Francais. When I joined the Harvard Faculty in 1969, I befriended Professor of History Patrice Higonnet from whom I learned

a great deal.

15 These events (the Munich appeasement, the takeover of Prague, and Molotov-Ribbentrop Pact have been significant events in the development of international relations theorizing about signaling, power balancing, that influenced my thinking over the years as it appeared in the work of Robert Jervis, Hans Morgenthau, Henry Kissinger, Kenneth Waltz, David Lake, and many others.

16 Sands, Philip, East West Street. (New York: Knopf, 2016.) A brilliant book which by studying his own family history, he tells well the story of Hersch Lauterpact and Raphael Lemkin, developers of concepts of crimes againt humanity and genocide as well as the Nansen passport. They come from his home town, Lviv, along with Hans Frank the Nazi governor general of Poland.

17 Lanzmann, Claude, Shoah. I met Lanzmann once in New York though my college classmate Raye Linda Farr, who had become an expert on documentary film footage from the WWII era and worked for some years at the Holocaust Museum in Washington. It was she who steered me to the Document Library there where I found valuable material concerning my great Uncle Buka Fichman to which I turn in Chapter 9. I thanked Lanzmann for his inspiration to my research strategy concerning my mother.

18 On 16-17 June 1942, more than 13,000 Jews were crammed into this urban sports arena and most were shipped to Auschwitz and killed there.

19 Padura, Leon, Herejes, 2013. Translated as the Cuban Detective, trans. Anna Kushner, 2017 Moment Magazine, Washington.

20 Spitzer, Leo, Hotel Bolivia, New York: Hill and Wang, 1998.

21 Irving Abelia and Harold Troper, None is Too Many: Canada and the Jews of Europe 1933- 1948, (Toronto: Lester & Orpen Dennys, 1983; University of Toronto Press, 2012). The phrase is attributed to an unidentified immigration agent in 1939 asked how many Jews would be allowed in Canada after the war. The book's authors identify Frederick Blair as the head of immigration under Mackenzie King's government, thus the counterpart to Breckenridge Long in the US case and argues that he had the support of Vincent Massey, High Commissioner to the UK and of many Anglophone and Francophone elites in power. My thanks to Janice Stein, former colleague at McGill University in the late 1970s, who told be about this case, and from whom I learned a lot.

Chapter 8

The Miracle of the Visas and Coming to America in 1940

In the 21st century, I am not used to telegrams. With emails, fax, and electronic messaging of all kinds, telegrams seem obsolete. But such things did not exist back then, and the telegram continued to be a major instrument of communication. Suddenly, in early July 1940, a telegram arrived to the family in Toulouse to announce a dramatic change in their situation.   Dated 6 July 1940, it came from the Woytinskys, who were in Washington.

> "Whole family authorized visit United States. Contact American Consul Marseilles. See you soon here. Emma."

Again, it is Uncle George who kept the telegram reproduced here.

What produced this life saving telegram? Answering that question constitutes an important goal of this narrative: My family got emergency entrance visas to the US because of the American Labor Movement.[1]

In the late spring 1940, several American labor leaders asked the Roosevelt Administration to grant visas to European trade union leaders trapped in France. A letter addressed to Cordell Hull, Secretary of State, dated July 2, 1940, on the stationary of the American Federation of Labor, signed by William Green, as President of the AFL, David Dubinsky, President of the International Ladies Garment Workers Union, Alexander Kahn, as General Manager of Jewish Daily Forward, and Isaiah Minkoff, the Executive Secretary of the Jewish Labor Committee notes, in the second sentence, the dangers posed by both the Nazi Occupation of France, where it was very well known to labor leaders around the world that the Nazis were destroying labor unions, but also the Soviet seizure of Lithuania in 1940 about the time of the fall of France, which together

> "have placed in jeopardy the lives of a great number of men and women prominent in the democratic and labor movements in Europe. ..... And "..unless these men and women find immediate temporary haven in the United States, they are in danger of being imprisoned, placed in concentration camps or shot, whether it be the Gestapo or the GPU. ....their loss would be irreparable for the civilized world. "[2]

The letter addresses the evils of both the USSR and Nazi Germany. When the letter was written, those two countries were allies. A list was attached to the letter providing the names of the people who were to receive these visas, among whom were my family members.

More questions can be asked about this letter. What motivated its signatories? Why did it provide the intended result? On the first question, several elements contribute to an answer. Some of the signers we know came from backgrounds that gave them sympathy and familiarity with what was happening in Europe. Dubinsky, head of the ILGWU, was born in the Russian Empire and had been a socialist worker in his youth and a staunch anti-Communist leftist. He and the other union leaders were building an American labor movement during the New Deal years and identified strongly with the endangered Europeans whom they saw as allies in the US. These very characteristics gave

AMERICAN FEDERATION OF LABOR

Executive Council
President, WILLIAM GREEN
Secretary-Treasurer, GEORGE MEANY
A. F. of L. Building, Washington, D. C.

First Vice-President, WILLIAM L. HUTCHESON,
Carpenters' Building, Indianapolis, Ind.
Second Vice-President, T. A. RICKERT,
Room 431—43 Astor Place, New York, N. Y.
Third Vice-President, MATTHEW WOLL,
670 Lexington Ave., New York, N. Y.
Fourth Vice-President, JOSEPH N. WEBER,
1440 Broadway, New York, N. Y.
Fifth Vice-President, G. M. BUGNIAZET,
1200 Fifteenth St., N. W. Washington, D. C.
Sixth Vice-President, GEO. M. HARRISON,
Railway Clerks' Bldg., Cincinnati, O.
Seventh Vice-President, DANIEL J. TOBIN,
121 East Michigan Street, Indianapolis, Ind.

Eighth Vice-President, HARRY C. BATES,
815 Fifteenth St., N. W., Washington, D. C.
Ninth Vice-President, EDWARD J. GAINOR,
404 A. F. of L. Building, Washington, D. C.
Tenth Vice-President, W. D. MAHON,
260 Vernor Highway, East Detroit, Mich.
Eleventh Vice-President, DAVID DUBINSKY,
3 West 16th Street, New York, N. Y.
Twelfth Vice-President, GEORGE E. BROWNE,
...
Thirteenth Vice-President, EDWARD FLORE,
...
Fourteenth Vice-President,
Fifteenth Vice-President,

NCE TELEPHONE NATIONAL 3670-1-2-3-4
CABLE ADDRESS, AFEL.

Washington, D. C.
July 2, 1940.

Hon. Cordell Hull,
Secretary of State,
Washington, D. C.

Honorable Sir:

   In the name of the American Federation
of Labor, the Jewish Labor Committee, and representatives of organized labor in the United States, we wish
to appeal to you in a matter of great urgency.

   The Nazi occupation of France and the
Soviet seizure of Lithuania have placed in jeopardy the
lives of a great number of men and women prominent in
the democratic and labor movements in Europe.

   Permit us to impress upon you, Honorable
Sir, that unless these men and women find immediate
temporary haven in the United States, they are in danger
of being imprisoned, placed in concentration camps, or
shot, whether it be by the Gestapo or the GPU.

   The men and women in whose behalf we are
now appealing are world-famous writers, editors, labor
leaders, former government officials, and ministers.
Some of them are in intimate contact with the trade union
movement, and are well-known to organized labor in the
United States. Should they fall into the clutches of the
German Gestapo or the Soviet GPU, they will face certain
death, and their loss would be irreparable for the
civilized world.

   Because of their opposition to Fascism,
Nazism, and Communism, the majority of these men and
women were forced to flee their countries - Germany,
Austria, Czecho-Slovakia, Italy, Russia, Poland. Most of

Do

99

them were until recently in Paris. Now they have found a temporary refuge in Toulouse and other parts of France. But, as you are undoubtedly aware, the present French government, acceding to the demands of the government of Germany, has agreed to hand over all these pro-democratic refugees to the Gestapo.

This, Honorable Sir, will be the fate of great and noble men and women, whose only crime is their firm belief in Democracy, Freedom, and Tolerance, unless they find an immediate place of refuge in the United States the traditional haven of all hunted and persecuted, and the only remaining one in this sad and tragic world.

Similar will be the fate of those who are stranded in Lithuania, which, for all practical purposes is now a Soviet dependency. Those in Lithuania were originally forced to flee Poland, because, as prominent leaders of labor unions and anti-Nazi and anti-Communist organizations, they were faced with the severest punishments in the areas occupied both by Germany and Russia.

In view of the above, we earnestly appeal to the State Department and sincerely urge you, Mr. Secretary, to do all within your power, in line with American tradition to make it possible for these people to enter the United States as visitors.

Enclosed kindly find a list of names, on whose behalf we appeal:

Sincerely yours,

President,
American Federation of Labor.

President, International Ladies'
Garment Workers' Union.

General Manager,
Jewish Daily Forward.

Executive Secretary,
Jewish Labor Committee.

the person in charge of granting visas at the State Department, Breck-enridge Long, a negative frame toward them. Long is notorious in the literature on this period as an anti-Semite, anti-East and Southern European, anti-Leftist, opposed to giving out visas to anyone who was not from Northern or Western Europe and politically "unreliable".

AMERICAN FEDERATION OF LABOR

Executive Council
President, WILLIAM GREEN
Secretary-Treasurer, GEORGE MEANY
A. F. of L. Building, Washington, D. C.

First Vice-President, WILLIAM L. HUTCHESON,
Carpenters' Building, Indianapolis, Ind.
Second Vice-President, T. A. RICKERT,
Room 211-43 Astor Place, New York, N. Y.
Third Vice-President, MATTHEW WOLL,
570 Lexington Ave. New York, N. Y.
Fourth Vice-President, JOSEPH N. WEBER,
1440 Broadway, New York, N. Y.
Fifth Vice-President, G. M. BUGNIAZET,
1200 Fifteenth St., N. W., Washington, D. C.
Sixth Vice-President, GEO. M. HARRISON,
Railway Clerks' Bldg., Cincinnati, O.
Seventh Vice-President, DANIEL J. TOBIN,
222 East Michigan Street, Indianapolis, Ind.

Eighth Vice-President, HARRY C. BATES,
918 Fifteenth St., N. W., Washington, D. C.
Ninth Vice-President, EDWARD J. GAINOR,
602 A. F. of L. Building, Washington, D. C.
Tenth Vice-President, W. D. MAHON,
260 Vernor Highway, East, Detroit, Mich.
Eleventh Vice-President, FELIX H. KNIGHT,
400-403 Chrisman Bldg., Kansas City, Mo.
Twelfth Vice-President, GEORGE E. BROWNE,
Room 603-680 Fifth Ave., New York, N. Y.
Thirteenth Vice-President, EDWARD FLORE,
630 Woodbridge Avenue, Buffalo, N. Y.
Fourteenth Vice-President
Fifteenth Vice-President

NCE TELEPHONE NATIONAL 3670-1-2-3-4
CABLE ADDRESS, AFEL

Washington, D. C.
July 2, 1940.

Hon. Cordell Hull,
Secretary of State,
Washington, D. C.

Honorable Sir:

Do

99

In the name of the American Federation
of Labor, the Jewish Labor Committee, and representatives of organized labor in the United States, we wish
to appeal to you in a matter of great urgency.

The Nazi occupation of France and the
Soviet seizure of Lithuania have placed in jeopardy the
lives of a great number of men and women prominent in
the democratic and labor movements in Europe.

Permit us to impress upon you, Honorable
Sir, that unless these men and women find immediate
temporary haven in the United States, they are in danger
of being imprisoned, placed in concentration camps, or
shot, whether it be by the Gestapo or the GPU.

The men and women in whose behalf we are
now appealing are world-famous writers, editors, labor
leaders, former government officials, and ministers.
Some of them are in intimate contact with the trade union
movement, and are well-known to organized labor in the
United States. Should they fall into the clutches of the
German Gestapo or the Soviet GPU, they will face certain
death, and their loss would be irreparable for the
civilized world.

Because of their opposition to Fascism,
Nazism, and Communism, the majority of these men and
women were forced to flee their countries - Germany,
Austria, Czecho-Slovakia, Italy, Russia, Poland. Most of

them were until recently in Paris. Now they have found a temporary refuge in Toulouse and other parts of France. But, as you are undoubtedly aware, the present French government, acceding to the demands of the government of Germany, has agreed to hand over all these pro-democratic refugees to the Gestapo.

This, Honorable Sir, will be the fate of great and noble men and women, whose only crime is their firm belief in Democracy, Freedom, and Tolerance, unless they find an immediate place of refuge in the United States the traditional haven of all hunted and persecuted, and the only remaining one in this sad and tragic world.

Similar will be the fate of those who are stranded in Lithuania, which, for all practical purposes is now a Soviet dependency. Those in Lithuania were originally forced to flee Poland, because, as prominent leaders of labor unions and anti-Nazi and anti-Communist organizations, they were faced with the severest punishments in the areas occupied both by Germany and Russia.

In view of the above, we earnestly appeal to the State Department and sincerely urge you, Mr. Secretary, to do all within your power, in line with American tradition to make it possible for these people to enter the United States as visitors.

Enclosed kindly find a list of names, on whose behalf we appeal:

Sincerely yours,

President,
American Federation of Labor.

President, International Ladies'
Garment Workers' Union.

General Manager,
Jewish Daily Forward.

Executive Secretary,
Jewish Labor Committee.

the person in charge of granting visas at the State Department, Breckenridge Long, a negative frame toward them. Long is notorious in the literature on this period as an anti-Semite, anti-East and Southern European, anti-Leftist, opposed to giving out visas to anyone who was not from Northern or Western Europe and politically "unreliable".

Reading Long's letters confirms this interpretation of his views.[3] The Roosevelt Administration has come under very severe criticism for not doing more to save Jews and other people in danger.

Indeed, when I visited the Holocaust Museum soon after its opening in 1993, I found some people there skeptical of the story I told them about these Emergency Entrance visas that have been given in response to labor movement lobbying. This led to an interesting exchange I had with a member of the museum staff.

Overall, I was very moved by the museum's role as a repository of memory and found the exhibits impressive. I had on the occasion of my visit an extra mission in seeing as well a side exhibit on Varian Fry and the Emergency Rescue Committee he led in Marseilles that helped save many famous people from the Nazis. Fry came from an establishment East Coast family, a graduate himself from Hotchkiss and Riverdale Country Schools in the New York City area, then Harvard, altogether an upper-class pedigree. In the summer of 1940, he was sent to France to help save prominent artists, intellectuals, and political figures, both Jewish and non-Jewish, known to be in danger. He went to Marseilles, supplied with some visas from the US, a small amount of money, and staff support from the Unitarian Service Committee and what became the International Rescue Committee. The group forged identity papers, smuggled people across the French border with Spain` with guides to get over the mountains or by train where permits could be secured, and on through Portugal to the US. Some quite famous people were rescued this way: among them Hannah Arendt, Marc Chagall, Max Ernst, Arthur Koestler, Wanda Landowska, Claude Levi-Strauss, Jacques Lipchitz, Alma Werfel, Golo and Heinrich Mann, and Max Ophuls.

As part of the Fry exhibit, I noticed a reprint of a long article in a NY newspaper interviewing noted author Lion Feuchtwanger on his escape in late summer of 1940 through southern France over the mountains, with guides and routes, then to Madrid, Lisbon and out. I was shocked that this detail was published while the rescue operation was still underway. It endangered the whole network and puzzled me as to why Feuchtwanger would give the interview and why the NY paper would publish it.

It so happened that the person who had become my father-in-law, Albert Hirschman, was featured in this exhibit because he had worked with Fry in Marseille. Hirschman had actually known my family a bit through links in Berlin, where as a young man, he had joined the same group—SAYot (Social Democrat youth movement)—as my parents. This exhibit had some photos of him under the pseudonym he had used in Marseille, Albert Hermand.

A college friend, Raye Linda Farr, had been working at the museum as an archivist. She had become quite an expert in WW II documents through her work with Granada Television in London, where she hunted down film footage all over Europe that was used in the famous television series, *The World at War.* Raye introduced me as a Hirschman relative to one of the people who worked on the Fry exhibit. That person was quite friendly and excited to have a relative of someone depicted in the exhibit. When I narrated my family story, and the Labor movement's action to get the visas, she was very sharply dismissive. I must be wrong, in her view, or at least greatly exaggerating the story. There could not have been more than a small handful of visas gotten this way. The FDR Administration was so prejudiced this could not have happened as I had understood it.

This response startled me as, of course I had understood the family narrative quite differently. Some months later, I spoke about this encounter to my cousin Helen Garvy. Helen jumped up, went to the closet, and pulled out a box, in which she promptly found her father George's actual visa, the very item being discussed. It was quite a remarkable thing to look at. It notes the date of the telegram from Emma Woytinsky and says he intends not to immigrate to the US, clearly a requirement for a non-immigration visa. It then shows many stamps and signatures of the various consulates and border officials marking their progress with precision out of France, across Spain to Portugal, a document of the difficulty of legal exit and entry at that time. We made a copy of the visa (reproduced here) and I mailed it to the Holocaust Museum staffer as evidence of the correctness of my understanding of the facts. I received a polite acknowledgement, but no comment on our disagreement. Here are portions of that visa.

Form No. 257
FOREIGN SERVICE
Revised Nov. 1936

64/

No. - 121-

American Foreign Service

At __Marseille, France__   Date __August 13, 1940__

APPLICATION FOR NONIMMIGRANT VISA

I, the undersigned APPLICANT FOR A NONIMMIGRANT VISA, declare that my full and true name is __George BRONSTEIN-GARVY__

That I was born __May 30, 1913__ at __Riga, Latvia__
(Date)   (City and country)

That I desire to go to the United States accompanied by the following persons included in my travel document:

(Names, relationship, and country of birth)

That I ~~am a~~ ~~citizen of~~ ~~(subject)~~ __have no nationality__ and am the bearer of [passport]
(Country)

No. _____ issued on _____ by _____
(Issuing office)

_____, valid until _____
(City and country)   (Date)

That I am {~~married~~ single}, and the name of my {wife husband} is _____

That {she he} resides at _____

That I {~~have~~ do not have} a residence abroad which I {~~do~~ do not} intend to abandon. My residence is at _____

__Marseille, France__
(Street, city, and country) (Strike out in cases of sec. 3(1) and 3(6) applicants)

That I arrived in __France__ on __March 1933__
(Country where applying)   (Date)

for the purpose of __accompanying my parents__

That my occupation for the last 2 years was __statistician__

and at present is __same__ That my purpose in going to the United States is
__visit my family__

That I intend to remain there for __1__ months and that my address in the United States will be
__5036 Massachusetts Ave., N. W. Washington, D. C.__
(Street, city, and State)

My references are __Telegram No. 83, dated July 6, 1940,__
(In United States: Names and addresses (give names of close relatives, if any))
__from Department of State, concerning my father Peter Bronstein-__
__Garvy.__
(Local) (Strike out section regarding references in cases of sec. 3(1) applicants)

That I do not intend to immigrate into the United States and that I consider myself to be a nonimmigrant under the provisions of the Immigration Act of 1924 on the following grounds: __I am a temporary visitor__
__and I intend to leave the United States in order to await the issuance__
__of an immigration visa.__
I offer for inspection the following documents in support of my claim: _____
__above-mentioned telegram.__

_____

_____

That I have never applied for or been refused a visa, either formally or informally, at any American consulate or diplomatic mission; that I have never been refused admission into the United States; and that I have never been deported or repatriated from the United States.

__- No. -__

(Applicant should here explain circumstances if he has applied for or been refused a visa, denied admission into the United States, or has been deported or repatriated from the United States) cealment of a material fact, shall be guilty of a misdemeanor and, upon conviction, shall be punished by imprisonment for not more than 1 year or by a fine of not more than $1,000, or by both such fine and imprisonment."

I realize that section 22 (c) of the Immigration Act of 1924 provides that: "Whoever knowingly makes under oath any false statement in any application, affidavit, or other document required by the immigration laws or regulations prescribed thereunder, shall, upon conviction thereof, be fined not more than $10,000, or imprisoned for not more than 5 years, or both."

I solemnly swear that the foregoing statements are true to the best of my knowledge and belief. I as une the obligation to leave the United States I soon as it is a sible for me to do so.

(Signature of applicant, with at least one Christian name)

Subscribed and sworn to before me this _____13th_____ day of _____, 1940

[SEAL]

Fee No. 1805

Passport visa No. 119

CONSUL'S FINDINGS ON STATUS. (Include statements regarding evidence presented that alien has a fixed domicile and that he has a right to be readmitted into the country in which he is applying or into some other country.)

Description of George Bronstein-Garvy

Color of hair: bro.
Color of eyes: brown
Complexion: medium
Height: 5 ft 10 inch.
Profession: statistician.

_____ of the United States of America.

Passport visa granted ____ t 13

19.40, as nonimmigrant under section 3 (2) of the Immigration Act of 1924.

Admitted at New York, N. Y.,

19.__, under Paragraph ___ Section 3, Immigration Act of 1924 for _____

Immigrant Inspector

No. 119

American Consulate at

Marseille, France
(Country)

SEEN
For the journey to the United States

of GEORGE BRONSTEIN-GARVY

(seal)
(fee stamp)

American ___ Consul

Date AUG 13 1940

Visa valid for presentation at United States ports at any time during twelve months from date provided passport continues to be valid for such period.

Visa granted as No. 119 class under Section 3 (2) of the Immigration Act of 1924

TEMPORARY VISITOR
(Classification)

U. S. GOVERNMENT PRINTING OFFICE   16—11268

1806   Fee: $9

Summary and Translation of Information on Visa:

Date of application: 13 August 1940

Date of Bingham signature: same

- Date of arrival in New York: 13 October 1940

- SEP Document: Office des réfugiés russes à Marseilles 17 August 1940
- French exit document: Department of Bouches-du-Rhones, Office of the Prefect, 30 august 1940, 10 francs
- Portugese Consulate, Marseilles, 31 August 1940 269.60 francs
- Spanish Consulate, Marseilles, 2 September 1940 1 1 0 0 francs.
- City of Marseilles, tax fee, 2 September 1940 2000 Francs
- Special Commission Cerbère, city at the French border) 7 Sept 1940 (denotes the date of passage)
- Directorate of Security, Port Bou, Spanish border, 7 September 1940 (denotes the date of passage)
- Directorate of Security, Valencia, Sept 1940 Transit
- Portugese customs "Aduana de Port Bou" 10 Sept 1940 3 1 0 0 Francs
- Portugal: Entrada Beira Marval: 10 September 1940 transit entry
- Portugal Visa: #1880, 14 September 1940, Valid 14 days
- Portugal Visa: renewal 25 September 1940
- Lisbon, embarquement, Nea Hellas, 3 October 1940

The details tell us something about the life of these refugees at this moment. For one, they must have been very busy rushing around Marseilles getting Visa stamps, paying fees, and getting documents from this or that official. This was long before the day of photocopy, fax, email, and other electronic shortcuts. My communication with the Russian FSB in 2017 was annoying but relatively fast.

Another striking detail is the cost. I add up the cost for George alone on this Visa, and it comes to 6400 francs. That was a good deal of money in those days. Where did they get it? They were penniless, without work, with no savings. I think this cost was born by the Joint—the Jewish Joint Distribution Committee and some labor groups, both in the US. It is these groups who paid the boat ticket for the large numbers who lacked the funds to pay their own way.

Another interesting detail: he promises to stay only one month, his purpose is to accompany his parents, he has no nationality, his residence is Marseilles (rather generic), and he does not intend nonetheless to abandon it. He plans to leave the US in order to reapply as the law requires an immigrant Visa, of which, thus, this is not one. His US reference is the telegram from the Woytinskys, and he lists what I think is their address in Washington.

Discovering at this moment the actual Emergence Entrance Visa Document used by my uncle as an exemplar of the kind each family member had obtained moved me greatly. Shortly after the Holocaust Museum visit in 1993, I went to the Tamiment and Robert Wagner Labor Archive at New York University. I discussed my experience in Washington with some staffers there. They reported tense relationships with the Holocaust Museum, precisely on the point of how much attention to pay to the labor story. The Labor Archive people thought the Holocaust Museum neglected the role of labor in order to stress the overall refusal of the State Department to issue visas to Jews.

Who was right between these two hard-working, respectable institutions— the Holocaust Museum or the NYU Labor Archive? Well, both.

Breckinridge Long and the US State Department certainly did not do remotely enough to allow people in danger to come to the US, as the Holocaust Museum people stressed. Yet, there were exceptions to this, among them emergency visas to labor leaders and to prominent intellectuals whom it was known the Nazis would persecute—thus the Labor Movement Story and the Varian Fry Story. The Museum featured the second, but not the first. It is important to me in this book to contribute to telling the first.

The NYU archive contained the actual list of people who were to get these emergency entrance visas. These included prominent labor leaders from several countries, mostly living in France. One of the pages of the list included my grandparents (Bronstein-Garvy) and their son, my Uncle George. And then my parents (Alexander Gourevitch and Sylvia Bronstein-Garvy Gourevitch). My dad Alex (Shura) was listed as a "Chemist and Volunteer" in the French Army, which I don't think was the case. Mother was listed as a "chemist," which was true at the time as she was pursuing a degree in that field.

Right after them on that list are two people famous in these particular circles: Boris Nicolaevsky (the person noted in the visit to the historian Nenarokov in Moscow), who became famous as the collector of manuscripts and whose name is on the archives at Stanford and

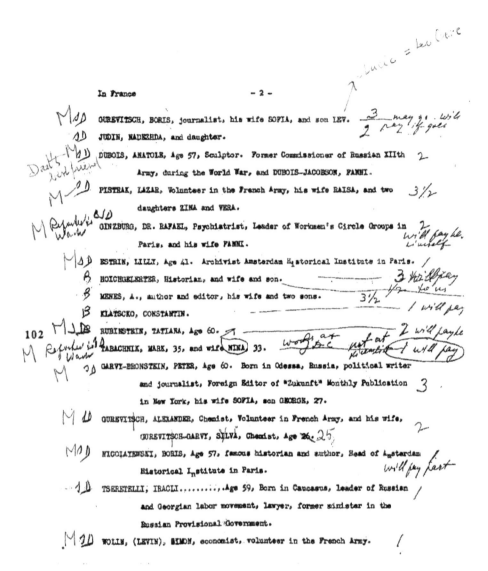

GUREVITSCH, BORIS, journalist, his wife SOFIA, and son LEV.

JUDIN, NADEZHDA, and daughter.

DUBOIS, ANATOLE, Age 57, Sculptor. Former Commissioner of Russian XIIth
Army, during the World War, and DUBOIS-JACOBSON, FANNI.

PISTRAK, LAZAR, Volunteer in the French Army, his wife RAISA, and two
daughters ZINA and VERA.

GINZBURG, DR. RAFAEL, Psychiatrist, Leader of Workman's Circle Groups in
Paris, and his wife FANNI.

ESTRIN, LILLY, Age 41. Archivist Amsterdam Historical Institute in Paris.

HOICHGELERTER, Historian, and wife and son.

MENES, A., author and editor, his wife and two sons.

KLATSCKO, CONSTANTIN.

RUBINSTEIN, TATIANA, Age 60.

TABACHNIK, MARK, 35, and wife NINA, 33.

GARVI-BRONSTEIN, PETER, Age 60. Born in Odessa, Russia, political writer
and journalist, Foreign Editor of "Zukunft" Monthly Publication
in New York, his wife SOFIA, son GEORGE, 27.

GUREVITSCH, ALEXANDER, Chemist, Volunteer in French Army, and his wife,
GUREVITSCH-GARVY, SILVA, Chemist, Age 26.

NICOLAYEWSKI, BORIS, Age 57, famous historian and author, Head of Amsterdam
Historical Institute in Paris.

TSERETELLI, IRACLI.........,Age 59, Born in Caucasus, leader of Russian
and Georgian labor movement, lawyer, former minister in the
Russian Provisional Government.

WOLIN, (LEVIN), SIMON, economist, volunteer in the French Army.

in Moscow; and Irakli Tseretelli, also noted earlier, a prominent figure in the Russian Revolution, the Menshevik leader of Georgia who sent Woytinsky to the West as Ambassador to the Vatican. The handwriting on the right notes who is paying their fares and who is not… and I note that my five relatives were not. The "M" on the left may refer to Menshevik, but then why not note it for Tseretelli?

So this was a list of people who would get visas to escape the Gestapo's jaws, the "Schindler's list" of the Menshevik and labor leader group. There were other "lists" of people who escaped the clutches of the killers. One such less famous than Schindler's list was that of the Kastner train from Budapest, on which Hungarians, mostly very wealthy ones, were allowed to buy their way out to Switzerland. Among them was Peter Munk as a child, who went on to make a fortune in Canada, and endowed, along with hospitals, the Munk School at the University of Toronto, where I taught as a visiting professor from 2011-13. These people were privileged and lucky. In the 1970s, I met a woman of Hungarian ancestry whose parents had survived Auschwitz. Her eyes flashed with anger when I told her my family story: "Why did your family get out and not mine?" she said. Did she prefer that my family not get out and suffer as had hers? Not exactly, but she understandably resented the suffering of her parents while others escaped. It does raise questions about victimhood. Schindler's list appears to have been constructed by the accountant who met Schindler by "accident." The "Kastner list" was constructed by him through contact among people with money. The "Labor list" was constructed by Minkoff out of the network of European labor leaders living in France. This was perhaps the only moment when being a labor leader conferred a moment of privilege that could save your life, having first increased your vulnerability.

Being politically active made these people more aware of the threat to their lives. It was not for being Jewish but for being labor people that they were targeted, and it was that which got them their emergency visas. Most of them were Jewish, but not all. Just after this 1993 visit to the Washington Holocaust Museum, I stopped by to see my mother in San Diego, where she lived near me, and she was being visited by Katia Ladjinskaya, herself a survivor of the same flight from Russia to Germany and France. When I told of the trip to the Museum, she, Katia, noted that, indeed, she was not Jewish (nor were Tseretilli and Nicolaevsky.)

The archive shows a typed list of names with many handwritten annotations. Who made the list? It seems to have been Isaiah Minkoff of the Jewish Labor Committee in New York, who played a major role in picking names, no doubt with input from people in Paris, such as Abramovich, Dan, and other leaders of the Foreign Delegation. The NYU archives show several versions and several lists of boats to which people were assigned; not all of these were totally accurate in my limited knowledge.

Having received the telegram from Emma, the family did go to Marseilles as instructed in August 1940 and got the visas, as well as the transit permits through Spain and Portugal. Before we resume their journey to the US, there are still more questions to pose about the evidence we have about causes and explanations.

Why were the visas issued?: The story of the Jewish Labor Committee, the American Labor Movement, FDR and Hiram Bingham IV

How did this very unusual granting of visas come about? We can see the hard facts: the visas were authorized, they were given to some people, and those people made it to the US, among them my parents. Yet the more one reflects on it, a number of questions arise about why these steps took place. Just why did the Labor movement in America, usually seen as isolationist, decide to put pressure on the FDR administration? Why did the FDR Administration give in to Labor pressure and grant the Visas? Why did the State Department actually issue them rather than passively obstruct them? Why did the French let the refugees leave France without exit visas? Why did Fascist Franco of Spain and right-wing dictator Salazar of Portugal let them pass through Madrid to Lisbon to board the boat?

None of these steps, each essential to the family's departure, are obvious. We have seen in the case of Grandpas Boris and Peter that the rules and bureaucratic procedures can produce a variety of results and interpretations. So let us ask similar questions of this situation as the family confronts decision-makers within a range of political systems, institutions and conditions. Asking this sort of question is what I have spent my professional life doing, so I can turn the lens inward and focus it on my own family.

Let us take these up in a causal sequence: First, why did the American Labor Movement choose to put pressure on the Administration in Washington to issue these visas? Right away, this rattles the conventional wisdom about the American Labor Movement. If it was so isolationist, as its reputation contends, why was it not behaving so in this instance? Indeed most of the time, American labor seemed distant from the intellectual and ideological struggles of European labor, proud of its domestic American concerns and its pragmatic commitments to unionism. American labor has generally been held up in contrast to its European counterparts, who are seen as transformative, interested in sweeping change, and engaging in the large social movements of the 19th and 20th centuries. Socialism, Communism, and even Christian Democracy, as practiced in Europe, had weak roots in the US. By and large, American labor did not send representatives to the great meetings, the various "internationals," to which even the least ideological European movements, such as the British, attended.

The emergence of the Jewish Labor Committee in the 1930s seems a break from this pattern.[4] It aimed to alert US decision-makers and the public to the evils of Nazi Germany and to Stalin's USSR. Its emergence reflects the sociology of the garment industry workers in the US and the background of their leaders David Dubinsky and Sidney Hilman, the former as head of the ILGWU, the International Ladies Garment Workers Union and Hilman for the men's garment workers union. Both were immigrants from the Russian Empire, of Jewish background, both radicalized in their youth as socialists, and both active in the labor movement of New York. The clothing industry in the US east coast had masses of poor immigrant Jews, refugees from the Russian, Austrian, Turkish and German Empires laboring in sweatshop conditions ripe for union organizing. Large numbers of other ethnic groups joined them, such as Italians and East Europeans.

Dubinsky and Hilman became important leaders of these garment workers' unions and, thus, major figures in State and national politics. Both became fully engaged in the many political conflicts of the period. Dubinsky fought more directly with the Communists than did Hilman, but both turned against the Bolsheviks. Both were active supporters of FDR's New Deal at home and his internationalism abroad.

They avidly followed European events, acutely aware of the double danger posed by the Nazis to Labor and to Jews. Both Dubinsky and Hilman saw the threat to the US in ways Churchill was to articulate later in the decade: an imperialist authoritarian regime would upset the global balance of power, menacing to all. So here, American Labor was an early ringer of alarms in the US about fascism, the Nazis, and the growing security threat from Germany.

So we see their motives in lobbying. Yet countless people lobby governments. Only a few are heard and have influence. This leads us to yet another question: Why did FDR, Secretary of State Cordell Hull and the anti-Semitic head of the visa office, Breckinridge Long, respond in the affirmative to the request for visas for this group of people?

The letter from the labor movement is addressed to Secretary Hull. Did FDR know about it, or was it all left to Hull and Long? The president does seem to have been aware, and there is talk of influence from Mrs. Roosevelt. Why would FDR care? Among other reasons, 1940 was an election year, where FDR would face the unprecedented move of running for a third term. Roosevelt needed labor support to carry New York, among other places. David Dubinsky was an influential political figure in NY as head of the ILGWU. FDR was very worried about isolationism in the US, an astonishingly powerful movement in Congress and the general public. From his defeat in 1937 on the plan to add justices to the Supreme Court, which was blocking legislation for the New Deal, FDR found the Southern democrats were deserting him on domestic politics, forming the alliance with conservative Republicans that has shaped US politics for many years since then.[5]

At the same time, the Southern conservatives were more internationalist than the Northern GOP and, indeed, more than many Democrats. This was due largely to their agricultural economic base: exporters of primary products such as cotton, tobacco, and sugar, they had been concerned with an open international economy since the 19th century, the core of free trade coalitions in American politics for well over a century, struggling with the protectionist industrialists of the older Midwest and Northeast. They were thus vital to FDR's policy of engaging the US in the growing international crisis, keeping alive the anti-Nazi policy, and helping the UK when it was at risk of collapse.[7]

On international issues, FDR was ahead of the political curve in the US, wanting more engagement than Congress and the public were willing to give him. He sought help where he could find it. That included the racist American South.

American blacks paid a great price for this: the cost of Southern support for the New Deal social programs such as the Social Security retirement, trade union recognition, creation of the Security and Exchange Commission (the SEC), price supports for agriculture, and many other programs, was that African Americans were excluded from many of these programs, as they were after WW II from Veterans' programs. Nothing was tolerated by Southern congressmen that could menace white control of the South. Katznelson notes that Nazis came to the South hoping to mobilize racism in support of the Nazi project.

The Nazis got nowhere in their efforts to attract Southern backing, and FDR had considerable support from the Southern racists for all his efforts to build up the military, Lend Lease to the British and international engagement, thus fighting Nazi racism.

The other victims of this bargaining were Jews. To ensure support for at least some internationalism, FDR avoided framing the combat with the Nazis in terms of saving Jews. He was cautious about making a foreign policy very general to avoid any kind of "special pleading."[8] That approach allowed some limited space for emergency entrance visas, people who could be framed in ways that did not disrupt the political balance in the US: the intellectuals, saved by the Fry operation, and the labor leaders, saved by the AFL efforts. The numbers were small, a total of 2500 or so for both groups. And even these provoked hostility, as intellectuals and labor were not popular categories. The visa office of the State Department knew it had Congressional backing to resist generosity of entry and pressed the consular corps not to help refugees even if they could, that is, even if there were slots available.

Given the isolationism and pressure against labor and intellectuals, we might expect no visas for intellectuals and labor, so why were even some granted at all? To the extent FDR was actively involved, I am inclined to think the decision was influenced by the election concerns he had as well as any humanitarian interests or sympathy he may have had as well. Why did Cordell Hull and Long agree to allow some visas? Catherine Collomp, French historian and author of an important book on the Jewish Labor Committee, thinks they were the key players at this point, more than FDR. She thinks they may have had a partial wave of sympathetic concern with the collapse in France, realizing disaster was happening, to take some limited action. Some responses to emergencies seemed appropriate, she thinks. It did not last long. By the early fall, they began to close the door again. I don't know how to prove the existence of this wave of sympathy, its presence or its lack, another example of uncertainty. I am skeptical. What sense of appropriateness or emergency would make them gesture toward groups about whom they, certainly Long, were normally quite hostile? I wonder if the decision-makers felt some kind of pressure, perhaps from FDR and labor, from the electorate, from Congress for at least a short period at the moment of the French collapse; perhaps they felt a moment of being watched by history, of some kind of accountability in this crisis moment and had to show some flexibility, albeit limited, and then that moment was gone and the door, open only a crack, for a few, closed up again.

We can see several steps in the politics of the granting of the visas that illustrate the connection between Jewish and non-Jewish support: First, the drafting of the letter, done by Minkoff of the Jewish Labor Committee; second, a broader union embrace, done by Dubinsky, head of one of the most important Jewish unions. At this point, they broaden the support base by getting Green, head of the AFL, which is step three. And step four is getting the top political decision-makers, the Secretary of State, Cordell Hull. I assume getting FDR is part of that process, though we do not have direct evidence of his involvement. Each step needs the other.

This raises yet another question of great consequence. Once the Secretary of State and the Head of the Visa Office make the decision to grant the visas, why were they actually issued by lower-ranking staffers of the State Department, the Foreign Service Officers, who do the actual work in supplying documents to those who ask for them? In our case here, this means the Consulate in Marseilles.

That the Secretary of State authorizes the visas does not guarantee they will be provided. We know countless examples of orders from on high not actually being carried out. Political science, public and business administration study just this sort of topic: principal-agent theory wonders what ability the principal (the person with formal authority) actually has in getting the agent (the staffer down the hierarchy, the hired employee) to carry out the desired activity. The equivalent for voters is how they monitor the behavior of the elected officeholders, for shareholders to monitor the directors and managers of firms, or in reverse, how dictators like Stalin or Hitler actually incentivize the lower-down staffers actually to do what is ordered.

In this specific case, there are plenty of examples of orders from the State Department or elsewhere not being carried out and quotas for visas not being filled by prejudiced officials. The State Department actually had the authority to grant more visas around the world than it actually did. Visas were by country quota. These were, in most cases, not filled. Long lines gathered in front of American consulates and embassies all over Europe, with desperate people seeking visas. Local consuls who filled the requests or not had great discretion. Most were operating under the restrictive order and prejudicial culture of the State Department elite, like Long, who advised his staff to make it quite hard to get a visa, not to fill the quota. At that time, the US Foreign Service was populated by the stereotype of the upper class, well-to-do WASPS from elite prep schools and private universities, just the group we know to have quite restrictive attitudes about immigration, the same dislike of Jews and Eastern-Southern Europeans as Long.

Why, then, did the Emergency Entrance visas get issued in Marseilles to this group of stateless, leftist, labor, heavily East European and heavily Jewish group of refugees? We would expect the Consulate to act like most of the others. Instead, a specific person behaved differently, out of the ordinary … a hero. He had an opportunity for discretion, of "agency", of choice, to go beyond the charge of his dossier to save people.

This was Hiram Bingham, IV, the vice-consul in Marseilles. The Consul-General himself was quite unsympathetic to the plight of the refugees; he fit the US State stereotype, and followed the official State line: that the US was not at war, had formal relations with the Vichy Government of France, and should not upset it by helping people escape against its wishes. Following that approach, Marseilles would have been as closed up as were most of the Consulates of Europe.

Hiram Bingham IV was different. To decipher why, one can probe his background and personality. His grandparents were missionaries in Hawaii and helped found the Punahou school to which President Barack Obama went many generations later. His New England Protestant religion was one of the roots of abolitionist sentiment in the 19th century and civil rights in the 20th. Bingham's father, as an explorer, helped find Machu Picchu in Peru, served as Senator and governor of Connecticut and married the heiress to the Tiffany fortune.

Bingham attended Groton Preparatory School and graduated from Yale in 1925, institutions which also turned out plenty of elitist conformists of the kind that populated the prejudiced elite in the State Department, but also turned out some non-conformists as well. Bingham grew up with a strong tradition of public service. But people of similar social backgrounds were not as sympathetic to the plight of refugees, so these are all hints, but perhaps not decisive.

Instead, Bingham might have gotten these values through travel or a specific person, some encounters, the specifics of his particular family culture and religion, or features of his personality. Bingham is described by one of his sons as a gentle man, a caring one. He had perhaps the independent money and personal character to resist career pressure from his superiors and the values and fortitude to do the right thing at that moment. He did pay for his righteous behavior by losing his career. The State Department expressed its displeasure with his behavior in Marseilles by assigning him to lessor posts in Portugal and Argentina and blocked his further advancement till he left the Foreign Service in 1945 to retire in Connecticut, where he and his wife raised 12 children. After he died in 1988, he was many years later recognized by Yad Vashem for his work, and the US issued a postage stamp to commemorate him.

During most of his life, he refused to talk about his past and kept the story hidden as if somehow he had done wrong. Letters and records he kept on these events were found hidden in his Connecticut home after his death, so somehow, he did not wish to publicize all this. Was he embarrassed to have disobeyed orders? Or to have failed a foreign service career? Was he at tension with his social circle for supporting this kind of refugee or being outside the regular path his sort took?

Hiram Bingham IV

Issued 2002 as part of series commemorating distinguished US diplomats

Bingham was not the only consul to have saved people, and some suffered harsher treatment by their governments, such as Mendes Sousa of Portugal, who was completely stripped of family assets by the harsh government of Portugal at that time. But Bingham's behavior was most unusual, and all the more so in the US consular corps.

Hiram Bingham plays a distinctive role in my family story. He is the exemplar of the person whose behavior was decisive to survival, life or death.

His actions could easily have been the opposite. They were not predictable from his position or background. He saved my family's lives and hundreds of others.

I have no family recollections of Bingham, no memories recounting their meeting him. He does seem to have met each refugee in the process, as verified by his signature, but aside from his signingthe Visa, I have no record of a Garvy or Gourevitch interaction.

The Third Flight: Crossing the Border and Ocean—Coming to the US August—October 1940

Bingham signed many visa papers, including those of my family. My Uncle's visa shows his signature in two places. The family situation was precarious in relation to the strict rules of procedure. They had no passports, as their citizenship had been stripped away by Soviet decree in 1931. They had Nansen passports, documents developed in the 1930s for people like them without a country: He got it even before the war broke out. It cost 38 francs—not a small sum back then.

The Nansen passport is but one example of the efforts they made to establish an identity. Uncle George had the dilemma of proving his demobilization from the army. Without that, the French authorities would make it difficult for him to leave. George managed to have such papers. They seem both generated by him and officially stamped. One document shows at the top "Centre de démobilization du Canton de Cusset", dated August 6, 1940. It shows him of having been mobilized September 2, 1939, his residence "avant les hostilités" at seven rue Jobbé Duval, the residence of his parents, and then his current address, in Toulouse, where his parents were at the time the papers were prepared. The document shows his signature and fingerprints, and then a signature of the Commander of the Center of Démobilization. And a note of payment of the tax for demobilization—200 francs, and on the back another stamp, paid on August 23, 1940, the sum of 800 francs, a second note of the demobilization sum required, stamped in Marseilles. Again, it seems like a lot of money, given their limited income. Another page writes out in hand the same document and shows handwritten signatures and stamps of both Uncle George, G. Bronstein-Garvy and the Commander of the Demobilization Center. We have then a third document prepared in the United States. It is a page notarized in New York on January 8, 1941 (two and a half months after George arrived in the US) stating that the Notary has translated and certified as accurate the demobilization document of George Garvy from the French Army. George drew on these documents when he applied in the 1940s to be a Ph.D. student at Columbia University and then again in the late 40s when he applied for regular immigration papers to the US.

Among Uncle George's papers is a statement from Hachette, a major publisher in France, certifying that he was an employee there, dated October 8, 1937.

Another interesting set of documents comes from the Office des Réfugiés Russes in Marseilles concerning my mother.

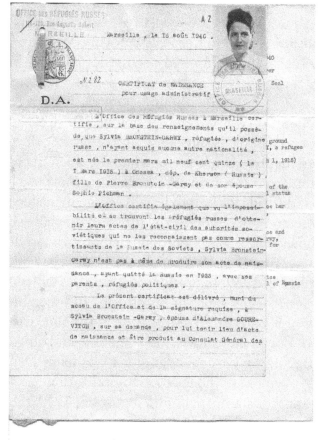

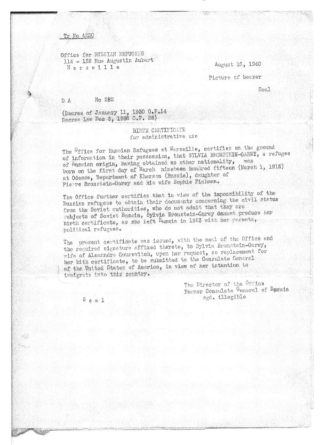

Dated 16 August 1940, it specified that Sylvia Bronstein-Garvy Gourevitch, having no official nationality, and in light of the impossibility of obtaining access to her civil documents from Soviet Russia, can consider this document as the equivalent of a birth certificate desired by the American consulate for purposes of entry to the US. It is interesting that George Garvy, who got a similar document, had his visa signed by Bingham on 13 August, thus before this certification. We can infer that Bingham was not too particular about details like this; perhaps the Nansen passport was enough for him. One source describes him as helping someone find any kind of proof; Bingham asks if she has a library card and takes that as sufficient. For my mother, this birth certificate document was perhaps considered useful as they thought of the next steps: crossing the border out of France, then Spain and Portugal and the US, and then establishing a life in the US. The more documents, the better. George obtains an identity card, so

important in France, dated August 30, 1940, from the Prefecture of the Bouches de Rhone, the department in which Marseilles sits.

The Nansen passports were valid from 20 May 1939 to 20 May 1940. We find a document dated 29 July 1940 from the *Haut Commission pour les Réfugiés, délégation de France*, located in Pau, France, addressed to the Préfect of Haute Garonne asking for an extension of the Nansen passports of the family. The copy of George's Nansen does not show any results of this request for an extension.

These materials so far all have to do with the groundwork for getting visas from the American consulate in Marseille. We can tell from the documents approximately when they reached that city and what they did while there. I have no notes about their feelings or state of mind. Here they were, having just barely escaped Paris, knowing the danger behind them. The Germans occupied most of France, so where were they to go? Mother was pregnant, as was her best friend Natasha Etkin. Suddenly the possibility of visas to the US appears. It seemed miraculous, and I do know they thought that. How did they spend their time?

This is not the same as knowing what they said, as a diary might tell us.

We can see something from the documents about the practicalities of their lives in Marseilles. They spent a good deal of time getting the permissions and documents that would need to traverse the various frontiers to reach the US. They went to each of the relevant consulates to get visas. Looking at the stamps on George's visa, we can see the following:

-30 August from the prefecture of the Bouches du Rhône allowing passage to Cerbère at the Spanish border.

-31 August, consulate of Portugal, for entry to Portugal.

-2 September, consulate of Spain, for entry there.

-7 September, the actual passage through Cerbère in France, Port Bou in Spain, and then into Spain.

Each of these stamps cost yet more francs. Once the visas were obtained, they did not delay too long in leaving, as the passage visas had time limitation dates on them and the boat passage was for a date certain, so they headed for the French border. They went by train. Reaching the border at Cerbère was a dramatic moment. People were often turned back often by French guards demanding the infamous exit visas. Walter Benjamin committed suicide after such an episode, apparently fearful of trying again. Many people, including the Etkins, had to hike over mountain paths to enter Spain, lacking the right documents. Natasha was pregnant and had to help her mother, a woman not in the best of health, who had trouble breathing. One of the major networks passed through the French town of Banyuls-sur-Mer. Its Mayor was a socialist, sympathetic to the cause. The famous sculptor Maillol worked there. His model and mistress, Dina Vierney, happened to be of Russian origin, from the same city as my grandmother, by coincidence, a friend of this Menshevik emigré group, and she played an important role in the escape system. There is a plaque of commemoration for them, the Mayor and Dina, in the town, and Paris has a museum she created after the war in honor of Maillol. The Etkins, Natasha, her husband Janni, and her mother made it on foot across the border.

Another vibrant piece of my Family Legend revolves around Grandma and the French border guard. Most of the family is passed through, but when the guard sees my uncle, he objects because George is of army age and should be back with the army despite the armistice. Grandma starts declaiming, "If he does not go, I am not going," threatening to camp out right there. The guard just waved them all through—was it the force of her personality, or my uncle's supposed discharge papers and all the stamps on the visa, and boat tickets to the US, or was it the guard's weariness in front of the stream of people clamoring to get by? They did pass by, and it became part of the Family Legend, yet another story about Grandma!

The family promptly boarded a train to Lisbon via Madrid. Why, yet another question, did Franco let them all through? A fascist leader who recently defeated the Loyalist Republican forces with the help of Hitler and Mussolini, one might imagine Franco would lack sympathy for these socialist and other anti-fascist refugees and be unwilling to let obvious enemies of the fascist regime escape. The most parsimonious explanation is that Franco's attention focused on establishing control within Spain, for which he had hundreds of thousands of prisoners already and did not need more.[9]

Franco held his distance from Hitler, refusing to join him in war. They met once at Hendaye on the Atlantic border with France. Hitler said he never wanted to meet Franco again, finding him cold and distant. Franco felt the same and refused to join up with Hitler much further. One interpretation is that Franco was a somewhat more traditional European conservative, old elite, army, business, aristocracy, and church. Hitler seemed wild, dangerous and risky, and too demanding and would dominate Spain, which Franco did not want. Franco was a devout Catholic suspicious of Hitler's attacks on Christianity. Some speculate he was part Jewish and knew it. He did allow Spanish soldiers to fight with Hitler against the USSR, but not against the Western allies. Whatever the reasons, the refugees were given passage to Portugal, provided they did not stay or linger.

My parents recall much damage and suffering in Spain when they crossed.

When the train stopped in Madrid, my dad went to get some food, and the train almost left without him. What panic must there have been for them and him as the minutes ticked away and he was not back on the train—a moment they all vividly recalled years later. George went for a swim near the Spanish border and got a fright watching German officers come down the road. In the 1990s, when I visited Spain to teach for a few weeks, my mother came to visit, and we did a little touring together, getting up the fortitude to visit the huge memorial Franco had set up in the Valley of the Fallen. Repelled as we were by his memory, we were too curious about history not to go. Spain still showed the legacy of those years of the Civil War. Spanish politics, movies and culture still process those, for example, with the movie *Parallel Mothers* (2021) directed by Almodóvar.

The stories told in the family about being in Lisbon involved waiting for the boat, somewhat bored, and playing cards—bridge, I think. George remembers the address in Lisbon—49 Rua Rodrigo da Fonseca Pansao Alentejo.

Lisbon also felt safe. The right-wing dictatorship cared little about the refugees, provided they were just passing through. Lisbon was legendary for being full of spies, agents, people trafficking visas, and information. They left on an old Greek ship, the Nea Hellas, which apparently sunk on the next crossing, torpedoed. Another incident of fate. In reading a recent novel by Colm Toibin, *The Magician,* based on the life of Thomas Mann, it turns out some of Mann's children were on the same crossing as my family, along with Alma Mahler and Franz Wurfel; in the novel, Mann meets the ship upon its arrival in New York. The novel makes no mention of Hoboken.

In New York, the family landed in Hoboken and was not processed at Ellis Island. They were met by the representatives of various Jewish

and labor organizations, who cleared their arrival and found places for them to live. Some

(such as the Etkins) had family here who helped materially. The Woytinskys had found for the Garvy menage a lodging house in the

West 70s, but I believe the family moved soon to the upper West 100s. Their economic condition was poor. My older brother was born in a kind of welfare hospital in February of 1941. They lived on private charity in a small apartment. They did have each other—the network of political refugees, including Mensheviks, many of whom lived in the same building. My dad got a job with Allied Chemical in New Jersey, requiring a long commute. Mother earned money hand-knitting fancy sweaters for well-to-do clients—well below her educational level, but it brought in income! George got a visa for Juliette, who arrived in November of 1941 from France. He enrolled as a graduate student in economics at Columbia and got a Ph.D. there.

Part of the family made it to the US and lived a good life there. But another part of the family did not have a favorable outcome, and I wish to turn now to their story: on the maternal side, mother's favorite uncle, Boris Fichman, Dadya Buka, was killed with his wife Olga in Auschwitz, and then on the paternal side, Boris Ber Gourevitch, my grandfather, was killed in Vladimir Prison near Moscow in 1938. And we need to backtrack for a moment to ask a question left hanging before: How did my father get out of the USSR in 1931 when his own father did not?

Endnotes

1 In the early stages of working on this memoir, I discovered the research being done by Catherine Collomp on the activities of the American Labor movement in this period, and met her in Paris. She showed me her manuscript, as yet unpublished in French. Its importance impressed me greatly. After its publication in France, I worked with her to find an American outlet. On the strength of her work, Wayne State Press has done it. A central contribution is to show the activism of American labor in foreign policy issues of the period, in raising alarm on the dangers of Nazi Germany. In this the Menshevik contact played a role in developing awareness which in turn may have helped them get the emergency entrance visas. Résister au nazisme: le Jewish labor committee, New York, 1934-1945 Paris: CNRS, 2016; translated as Rescue, Relief and Resistance: The Jewish Labor Committee's Anti-Nazi Operations, 1934-1945, trans. Susan Emanuel, Wayne State University Press, 2021.

2 Ibid.

3 Ibid.

4 Collomp, op cit. , Résister au nazisme.

5 Katznelson, Ira, Fear Itself: the New Deal and the Origins of our Time (New York: Liveright Publishing Corporation, 2013). He stresses the importance of the South to FDR's internationalism.

6 Williams, W.A., Roots of the Modern American Empire, Random House, 1969

7 Katznelson, op cit.

8 Breitman, Richard and Allan Lichtman, FDR and the Jews, Cambridge: Harvard University Press, 2013

9 Thanks to Pamela Radcliffe, Professor of History at UCSD, for advice on these issues

Chapter 9

The Tragedy of the "The Unsung Hero"

Dadia Buka and Auschwitz

When I showed my mother the copy of the train list from Drancy to Auschwitz, which bore the names of Uncle Buka and Aunt Olya, she began to sob.[1] "Why, " I asked her, "This is not new. You have told me all my life how much you loved him and that he had been killed there." "Yes," she replied. "But seeing in black on white on a printed page on a real historical document sinks the pain much deeper." Indeed. I felt a fragment of the same emotion, indeed much more than a fragment, as I found documents throughout the journey of doing this book. Finding them drew me closer to the specific person, especially the ones I never met. Without my choir, I would never have had the emotional courage to visit Auschwitz. I had told myself over the years that though I knew I was a deeply committed tourist, I could not bear to visit concentration camps. But when in 2002, my University of California San Diego-based choir toured the Czech Republic and Poland and arranged a trip to that camp, I thought there would be sustenance in going with them, and so I did it, as a pilgrimage to where Uncle Buka and his wife Olga were killed.

While the Bronstein-Garvys escaped France in the nick of time, Boris Fichman, Grandma Sophia's beloved brother, the uncle of Sylvia and George, and Boris' wife Olga, stayed behind. Dadia Buka and his wife, Teutia Olya, were dear to the hearts of this family. The notes written by my uncle George while in his 70s compliment my mother's oral comments to me about him. How warm and caring, how important Buka was in their lives when their parents were busy with politics or other things; I had heard about him my whole life. I quote at length to give voice to my uncle about his uncle:

"The younger brother, Boris (called Buka), was very close to ourmother (Grandma Sophia) and, in fact, supported our family all his life. He was the unsung hero of our life whose boundless devotion to Mother kept us literally alive for years. He accompanied her on a trip to Italy and Sicily after she broke with Parvus (with whom she had lived [they were not legally married]. In 1916, our father Peter was banished to Cherny Yar on the lower Volga (not far from Stalingrad), and Buka accompanied Mother and us children when she joined herhusband, and he stayed in Cherny Yar for some time. [Note: Sylvia says the conditions were so harsh that their mother returned with Buka to Odesa.]

Buka had an electric supply store and automobile agency, representing the German automobile maker Brennabor [elsewhere, George mentions they also sold bicycles]. Buka owned the store in partnership with a man of Greek extraction. The store was a spacious showroom on one of the main streets and looked not much different from similar stores in the US today. The store was located in the center of the city, but I did not find it when I visited Odesa.

Buka became a "Nep" speculator and then emigrated to Berlin (when we did). He married a divorcee (who emigrated to Berlin with him) who had a daughter much older than I (and the daughter emigrated to Brazil)… Uncle Buka went to Berlin in 1923 and then Paris in 1933."[2]

When the French front collapsed in the spring of 1940, Uncle George writes he stopped by to see Boris and Olga in the small town of Ussel, south of Paris, a bit west of Lyon. There is no explanation for why they were in this town. This is probably the last time anyone in the family saw them.

What decisions led to the sharp divergence in the fate of my grandma Sophia in contrast to her brother Boris Fichman and his wife, Olga? When the Bronstein-Garvys went to Toulouse, Boris did not go with them. When the family went to America, Boris and Olga went to Nice, leaving the German-controlled zone.

Nice appeared relatively safe at that time. It was under Vichy's jurisdiction. Prior to 1860, it had been Italian before Italy became a unified country and boundaries less clear, but Napoleon III took it as a price for helping the Italians unify against the Austrians. In the spring of 1940, when France was collapsing, Mussolini declared war on France and took some territories to the east of Nice. When the Allies landed in North Africa in November 1942, Germany took direct control of Vichy, and Italy took over Nice itself.

While Vichy helped turn Jews over to the Nazis, Mussolini passed several racial laws but did not turn people over to the Gestapo. So for three years, the bet on going to Nice seemed to work. It was large, warm, sunny, a port city, perhaps reminding the Fichmans of Odesa, with a large number of refugees, and relatively safe.

Then things changed very abruptly. The Allies invaded Italy and took Sicily in July 1943. Later that month, Mussolini was deposed by Italian leaders and arrested but managed to escape into German hands in September. His replacement in charge of the Italian government, Marshall Badoglio, opened negotiations with the Allies, which prompted the Germans to take control of Italy in full force. Nice now fell into the direct hands of the Nazis and the SS, who brought the full weight of terror to that city by rounding up all the Jews they could find.[4]

Some Nice residents fled when the Nazis came in. Among them, for example, were Stanley Hoffmann and his mother. Hoffmann was my thesis advisor at Harvard when I arrived as a graduate student in 1963, and thus an important person in my professional life and a prominent American-French intellectual. He did not talk much about this background when I first knew him, but as he aged, he published some materials reflecting on what happened in Nice.

Hoffmann's mother was of Viennese Jewish background; his father an American protestant, not connected to his child or the child's mother. The Hoffmanns were thus people in danger under Vichy and the SS. From the balcony of his apartment, Hoffmann saw a school chum be arrested and taken away with his mother, who rushed into the street attempting to save him, neither of them ever to be seen again. The Hoffmans waited a few weeks more and then decided to leave the city by train to a small French town, Lamalou-les-Bains (in the Occitanie region, to the west of Montpelier), where they knew people from holiday before the war. Quite a lot of Jews hid out in the French countryside, protected by the population. Hoffmann describes in moving terms a school teacher in Nice whom he suspects was anti-Semitic but who also did not wish to help the Germans; that teacher forged papers for them in case they were stopped on the trains. The Hoffmans made it successfully to Lamalou-les-Bains, whose townspeople protected them during the occupation. Other French towns did the same, most famously *le Chambon-sur-Lignon*, which protected several thousand people.[5]

Buka and Olga did not leave Nice for the countryside when the SS arrived, as did the Hoffmans. I had not known about Ussel (the town in which my Uncle George visited them) when I began writing this memoir, one of many discoveries, part of the process. Ussel is not far from Clermont Ferrand. It raised an interesting question about decisions: Why had they gone there, why did they leave it, and why did they not try to go back? Perhaps they did not think they could blend into the countryside with stronger foreign accents. The Hoffmann's spoke excellent French, better, I imagine, than Boris and Olga. It is also part of the Family Legend that Buka tried unsuccessfully to go to Switzerland to escape there but was turned back at the border. So they knew they were in danger. We will never know for sure what calculations they made.

Boris and Olga were arrested in Nice in September of 1943, shipped to Drancy and from Drancy to Auschwitz in October and killed there right away. The family in New York knew the general facts soon after the war as news of the camps circulated, and many specific fates became known

Over the years, I have discovered some details and documents to fill out the story. While visiting the Holocaust museum at the time of my discussion over the visas and the Varian Fry exhibit, I found some materials in the Museum's Documentation section, where I had gone on the urging of my college friend, Raye Linda Farr.

On a table, I saw a volume that said roughly, in German, *Victims of German Fascism*. I opened and found name after name, in the thousands, of people -- dates of birth, date of death. A bit stunned, I went to find the archivist to see if such a thing existed in France. While waiting to see her, an elderly man was ahead of me in line. "This postcard is the only thing I have left of my aunt," he said in a trembling voice with a strong Eastern European accent. "What will become of it when I die?" The archivist took it gently. "We will put it here in the museum for you, and it will stay here forever to commemorate her." She, he, I and others around us started to cry.

This is what the museum was about, I recall thinking. It is a repository of memory. It is not, as some commentary around museums of remembrance suggests, about making sure things like this happen "never again" by teaching about history, as it is not clear that visiting such places really does prevent people from doing such things again.

The circumstances and causes of horror are more complex. But remembering has meaning. Commemorating is a composite that makes a culture.

When it was my turn with the archivist, I asked if there were books like the German one which gave information about France. Indeed, it turned out there were such books: the "Memorial Volumes "produced by Serge Klarsfeld, who had become famous for having found in the French archives the lists of people on trains from Drancy to Auschwitz during the Vichy period. The French government and culture had long resisted acknowledging the complicity of the French state in the Holocaust. Much emphasis had been put on the Resistance and its accomplishments in fighting the Nazi German occupiers. Laval was executed for collaboration, though Petain was pardoned by De Gaulle as recognition for his role in WWI.

Over time, more and more had been done to probe the story, such as the Ophuls' movie, *The Sorrow and Pity*, and, in the academy, the research of Robert Paxton and other historians, American in his case, but also in France.[6] The Klarsfeld research burst a bubble by showing the active involvement of the French state in the roundups and the transport. Research comparing France to other countries did not favor France or even put it in the middling category, in contrast to Denmark which smuggled out to safety in Sweden almost all of its 8000 Jews. France as a "victim" proved a poor framing. This has, over time, agitated me as I began my professional work as a Francophile, and indeed I still am, but a more guarded one, with a deep disappointment about its behaviors in this period, and indeed others. Perhaps as I have aged, I have learned to be less severe in my judgments: of countries as well as people. France and the United States have made disturbing errors, as have people I love and as have I. One must come to terms with this.

The Holocaust Museum librarian found the Klarsfeld book for me, and I found a desk at which to study it.

From Nice to Auschwitz 1943

The Klarsfeld book showed train list by train list, departing Drancy for Auschwitz.[7] I sat down at a table and began turning pages, running my fingers to the "F's. After over an hour, suddenly, there it was. Fichman, Boris ; Fichman, Olga. And dates and place of birth. Instead of Orgev as birthplace, it said Orfer; instead of Boris, it said Bons-- transcription errors or misspellings. It gave birthdates which seemed approximately correct, given what I knew about my grandmother's dates.

Name	First Name	Date	Place
CREMIEUX	ALEXANDRE	23.03.77	MARSEILLE
CREMIEUX	ISABELLE	27.08.80	MARSEILLE
CREMIEUX	PIERRE	07.12.99	RAINCY
CREMIEUX	SIMONE	15.06.05	PARIS
CREMIEUX	RAYMOND	08.04.06	NIMES
CRESPI	MARCO	25.06.76	CONSTANTIN.
DACHNITZA	BARUCH	15.04.85	BOLZARKA
DACHNITZA	RACHEL	01.05.84	TEPLITZK
DALIEZ	ELIE	19.10.26	PARIS
DALIEZ	MAURICE	11.01.23	PARIS
DANA	SAUVEUR	25.03.00	TUNIS
DANCYGER	SARAH	01.03.98	PLOUSK
DARTBUIL	MAURICE	16.06.01	TOURNAI
DAWIDOWICZ	ADOLPHE	11.04.97	CRACOVIE
DEL PORTO	LUCIEN	02.10.92	PARIS
DE MINDEN	ROXANE	18.08.15	NANTES
DERKAUTZAN	ADRIENNE	02.10.86	NANTES
DEUTSCH	PAULA	29.07.83	VIENNE
DI ALUF MEDINA	ELIE	26.12.86	
DI ALUF MEDINA	SOPHIE	26.02.93	
DIAMANT	MAURICE	02.05.25	
DOBO	JEAN	11.08.05	DES
DONSKOI	HERSCH	09.83	CZECINKA
DONSKOI	PAULINE	08.85	FELESCH
DONSKOI	RACHEL	27.07.12	PARIS
DREYFOUS	MICHEL	13.05.23	NANCY
DREYFUS	GEORGES	21.06.85	MULHOUSE
DREYFUS	GEORGES	31.12.98	EVREUX
DREYFUS	JACQUES	09.01.92	PARIS
DREYFUS	JEAN MICHEL	19.02.97	OSTHOFFEN
DREYFUSS	CAMILLE	20.10.99	HALBSTADT
DREYFUSS	FERNANDE	27.09.05	HALBSTADT
DREYFUSS	IRMA	26.02.97	GEORGENSMIUND
DREYFUSS	SIEGFRIED	06.03.90	OCHRINGEN
DUNNER	HENRI	10.12.98	CRACOVIE
DYNER	ESTHER	71	VARSOVIE
DYZENCHANZ	ETKA	10.05.75	RADOM
DYZENCHANZ	JOSEPH	10.06.81	RADOM
EBER	DAVID	27.05.03	BERLIN
EBLIN	SIMONE	16.04.19	PARIS
EINSTEIN	JEANNE	07.12.96	MULHOUSE
EINSTEIN	JULES	20.11.90	MULHOUSE
EINSTEIN	MARIE	02.08.20	MULHOUSE
EINSTEIN	RAYMOND	29.01.22	MULHOUSE
ECKSTEIN	JOSEPH	24.07.95	DUBON
EDWARSKI	ERNESTINE	20.11.72	KATTOWITZ
EICHEL	HENRI	02.10.99	VARSOVIE
EISINGER	WALLY	04.02.97	BRUNN
ELZENBERG	GEORGES	02.83	KLIMONTON
ELAZAR	RACHEL	25.11.21	
ELFENBEIN	SALOMON	21.01.00	PARIS
ENGELSTEIN	ABRAHAM	84	CRACOVIE
ENI	JACQUES	01.11.06	
ENRIQUEZ	CHARLES	24.03.06	PARIS
ENRIQUEZ	EMMA	24.11.79	ISTAMBOUL
ENRIQUEZ	PAULETTE	24.03.03	PARIS
ERRIO	JEANNETTE	25.05.21	SOFIA
ESKENAZI	ROBERT	02.10.11	PARIS
ENSELMANN	COLETTE	09.05.26	NICE
ENSELMANN	EUGENE	19.11.85	MOSCOU
ENSELMANN	IRENE	10.01.97	MARMOUTIER
FASS	MOSES		
FEDER	ABRAHAM	15.10.79	LODZ
FEDER	ANNIE	15.10.79	PARIS
FEDER	RACHEL	09.01.07	PARIS
FEIBELSOHN	HUGO	04.02.72	BRESLAU
FEIST	PHILIPPE	21.07.90	FRANCFORT
FELDBAU	JACQUES	22.10.14	STRASBOURG
FELDMANN	ANNA	78	KHUCHINCK
FELDMANN	CHINKA	17.07.60	ZOLYNIA
FERNANDEZ	HENRIETTE	25.09.89	ISTAMBOUL
FERNANDEZ	MAURICE	21.10.84	SALONIQUE
FEUERSTEIN	LEON	29.04.76	CZERNOWITZ
FICHMANN	BONS	07.07.80	ORHER
FICHMANN	OLGA	18.09.89	CHISINAU
FINKELSTEIN	FRIEDEL	14.05.82	CRACOVIE
FISCHBACH	DAVID	20.05.05	KOLOMEA
FISCHBEIN	ELIE	29.11.97	STRYJ
FISCHER	EDOUARD	05.02.03	VIENNE
FISCHER	MAURICE	02.04.06	GEGENY
FISCHHOF	LEO	27.07.85	VIENNE
FISEL	FISEL	26.01.89	JASSY
FLEISCHNER	EUGEN	18.06.91	VIENNE
FOLKS	MAURICE	12.07.23	PARIS
FRANCES	OLGA	15.12.91	RHODES
FRANCES	ROBERT	04.12.19	
FRANCO	ISAAC	12.07.88	SMYRNE
FRANDJI	HAIEM	15.03.08	ANDRINOPLE
FRANDJI	ROSA	03.82	ANDRINOPLE

Name	First Name	Date	Place
FRANK	HEDWIG	28.07.81	TREVES
FRANK	MEYER	10.05.73	CHALONS S/ MARNE
FREI	LADISLAS	04.03.09	
FREIDENBERG	ABRAHAM	24.01.65	NICOLASEFF
FRIDMAN	HENRIETTE	10.05.99	GALARZ
FRIDMAN	JACQUES	23.04.99	TCHIEGA
FRIDMAN	SIMONE	11.06.35	PARIS
FRITMAN	LEA	30.12.82	SKALAT
FRIED	ANNA	01.11.96	SARREBRUCK
FRIED	EMILE	10.03.83	TUCENHEIM
FRIEDLER	JACQUES	12.06.78	BENDZIN
FRYDMAN	ABRAHAM	05.01.13	VARSOVIE
FRYDMAN	CHANA	03.10.12	PIATIKOW
FRYDMAN	ESTHER	02.11.09	PARIS
FRYDMAN	JEAN	02.03.36	PARIS
FRYDMAN	LIPA	08.08.13	CARVOLIN
GABAI	VIDA	15.02.89	ISTAMBOUL
GABRIELEFF	ELKA	.74	WINGBOW
GAGAOU	MALKA	07.12.13	EDWITE
GARFUNKEL	BERNARD	24.09.30	PARIS
GARFUNKEL	IRENE	19.03.36	LE PERRAY
GARFUNKEL	ISRAEL	28.08.04	
GARFUNKEL	MARY	06.11.05	RIGA
GELBSMAN	CHAIM	24.07.90	LUBARTOW
GELDZALER	LACA	13.02.78	MANOW
GELRUD	LEISER	27.07.93	BERDICHEFF
GILBURT	ICEK	10.03.03	
GILDIN	IGNACE	01.10.98	DRISSER
GINSBURGER	JULIE	15.06.79	HEGENNEIM
GINSBURGER	MARX	11.03.72	HATTSTATT
GLASBERG	JACOB	07.06.00	TARNOW
GLUCKMANN	PAUL	23.02.23	ROMAN
GODCHAUX	YVONNE	22.02.92	
GOLDAB	SZMUL	10.05.99	LODZ
GOLDBERG	ALTER	29.12.94	VARSOVIE
GOLDBERG	ARMAND	05.01.25	
GOLDBERG	CHAYA	05.07.99	VARSOVIE
GOLDBERG	DANIEL	18.11.86	PARIS
GOLDBERG	LEON	25.05.07	PARIS
GOLDBERG	MAURICE	22.10.86	LANDRECIES
GOLDBERG	REGINE	13.07.29	PARIS
GOLDENBERG	MOISE	07.07.01	VARSOVIE
GOLDENBERG	JULES	10.03.00	LIPODTZ
GOLDHABER	PERLA	15.10.72	BZEZZANY
GOLDHABER	SIMON	05.05.72	ROZYSZEZA
GOLDSCHMIDT	PIERRE	04.03.07	
GOLDSTEIN	COLETTE	31.03.40	PROVINS
GOLDSTEIN	MAURICE	01.10.01	PARIS
GOLDSTEIN	SIMONE	13.08.09	TOURS
GOLDWASSER	ALFRED	28.09.79	VIENNE
GOLDWEIN	HANS	19.08.23	
GOLSCHMANN	BORIS	25.11.06	PARIS
GOLSCHMANN	CHRISTINE	21.02.13	VARSOIVE
GORDON	MARCEL	11.06.94	PARIS
GORENBUCH	MOISE	22.01.99	KICHINEFF
GRADSZTEIN	NECHEMIA	12.03.01	VARSOVIE
GRINBERT	LEON	10.11.97	PARIS
GRINBERT	YVONNE	21.03.01	DUNKERQUE
GROSS	SAMUEL	05.05.01	
GRUNAPPEL	CELINE	18.11.74	KIRCHEN
GRUNFELD	JEAN	30.06.18	BUDAPEST
GRIMSPAN	DORA	.77	PIASKOW
GRYMAN	MORZEK	10.03.19	POLTTE
GRYNBERG	JOSEPH	30.06.92	VARSOVIE
GRZYSOWSKI	JOSEPH	03.02.24	PARIS
GUERCHON	HAYA	17.07.85	ORSHA
GUERIN	ROSA	11.10.99	BRUNSWIG
GUETSCHEL	BERNARD	19.10.72	NICE
GUETSCHEL	JULES	23.09.94	VICHY
GUETSCHEL	JULIE	05.08.76	PARIS
GUETSCHEL	SIMONE	04.11.06	MENTON
GUETZOMITCH	BENJAMIN	22.12.94	KIEV
GUTSZMIDT	JACQUES	17.11.99	VARSOVIE
GUZIK	JOSEPH	14.08.17	
HAAS	CELINE	01.09.88	MULHOUSE
HAAS	RUTH	01.03.11	COBLENCE
HAGGAI	ISIDORE	08.07.11	
HAGUENAUER	GEORGETTE	09.05.95	PARIS
HAGUENAUER	PHILIPPE	26.04.25	PARIS
HALBRONN	FANNY	07.11.70	STRASBOURG
HALBRONN	MARCEL	29.01.01	STRASBOURG
HARBAND	HEINRICH	13.11.10	VIENNE
HASSAN	MICHEL	03.03.17	SMYRNE
HAUS	SALOMON	19.11.18	VARSOVIE
HAZAC	JACQUES	13.10.98	CONSTANTINOPLE
HAZAC	HENRI	02.06.23	
HECHT	ALBERT	16.11.27	DIERBUK
HEIMENDIGER	LEON	12.07.13	GRUSSENHEIM
HEIMRATH	PIERRE	25.02.22	VIENNE

It said "Convoi #60," and its date of departure was October 7, 1943, from Drancy, the suburb near Paris in which the French were holding Jews to be shipped east to the camps. The Klarsfeld volume provides details on the transports because, in most cases, a few people survived and described their experiences. The train arrived in Auschwitz Oct 10, and they were killed that day. Stunned, I made copies of the train lists and called my mother to ask if the dates and places sounded right. She said yes.

When I returned to San Diego, I went to see my mother. She was quite agitated. In working on the materials for this manuscript, I found in my papers a memo I wrote to myself at the time of this conversation with her. Dated October 9, 1993, the memo quotes her as saying

" I know why I have been so agitated this week. Seeing the list makes me see them, my Uncle and Aunt, the two of them in that situation. It makes it concrete."[8]

"Talking to me, and seeing the documentation, brought back her feelings when the family learned definitively they had been killed, the sadly all too familiar "survivors' guilt." Could the family in New York have done more to persuade them to come? The Fichmans did not wish to be a burden on the family, with small children, mouths to feed. They were tired of running, said a postcard from them.

There is as well the power of documents on emotion, the physical "black on white" of that train list. The fact of the killing of her favorite relative was not new information to my mother but seeing that train list was new. My words in the notes memo from 1993 observed that "I, Peter, felt that way at the museum standing at the boxcar they had put on display, thinking of these two people whom I had only heard of. For my mother, knowing them and feeling about them as she did is so much harder." In 2015 while visiting Paris, I went out to Drancy to see the small monument and museum and the apartment blocks, now used as they had been intended for housing.

"The complexity of feeling emerges with Mother's reaction to my summary of the Museum encounter with the Varian Fry exhibit curator. Mother was agitated," my notes say.

"She remembers clearly going to the American Consulate in Marseilles in 1940, that these papers were given by them, that they had made big stamps and ribbons on them to make them impressive to the border guards, to counter that obstacle that the family was stateless and had no passports."[9]

At about this time, I found in my mother's papers the document noted above from the Office of Russian Refugees as a substitute identity paper.

A further comment on the memo about my mother: a bright, lively woman, my notes say she wanted to change the subject and talk about what was happening in Russia at this time—by coincidence, it was the period of the battle over the Russian Parliament, the fighting in the streets between Yeltsin and the old guard, which marked the end of the regime which had thrown her out so many years ago. My talking about the Holocaust coincided with that event in Russia, blending two huge historical processes that shaped our lives. She wanted to talk about 1917 and 1993, not so much about 1940-43! Hitler, for her, was just pure evil. Lenin and Stalin were the betrayers of a noble ideal of social democracy.

Back in San Diego, having absorbed finding this page in the Klarsfeld volume, I contacted Klarsfeld directly to see if there was more information on Boris and Olga Fichman. I wrote a note of thanks for his efforts and sent a check as a contribution to his work. He wrote back a handwritten note and included a booklet he had published: "Les Transfers de Nice à Drancy"[10] which contained more train lists from that city to the transit center and a history of his family experience. In his text, I saw that his own father had been seized in Nice at about the same time as my great Uncle Boris. When they came to the Klarsfeld apartment, the father told his family to hide, saying that he was young and strong, that he could deal with whatever would happen, and that by taking him, the police would not look for the rest of the family. The Fichmans were on Convoy 60 to Auschwitz; the Klarsfeld father was on Convoy 61. I realized the major researcher of the Vichy complicity in deporting Jews from France was in the same place at the same time as Uncle Buka and Teutia Olya, sent to Drancy and Auschwitz at the same time, and did not survive. This gave me an emotional tug of connection to Klarsfeld and gave me more information than I might otherwise have gotten about my relatives.

In the booklet were their names, but also that they resided at the Hotel Garden, that Olga's maiden name was Karchansky, that she was born in Chisenau (Kichinev) on September 18, 1889, and he on July 7,

79	FRENKEL	Chéry	5164	"Nice	18.2	s.20.9.93
80	WIENER née Lehmann	Hermann	65		18.2	
81	MOSSER	René	66		18.3	
82	SCHWARTZ	Robert Albert	67 B		18.3	2.2
83	RAVITCH	Emmanuel	68 C4		—	15.4
84	GRYNBERG	Joseph	69 B		—	2.2
85	ZASTOFF	Henri	70 B		—	8.4
86	KELBERINE	Léon	71 C4		—	15.4
87	BLESCHAR	Judecka	72 B		—	8.2
88	ALGRANATE	Isaac Ralph	73 C4		—	15.4
89	SADOUN	Sauveur	74		17.3	
90	TORONOFF	Serge	75 C4		-.	15.3
91	FICHMANN	Boris	76 C2		,	19.3
92	née Kaigchowsky	Olga	77 C2		18.2	2.2
93	GUETSCHEL	Bernard	78 B		18.3	8.2
94	née SALOMON	Julie	79 B		18.2	8.1
95	—	Simmie	80 B		—	8.1
96	CARACO	Albert	81 C4		18.3	15.4
97	GOLDHABER	Simon	82 B		18.3	8.2
98	GOLDHABER née	Perla	83		18.2	
99	RASINGER	Coloman	84 B		18.3	2.4
00	LATALSKI	Paul, Lucien	85 B		—	8.2
01	née HERTZMANN	Fromma	86 B		18.2	8.3
02	LATALSKI	Jeannine	87 B		18.2	8.3
03	PRESSER	Simon	88 B		18.3	8.4
04	HELLREICH	Heinrich	89 B		18.3	8.4
05	STIMLER	Salomon	90 B		18.3	5.4

1880, in Orher (again, a mistyping of Orgev.) The Nazis had trouble telling Russians apart, so they hired East European emigrés to select who was Jewish and who was not. In *Schindler's List*, Spielberg uses Polish extras to play Jews in a camp scene, so similar did they look, but in one scene where they are nude because they are being selected for deportation and the guards want to see who is healthy, the film extras are shown running in a circle, naked ,and the men are not circumcised. What selection technique did the filmmaker use to sort out which

Poles otherwise looked Jewish enough? How monstrous the whole process of sorting is!

Then yet another startling coincidence took place, which gave even more information. I had narrated the paper trail discoveries to a friend, Mary Katzenstein, whom I had known with her husband in graduate school days in Cambridge, Ma., who told me of a professor in the San Francisco bay area who had written a biography of a German Jewish artist named Charlotte Salomon. Salomon was not known to me then, but she has since become better known with some major museum shows, books, and an opera about her life. Her most famous work *Leben? Oder Theater? Ein Singspiel (Life? or Theater: a Song play)*[11] is a unique combination of gouache painting, text with captions, all with notes about the appropriate music. It is a kind of fantasy autobiography commenting in various ways on her family life. Quickly I traced down the biographer: Mary Lowenthal Felstiner, and the book, *To Paint Her Life*.[12] Felsteiner tells us that Salomon, a native of Berlin, fled the Nazis and went to Nice, where she lived with her husband. The book describes the relatively safe, quiet existence in Nice under Vichy. Then all hell breaks loose as the SS arrive, led by Alois Brunner. Felstiner structures the book around the lives of these two figures, Brunner and Salomon, who cross paths in Nice at this moment. So my great-uncle was living where a famous person had attracted the attention of a historian who hunted down the story and provided valuable detail about the circumstances that were relevant to the story I wished to explore.

In the fall of 1943, Brunner unleashed the SS on the large Jewish population that had taken refuge in Nice. Salomon was seized with her husband and sent to Drancy, put on Convoy 60 with my uncle and aunt, and, like them, were then killed in Auschwitz. She was pregnant. The biography notes that at Drancy, people were asked if they had money. If they did, it was taken and a receipt filled out, written in what was called the *Carnet de Drancy*.

Astonished at the coincidence, I tracked down Felstiner and called her. "Where," I asked, "are the 'carnets de Drancy?' I would like to see if my uncle had any money taken from him." She asked my great-uncle's name, asked me to wait on the phone, went to her notes, and came back to tell me: "Not only were both on Convoy 60 but both in the same wagon. "It turns out records were kept even of that, arranged by where in the Drancy apartment complex one was put while waiting for the train. My uncle and aunt were on the same apartment floor as Salomon and her husband and therefore loaded into the same train wagon.

I visited Drancy in January of 2015 to see what it looked like and to visit the museum there: it is, as described, a plain apartment complex used today as low-income housing. As a monument to the deportation, it has a railroad car, a cattle car, the type on which people were put, placed near the entrance to the apartment complex. Across the street, there is a museum, where the staff provided me with some more detail about just which apartment block the Fichmans were in.

What terrible drama took place in that location, people loaded into crowded cattle cars, fearing for the future. Again, as I saw such a car at the Holocaust Museum in Washington, I wondered about this beloved Uncle and his wife and their specific feelings at that moment.

From Felstiner, I learned that the "Carnets de Drancy "are stored in the *Musée de la vie juive contemporaine* in Paris. On my next trip to Paris after the phone call, I went to the Musée and asked to see the "Carnets." As with the Holocaust Museum in Washington, I sat at a desk and turned pages. Suddenly there it was,

"received from Boris Fichman at 1 rue Balégrier, Cannes (another address, new to me), 13, 440 francs, the 20th of September 1943."[13]

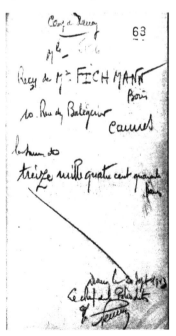

Again, I was stunned: that "they" (Vichy police) had taken money, made a receipt and that this document still existed – what bureaucratic correctness, how complete the ruse. Also, the sum of money was startling. Almost all the other receipts I saw were for modest sums like 25, 50, 100, and 200 francs. This was rather a lot of money. In current purchasing power terms, it was like US $10,000 or more. I tried to imagine the situation. They know they are in trouble. It seems he had tried to go to Switzerland and had been refused. Now he took much of what he had, if not all, hoping for what? That he could bribe their way out? That money could be useful in some other way, for food or medicine.

Whatever he thought, it did not work. The Fichmans and the Salomons left on Convoy 60 on 7 October 1943, a trip which took three days and were killed at Auschwitz right away on October 10. This good and gentle man and his lovely wife were gassed in that hell hole on earth.

Almost 60 years later, in 2001, I found myself in Cracow, Poland, not far from Auschwitz. I had gone there with the La Jolla Symphony and Chorus, a choir I joined after my first wife died in 1999. I had never wanted to visit a concentration camp. Having read much about them, I thought it would be too hard to see, though I am a relentless tourist who wants to see everything; (I drove my parents a bit nuts as a child wanting to stop for every historical road sign along thehighway, especially at the site of the Battle of Gettysburg a central event in the American Civil War in Pennsylvania we passed annually on the way to Washington to visit the Woytinskys; eventually, we did do it, and I was fascinated. As an adult, many years later, I made my wife and children do the same and could not quite understand why they did not share my infatuation). As the choir was visiting Cracow on a performance tour and offering a side trip to the camp, I decided to do it, hoping for emotional safety in the company of my fellow choristers.

After a tour of the Auschwitz museum, we took a short bus ride to Birkenau, where the infamous gate sits with its cruel words "arbeit macht frei", and the barren, barn-like structures that housed inmates were located. Auschwitz itself sat in an old Austrian army barracks, solid brick from the old empire. Survivors of Auschwitz disproportionately came from there, as one could imagine lasting winter in a solid building, but not in the non-insulated, many-holed wooden boards of Birkenau, more like barns than housing for people. This is where trains arrived, and the infamous selection took place, where a few went to labor detail, and most were sent to the gas chambers.

I pulled out Xerox copies of the Kaddish I had brought with me and asked my friends if they would recite it with me standing there on the platform. I am not a religious Jew. I knew Dadya Buka was not. I had not read the Kaddish, the traditional Jewish prayer of mourning, at the funerals of either of my parents, my brother, or my wife.

Buka was killed for being a Jew. I wanted to "close the circle" somehow, the link to my mother, uncle and grandparents he represented. He was why I was there. This seemed appropriate. I asked a choir member whom I knew often sang as a Cantor in Jewish services if he would lead us, as he would know the words in transliteration. "What are we doing?" I heard one of the group ask, very few of them, as it happened, being Jewish. I explained what it was and why we were doing it. We chanted the words. I found it very meaningful to remember Dadia Buka and Teutia Olya in this way. It was indeed a horrible place to visit, but I felt it was the right thing to do, bear witness , and have a deeper sense of its structure, horrors, and atmosphere. One of our group was gay and in a wheelchair. I asked if I could push him along at the museum. He understood immediately, saying, indeed, "It would have been both of us."

In this spot, I lost my family's beloved uncle and brother, the person everyone said was their savior and bedrock and warm and loving. And so my childhood was poorer for not having known him.

Many years later, in 2015, in France, I discovered through the suggestion of Catherine Collomp a remarkable book by French historian Ivan Jablonka with the brilliant title "*L'histoire des grands parents que j'ai jamais eu,*" which was translated and published by Stanford Press in 2016 as the "history of the grandparents I never had."[14] The title expressed my feelings noted at the beginning of this book: I missed knowing some people in my family tree who were important to my parents and family. Jablonka's book reconstructs the life trajectory of a non-famous, non-prominent person, someone in a network of family and friends with some politics but at the bottom of hierarchies. We usually know little about people like this as we lack letters, books, journalists or other cultural statements. Jablonka realized documents do exist by tracking down police records. He is able to reconstruct what happened to his grandfather, how he fled a Poland hostile to him both as Jew and Communist, how France was hostile to him as a foreigner, Jew, Communist, low skilled and employed, how hard it tried to drive him out of the country. This was true under the Third Republic long before Vichy replaced it, as dislike of foreigners in general and Jews, in particular, was quite real. Vichy had much to draw on when it turned savage. This is generally known, but Jablonka makes it vivid. When WW II started, France decided it needed every male it could get, so it let Jablonka's grandfather enroll in the French Foreign Legion. After the French defeat in 1940, the Jablonka Grandpa was in Paris, now with tiny children. As the police sweeps got stronger, he sent the two children west toward Brittany for the protection he had arranged. The children survived, and one became Ian Jablonka's father.

Jablonka probes what happens to the grandfather shipped to Auschwitz. He survives for a while and is then gassed. Jablonka does eloquently what I would never dare to do: put in words what happens to someone who is gassed. Admirably, he takes his effort to connect to the grandfather he never "had" to the very end of his life into the gas chamber itself. I cannot do that, but I urge readers to examine Jablonka's book. He gives voice to the mass of people killed, from which we usually hear very little. I have tried here to reconstruct some voices for this beloved family member on my mother's side.

Sometime after my visit to Auschwitz, I learned the French government had a program to compensate those who had lost possessions in the Holocaust. I decided to request the funds taken from Buka at Drancy. It was not for the money but to get some kind of formal acknowledgment of the complicity of the French state in his destruction. As a Francophile, this was a challenge for me. I felt angry. I wanted something in writing from the French state about its role in this process. I found the forms for the Compensation Program and filled them out. At a key moment, some hearings were held in Paris, and, as I could not attend, my friend and colleague Patrice Higonnet, a prominent French historian at Harvard, agreed to attend in my place. I had to prove I was a relative and that there were no other descendants. They awarded a modest sum to me and the others I had listed: my brother's twin daughters, Sasha and Becca, and my cousin Helen Garvy. I sent some of the money to the *Centre de documentation juive* in Paris in appreciation for their work in guarding the Carnet de

Drancy and the memory of those who had perished.

Buka and Olga died because they were Jewish. Circumstances accentuated their vulnerability. They were stateless in France. Had they been of French nationality, their chances of survival would have been somewhat higher; though Vichy and the SS killed many French Jews as well, they were particularly keen on quotas for foreigners. Had Buka been politically active, he might have sensed danger earlier and been more active in leaving. He might have had networks, such as the labor one, to sensitize him to the menace and to help him with visas.

Sadly, it is possible that Buka and Olga were psychologically exhausted, reluctant to flee once again, a third time for a fourth country, concerned about a new life and burdens on his family. Could the family have managed to get him out, as they always wondered?

Visas were indeed hard to get: could they have gotten emergency entrance as a vulnerable relative of the labor group? I don't know. He is one of the most important relatives I never met. The next chapter seeks to give voice to another important person I never met, my father's father, Boris Naumovich Ber-Gourevitch.

Endnotes

1 Klarsfled, Serge, Index to Memorial to the Jews deported from France. Microfich, Teaneck, N.J. Avotanyu, Inc. 1989

2 George Garvy, "Memoir notes: Typescript from handwritten material", by Helen Garvy, 1980s.

3 This shift in power is vividly described by Mary Fehlsteinter in her book on Charlotte Salomon. Felsteiner, Mary, To Paint her Life (Harper Collins, 1994.)

4 I probe some of the parallels and contrasts between the experience of the Hoffmanns and that of my family in an essay published in honor of Hoffmann upon his death. See. "The Origins of the Stanley Hoffmann We Knew: Some Comparisons of his Vichy Years with My Family Story", for French Society and History, 2017; "Essays of Obituary for Stanley Hoffmann", with Robert Keohane for the American Philosophical Society 2017, "Stanley Hoffmann as Leader", Commentaire 2017. http://www.washingtonpost.com/blogs/monkey-cage/wp/2015/09/15/stanley-hoffmann-has-died-he-changed-how-america-thinks-about-france- and-europe/ -- http://duckofminerva.com/2015/09/stanley-hoffmanns- approach-to-studying-politics-in- memori-am-1928-2015.html#more- 27870

5 Movie on Le Chambon-sur-Lignon: Weapons of the Spirit, Pierre Sauvage, filmmaker, 1987.

6 Ophuls, The Sorrow and the Pity. Robert Paxton and Michael Marrus, Vichy France and the Jews, New York Basic Books, 1981; Robert Paxton, Vichy France: Old Guard and New Order, 1940-44, New York: Knopf, 1972. The French Village TV series, 2009-2015.

7 Klarsfeld, Serge, Index to Memorial to the Jews deported from France. Microfich, Teaneck, N.J. Avotanyu, Inc. 1989. This is also available as a book volume in various libraries, usually in French.

8 Peter Gourevitch, "Notes on Conversation with Sylvia Gourevitch," mimeo, in author's papers.

9 Gourevitch, Ibid.

10 Klarsfeld, Serge, op. cit. the Monument, but also les transfer de Nice à Drancy which was later incorporated into a larger ensemble volume. Klarsfeld, Serge Les transferts de juifs de la région de Marseille vers les camps de Drancy ou de Compiègne, en vue de leur déportation, 11 août 1942-24 juillet 1944, Paris: Association "Les Fils et Filles des déportés juifs de France." 1992.

11 Charlotte Salomon, Life? or Theatre? : a selection of 450 gouaches, Koln, Taschen, 2017.

12 Felsteiner, Mary, To Paint her Life, (Harper Collins, 1994).

13 Les Carnets de Drancy, p. 69.

14 Jablonka, Ivan. L'histoire des grands-parents que j'ai jamais eu. Translated, Stanford Press, History of the grandparents I never had. 2016.

Chapter 10

The Song of the French Rooster Boris in USSR 1934-38

Boris was the relative I most wished I had met, though I would place the other Boris, Fichman, whom I call Buka here, my grandmother's brother, a close second. These are the men who had a great impact on the evolution of my family: Buka as the Garvy savior, Boris Ber as the authority figure for my father and the Gourevitch flock, to whose memory they remained loyal and bonded.

While the Garvys had arrived in France in the late winter of 1933 and begun to build a life there, with what we know is the shadow of WWII looming ahead in the distance, the life of Boris is reduced to us largely to the letters we have, along with one or two incidents that burst into public view, some research by specialists, and the knowledge of the purges to come. My desire to know him narrows in its sources and grows in its intensity. I reflect on the materials I have and from which I can learn. My research does turn up some material new to me, notably from the prison archives of the former KGB.

Perhaps most stunning is the photograph accompanying the dossier from his final prison term in Vladimir. I stare at this photograph. I form an opinion of this person looking at it. He appears resolute, determined, solid, strong, and at the same time warm and friendly. I can see him saying, "Nyet!" ("No!" in Russian) to those interrogators who want him to betray his ideals. I can see him resisting torture. I can see him playing with grandchildren or great-grandchildren. I can see him reprimanding his children, embracing his wife—being a human. But I draw out from the letters the image of a strong, loving human in that portrait as I draw out from the letters. The photo came

SEQ Figure * ARABIC 2BER-GOUREVITCH, Boris
Naumov. Vladimir, 1937.

late to me. I had read all
the letters and written
much of my thoughts
before the dossier ar-
rived before it told me
of how they had tried
to force him into the
classic confessions that
he had hatched a plot
to kill Stalin and oth-
er absurdities hurled at
people in this period of
trials.

These are my projec-
tions. Turning to the specific evidence we have before us, what we have are
the letters that Boris mails
to continue contact with
the family in Western Eu-
rope. In the Chapter on
Berlin, we followed these
from the moment Shura
left Russia in November
of 1931 through his de-

parture from Berlin in 1934. We reconnect to that point here.

In the last letter we examined from March 27, 1933, Boris continues to worry about where the Berlin family will go, including issues
about getting a visa for entry elsewhere, with an allusion to the possibility of Palestine.

A recurrent theme is isolation from Shura. Boris frequently complains that he hears nothing. At times this could be the irregularity
of the mail, that various things interfere with the arrival of letters,
especially the weather, creating mud, storms, or ice floes that block
the delivery vehicles. At other times, it is most likely that Shura does
not write as frequently as an isolated Boris would like, and it reveals
Boris' desperation at being cut off and remote. Political turmoil generated anxiety. Boris had some knowledge of the German and Russian

situation, and so did the silence indicate something sinister. And how much did lie on Shura's side? He was not when I knew him a "talker", a raconteur, someone who liked to reminisce or express his thoughts on this or that. I can imagine writing letters did not come so comfortably to him. So the boy and his Dad, and the situational elements of great distance, country, and circumstances, there are many variables at play.

Boris is often desperate at not having work. I expect this is a mixture of boredom and money. House arrest did not likely come with a stipend. So somehow, he had to earn something to eat and live. And surely he needed stimulation to be active, busy, and to exercise his brain. Here was a well-educated person, an intellectual, a revolutionary, full of energy and commitment. He was deeply engaged in theoretical debates about social change, democracy, capitalism, tyranny, liberty, and all the issues of the day. He had played a leadership role based on a combination of personal and intellectual skills. Now, suddenly he was cut off, forced into internal exile, banished to provincial places, and deprived of any ability to use his skills, engage in politics, write, or do much of anything.

At times he seems to have been able to use at least some of his skills: he did translate from German or French into Russian. It is not clear what texts he was asked to do. These stimulated him somewhat, depending on the subject and earned a bit of money. It seemed sporadic as employment, and as time went by, there were no longer references to him getting such offers. At another moment, in the city of Vladimir, where he was living in 1936, he got work doing the accounts of a business, a state enterprise, no doubt, where a manager needs someone to do the books. In one of the remoter places in the wilderness, he takes on work making duck or other animal decoys for hunters! This was a kind of manual, or artisanal labor, which could not have been very satisfactory, though he seems to have enjoyed it, and it was better than nothing.

In reading about Nelson Mandela, or other such figures, it is being deprived of the opportunity to read or write or to do things that engage their personalities and skills that always seem among the worst aspects of confinement. This happens to Boris from the age of his early 40s on, at the peak of his talents and energies. The financial situation is a large puzzle to me. Unable to work, how does he support himself or his family?

Packages do arrive. He sends thanks for books, magazines, and clothes. He notes these can be traded for items that fit better or which are more needed. Some sort of barter economy does exist, whatever the state planning policy is!

The letters often express an aching loneliness. Boris is cut off from family, friends, and political affiliates. He has, in some places, colleagues who share his status and with whom he can talk. The letters do not make reference to these people, but that may be for prudential reasons. He likely had some opportunity to talk, but most of the time, he did not have family around. I am not able to reconstruct just when and where he had the company of his wife and children. At times he did, as in Tashkent toward the beginning, where we have some photos. At other times, they did not live together, as when they were upset Shura was not accepted into a school. Boris often writes that he waits for letters with such ache. The loneliness is so palpable.

Overall the letters convey a powerfully observant and caring father, in exile, cut off from his family. He looks carefully at his children, the oldest, especially Shura. He engages, and he is frank and direct. These themes become more intense as the letters taper off after Shura has left for the West and his isolation increases. For a year or two, we get a lot, then less and less.

A letter from July 1934 is of considerable political interest because it is the moment when Boris was used by Stalin to intervene in French politics to promote the Popular Front. This produced the Kazan telegram discussed in the French chapters above. It is the only overtly political passage in all his letters. It was   perhaps the only moment when he could say something in public where his beliefs coincided with those of the Soviet regime. It is a moment when he was connected from his internal exile and isolation to the community outside, to his peers living a free life in the West, engaged in political activity there. Boris' writing on the Popular Front is lyrical. How passionately he believes in its hopes.

July 14th, 1934

Today is the 14th of July. I'm eagerly awaiting the letter about how your (plural) day went today. Against the background of senility and wild reactions, sweeping up a large part of Europe, after the defeats of the last years, progress—a lot over there in France, to the extent that it's possible to judge from here the progress of the "single front," achievements of the only working-class progress and developments from this wide base of anti-fascist movement brings joy, hope for the future, maybe even the beginning of the new, brighter day. What's happening in France right now, from my perspective, has great meaning. France is becoming the springboard from which a decisive approach to the fascist reactions will be made, and when taken with all the capitalistic systems, not only on a national scale. The outcome of this struggle depends on the direction of the social and political development in all of Europe, in the whole world. I am deeply convinced that defeating the anti-fascist movement in France will not only suspend the further enhancement of the development of fascism and save the existing limited democratic freedoms, for the victorious French people, in the name of heroic revolutions. I am sure that this victory will be a great starting point for a historical fracture, the start of new and mighty revolutionary ascension that cannot be confined only to the protection of bourgeois democracy but that will pose the question of the liquidation of capitalism—and not only in France but in all of Europe. The basic condition—the implementation of a single worker's movement and a clear, bold program of action capable of rallying around the wide proletariat people, can lift the people's movement. I'm certain that with that, the conditions of progress will be inevitable, and victory will be realized. And then the song of the French rooster will signal the beginning, the start of the socialist revolution in all of Europe.

***

The date of the letter precedes what becomes the "Kazan telegram," but by only a few weeks, and I wonder if Boris knew something was in the works.

The enthusiasm is so strong!! There is no other letter quite like it in the dossier. It reveals Boris's energy, commitment, a kind of yearning and hope, the spirit of the revolutionary he once was. Or was this aimed in part at the police apparatus that was reading his letters in connection to communication with the Mensheviks in Paris? Was this to gain some better treatment? Or a combination of all of these things? The Kazan telegram event had not been part of the Family Legend discussions when I grew up, though it was not a secret. When I discovered it by reading Liebich's book, it seemed very dramatic!

Last letters from Boris

The Kazan telegram event took place in the summer of 1934. (This precedes the French Popular Front itself, which occurred after the elections of 1936.) Boris's letter in November 1934 narrates that Boris and his brother Asrunia have discussed Shura going to the Sorbonne for chemistry, which is what, in fact, he did. Boris appreciates the significance of this and sends some fatherly advice, hoping that Shura does not take offense from it!! Shura, at this point, is 18 years old, starting what in the US would be an advanced college program at an elite institution.

November 13, 1934

> Shurik, my dear! Anya writes that you decided that you would go to Sorbonne for chemistry. … And I think that is the best decision…What is the situation from a materialistic standpoint? … Shurucya, don't get mad that I'm reciting "morals" to you, but you are infinitely important to me.

***

This next letter describes travels. I don't know what led to them. For some period, Boris did live with his family, Lyalya and Galka. At other times, they were clearly not living together. I don't know if they are being forced apart or if they have separated. At some point in these years, Boris and Lyalya did separate, and he formed another attachment, but I don't know just when or much about with whom.

In 1935 Boris wrote from the city of Vladimir, not far from Moscow, where he is allowed to live. He has some freedom there and is allowed to go visit his mother in Moscow. His greater freedom is likely a reward for participating in the Kazan Telegram of 1934. This is the interpretation given in the history I have read,[1] though it does make me wonder: since he lacked freedom, did he have a choice? Could he have refused? Perhaps. I think supporting the Popular Front fit his ideas, so he did not feel compromised by agreeing. Indeed it is interesting that overall he was not treated even worse during these years. He could have been killed at many points along the way; he could have been one of the accused in the Menshevik Trial of 1931 when several members were condemned and executed. Was he allowed to live because, at the end he was protected by an old friend of the inner circle? Or too potentially useful for just such a moment as the Kazan

Telegram?

He writes with worry about his brother, who was arrested in Berlin for a time. There are references to the visa situation of Grandmother Styssia, who was in Berlin. They sought a visa for her to live outside the USSR but were not able to find one, and she returned to the USSR, where she died in 1939.

The last letter from Boris is August 1935; it seems to be from Vladimir. The last letter from Lyalya is March 1936, from Cherdyn. Why, after all the years of house arrest in Siberia, then to the city of Vladimir, was he now taken to prison in Vladimir? This is the height of the purges, so repression has been accentuated. Being a Menshevik protected him from nothing, as Bolsheviks were also being killed, including his next youngest brother, Mayor, who died shortly after his release from imprisonment, likely as a consequence of health issues deriving from it.

What do we know of what happens to him? My Dad stopped hearing from either of his parents by 1937. The evidence we have from *Memorial* says he was arrested in 1937 and died during an investigation, "na voprosi", "under questioning," in 1938. This sounds ominous: a heart attack under torture, being beaten, or under sheer fatigue, stress and ill health? The notes from Vladimir Prison stop suddenly, so I suspect beating or some other form of torture. One of the citations in the Memorial biography lists his death as 1937 in Vladimir Prison, but the dossier from Vladimir says 1938, as do other sources.

The KGB file from Vladimir itself (not from the archive in Lubyanka, Moscow) specifies arrest and prosecution for counter-revolutionary activity: discontent with Stalin and the regime, contact with the Foreign Delegation, conspiring with dissident groups inside USSR, and contact with his family in France and Germany -- so the fact he was writing all the letters we have been reading was used as evidence against him. The file contains the kind of forced confession of treasonous intentions toward Comrade Stalin that are familiar to all the literature on the great show trials of the Communist era. It cites some alleged confirmation from supposed witnesses.

Decades later, Boris Naumov Ber Gourevitch was rehabilitated, years after Stalin's death and years after the famous Krushchev speech of 1956 which denounced Stalin's crimes: Officially, "On the Rehabilitation of Victims of Political Repression on October 18, 1991" on the conclusion of the Prosecutor General of the Russian Federation, November 24, 1997."[2]

The rehabilitation seems a strange gesture to evaluate. It evokes many current conversations around the world on what to do after atrocities: in South Africa about apartheid, in Rwanda, the massacre of the Tutsi, and Argentina's "disappeared", for some examples. The discourse over the past matters in how we think about the future. In the summer of 2015, a serious debate developed in the US over the display of the Confederate battle flag, following the killing of several African Americans in Charleston, South Carolina, by a man wearing that flag on his clothing. The argument continues about moving monuments in the American South that honor Civil War generals who fought against the Union. And in renaming Calhoun College at Yale and the Woodrow Wilson School at Princeton.

The Putin regime's crackdown on dissent adds to the pain of the families who lost relatives during the Stalinist era. Putin's regime did not commemorate the 100th anniversary of the Russian Revolution. He seeks to avoid linkage to the Revolutionary past and resistance to authority. The Memorial organization, so valuable in reconstructing the lives of the dissidents to Stalin, has been shut down. The grip of the past still holds in the archives. There remain pages stapled shut in the files of my grandparents. There are things I still am not able to learn.

Boris Nahumov Ber Gourevitch is certainly a Grandfather I would like to have known, as was Peter Bronstein Garvy, whom I met technically but did not know.

Lyalya's fate

As fortune allowed, I did have the great pleasure of meeting Lyalya. She was an extraordinary person. I met her only once—the week I spent in Moscow with my father in the summer of 1966. It saddens me that my drive to probe the details of the family story did not happen when she was still alive, and I lost the opportunity to learn more. As a result, I realize that my knowledge of her story is fragmented and uncertain. I have some different accounts of what happened to her in the years between the arrest and death of Boris in 1937-38 and her discovery of my father's whereabouts in DeWitt, New York, in 1961.

I have two stories of Lyalya's life in these years. For many years, I was convinced of the utter certainty of the version I had understood after my parents met her in Moscow during the summer of 1963: that she was sent to Siberia in 1937/38 when Boris was hauled into Vladimir Prison as the screws of the purges tightened in 1937-38. She stayed there till Stalin died in 1953, after which the screws loosened, and she was released, though confined to residence in small towns and obligated to report to the police weekly. Finally, in the early 1960s, she was free enough to travel to Moscow and consult the Russian organization that helped her track my father down. I conferred with some relatives on this story, and that was how they understood it as well.

Then, when I began systematic work on the family story, I sought archival evidence to provide some detail for this account; I was confounded, not so much by evidence but by its absence. When we, that is, my research assistants in Russia, searched the records, we could not find material that showed arrests, releases, or her location clearly. The archives just did not tell us much. What to do?

The Russian archives were suspect to me. In my grandfathers' dossiers, some files were stapled shut, and some were left open. Things are being covered up. Between an oral account as narrated through the family and fragments of what could be found in the files—well, I was going to believe the family story. Arrogant on my part, perhaps, but = nothing in my story really turned on being right or wrong on many of these details.

Then suddenly, while reflecting on this decision, I found among my mother's papers some documents I had overlooked, letters of Lyalya she had given my parents in the 1963 visit or mailed to them. I saw they were letters from the 1940s, from her to her sister and back, as well as some correspondence to other people. There were numerous references to Galka, the daughter of Lyalya, my father's half-sister, with Boris as their biological father. This was important, and I asked my assistant Olga for a careful translation.

The letters turned out to be an account of how Lyalya came to learn of the death of her daughter and how it came about. Galka was killed during a battle with the German army by a bullet on December 14, 1943, near a village called Gorki, near Novosokolniki, Vitebskaya oblast, today in Belarus, then in the heart of the USSR between Smolensk and Vilnius. This incident was witnessed and described in a letter sent to Frida, Lyalya's sister, whom we have encountered often in helping Lyalya with Shura and Galka as children. A battle was beginning, and Galka was slightly wounded. As she walked from one position to another, not crawling, she was hit by a machine gun burst, right at her Komsomol ID and her medal for bravery, and died instantly. No suffering. At night they were able to retrieve her body and bury her in place, as was the practice.

Frida received this information and a military report in the summer of 1944, but she and some friends of Galka had not wanted to tell Lyalya what happened. Frida writes that Lyalya's doctor thought it could be harmful to her health. Finally, in 1948, Frida does inform her. Her letters do not fully explain the reasons for deciding to write in 1948.

The letters convey information about Galka: her friends, her life, and her character. Mixed with the bundle are several letters from Galka to Lyalya from 1943. She describes a bit of her life, noting that they have not been in communication for at least two years, that she was apart from Frida as well, and finally found a working address and re-established contact with Frida, suggesting that it took time for Frida to find Lyalya --- so for some years there has been some force separating them and they are being indirect in talking about it. This seems evidence for the Siberian confinement of Lyalya or at least some kind of house arrest or imprisonment as forced separation.

Galka writes of being in school, studying and working when the war burst forth—that is, the German invasion in 1941. She graduated in 1942, though it does not specify just where she is. She has mixed grades, it seems. At a certain point, school seems suspended, then resumes. She applies via the Komsomol (Soviet Youth Organization) to enter the Army. At the time of the letter, in the early summer of 1943, she has been in the Army unit for 10 months. They are in a forest near a river, which allows them to bathe. They have plenty of food, and she complains of being fat. She notes that Friday, she is moving, and that will likely improve her food and housing situation—by implication, poor wherever she is. By inference from the other letters, she is moving to Sverdlovsk, which implies this is a better situation than in many other places, as are the conditions for sleeping. Soon she hopes they will be free!!! The friends articulate Galka's honesty, energy, and probity. When the war erupts, she is eager to fight and joins the army.

The location of her death is moderately far north, somewhat west of Moscow, and already at the time when the German army is being pushed back, not the original invasion of 1941. There are references to Galka talking about and wondering about Shura. There are references in Lyalya's exchanges with Frida about having no news about Shura either.

What was learned from these letters? Something about Lyalya's life. It told us: that she lived apart from her daughter and sister in the '40s and that she had not heard from Shura. I know from family sources that Boris separated from her in the mid-1930s at some point, so I don't know if she is officially his widow. The contact with her sister Frida was in 1948. Shura reports he had not heard from her since 1937.

The next data point we have is her going to the Russian Red Cross relief agency (a political organization, not the relief group we think of in the West) in Moscow in the early 1960s looking for information on Shura. It is this which proves successful. When I first heard about it and the chronology of her Siberian imprisonment, I simply took its timing for granted. She went when she could after being released. But if the alternative story is accurate, then she was free in her late forties and could have gone to explore then. Why had she not done so? Possibly the political climate made it risky. But was it less risky in the early 1960s? Perhaps. The political thaw was beginning, and there was some talk between Russia and the US, so she tried, and it worked.

It seems quite possible that had she tried in 1946 or 1950 to find him, she would not have done so. Shura was not an accomplished biologist at that point, not having finished his Ph.D. nor started a program of research and publications. So an inquiry into Whos who of Science or Medicine would have revealed nothing! And recall that the reason his name did appear there was because of the decision taken in Germany in 1931 to have my father pursue the academic university track, which led him eventually to the Ph.D. and research accomplishments that put him into the *Who's Who of Science* so that he could be found. Laylya wrote the letter to my parents I noted earlier, which arrived in 1962.

The family arranged to visit the USSR to see Lyalya. The visit took place in the summer of 1963. I had a summer job in Washington   an internship at the State Department, and I did not think I could take a week off from work. I regret that decision to this day. What a unique occasion to be at the reuniting of my father with his family after 25 years! It was an amazing summer to be in Washington. I was at the Martin Luther King "I Have a Dream" speech at the Lincoln Memorial, a deeply moving, memorable occasion that stays with me to this day. And the program took the interns to a press conference given by President Kennedy. So I thought I could not leave the internship, but I regret not being in Moscow for the reunion.

My parents did go in the summer of 1963 with my older brother, Sergei. They met Lyalya, Mosei (one of the younger brothers of Boris), with whom Dad had lived in Moscow before going to Berlin, the children of Mosei, Vove and Valia, two boys, and the wife of Mosei. I don't recall who else they met. There was indeed much emotion in the trip. Lyalya told them about her experiences and what she knew about the family. She told my parents that the description of a Siberian prison camp in the recently published Solzhenitsyn short story, *A Day in the Life of Ivan Denisovich,* which had generated a great sensation, was, if anything, too soft, as life in those campswas cruelly hard.

During imprisonment, Lyalya passed the time with embroidery. She put together some pieces of cloth from scraps to form a dark background and collected scraps of colored material to make threads. She then created items, some of which she gave to my parents. One, the largest, about 18" by 10", evokes a scene something like the top of famous Russian lacquered boxes: a woman and a man each dressed in fantastical costumes, the woman, something like a fairy princess, the man in peasant garb, all very colorful, vivid, and evocative. It hangs in our family entrance, my most prized possession, often drawing questions about its provenance. Another embroidery Lyalya made is of Mayakovsky, the famous poet, with a scowl on his face, a look taken from a famous photograph. So accurate is it that knowledgeable people, usually of Russian background, ask about it when they visit and are astonished when I say she had no photograph of Mayakovsky when she did it. A third piece is a depiction of Maxim Gorky, another famous writer from the 20s and 30s; recall that it was Mme Gorky who ran the special Red Cross organization to which Boris and Lyalya wrote for help in 1928 and 1931. Again, the people who know them always recognize his portrait.

At this meeting in Moscow in the summer of 1963, Lyalya gave my parents these embroideries and some family photos. Possibly some letters were added to the file. In the summer of 1966, I was able to go with my Dad to meet her and other relatives. Dad was invited to attend an International Congress of Microbiologists. I went with him. It was an early moment in the thaw between USSR and US, and the Soviets were eager for good relationships. I wondered if my parents had been concerned about traveling in 1963, as they had both been declared while children as enemies of the Soviet state. At this point, they had American citizenship, and in the end, nothing happened. In 1966, my Dad and I were part of a delegation of scientists, and we felt safe they would not wish to jeopardize scientific exchange as the USSR was slowly embarked on a thaw in foreign relations.

Meeting the family was very moving for me. After all she had been through, she had energy, engagement, and rapport. One night we went to the theater to see a play called "Black Dragon." On coming out, we looked for a taxi to take her back to the home of Moisei, where she was staying during our visit. The taxis would slow down, ask where you were going, and if they did not like the location at that time of night, off they went, leaving people stranded very much; the way I have seen can happen in NY between taxi driver shifts. Lyalya was irate. She walked over to the famous Bolshoi ballet building across the street and found a policeman on duty, an enormous fellow twice her size; she grabbed his arm, pulling him with her, yelling, "You must help these people and make those cab drivers do their duty." And lo and behold, he obeyed her, restored order to the cab ranks, and most people got cabs. Despite everything, she still felt committed to improving the world in which she lived. Then, having helped everyone else, there were no cabs left for her. Dad decided to take her with us back on the special Conference bus to the Conference hotel where we were staying, at Moscow State University. My father arranged with fellow delegates on the bus to make a lot of noise when we arrived, as a distraction, so we could sneak her past the guards. It worked! We got her through. The delegates on the bus were French, my Dad switched to that language which he also knew, and they enjoyed the whole thing. I slept on the floor while she took my bed!!

Imagine now a sharply contrasting scene that happened to me fifty-one years later, in January 2017 to be precise, at the very same spot in Moscow. I am attending a conference to which I have been invited and also doing research in the KGB- FSB archives, as I have described in Chapter Two. The conference, the Gaidar Forum, has offered me tickets to see Swan Lake at the Bolshoi, thus, the most classical ballet at the most classic location it can be performed. Of course, I accepted, as did a colleague who is also an old friend, also giving a paper at this conference. The performance was outstanding. During one fifteen-minute period where the two principals do a duet, the audience was so intensely absorbed, people became so still, so quiet, so involved, there was not a sound, not a movement, not a breath, the proverbial pin could drop and smash loudly. This knowledgeable audience appreciated perfection, and I was greatly moved by the performance, the sophistication and the engagement of the people around me, by the entire experience.

When the performance ended, and we descended the stairs into the theater lobby, we were met by the two young university student guides who had been assigned to take care of us. They had reserved a car to take us back to the hotel. As we walked outside to find our designated limo, we saw dozens of taxis and a clutch of people shouting at us, "Taxi, Taxi, Taxi, Taxi." How stunned I was! The contrast between the two moments, 1966 and 2017, swept over me in this wave of light, noise, machines and the aura of the modern marketplace; cellphones, automatic car calling, and taxi-wolves hustling for business. Of course, I thought of Dad and Grandma back in 1966 and what they, especially she, would have thought. The change in Soviet society from then until today is expressed via the indicator of the taxi system: the more taxis, the less the regime can control visitors, as they have greater freedom to travel without the supervisor-guides. This is something I had noticed in travel to Beijing in the 1980s and 1990s: the increase in the number of taxis coincided with a loosening of the regime's grip and the growth in the market economies. It was all the more vivid to me in contrasting Russia over these two visits, thinking about my family.

Recalling the mental space of 1966, I remember being mostly with my Dad and relatives. One afternoon I met Lyalya at the department store known as "Detsky Mir," Children's World (the very spot fifty years later, I met my research assistant in January 2017). We walked thru the huge building of GUM, a famous building and store of the Soviet period.

I connected with some of the other relatives: We bonded over small things: Great Uncle Moisei appreciated my enjoyment of local food specialties, like the Georgian mineral water *Barjomi,* and various soups, *okroshka,* for example, or drinks like *kvas* which foreigners usually don't like.

One relative did not come to the 1963 meeting but attended the 1966 one. He was closely watched because his work had security implications, and had to be cautious. Another relative came the first time but not the second: he had been captured by the Germans as a soldier and survived that only to be put into prison by Stalin, who thought that all who survived German captivity were traitors not to be differentiated much from those who fought actively on the German side. His brother got him out of that imprisonment, but he spent the rest of his life as a bus driver, considerably below his educational level. The other brother became a technical professional, had a successful career, and was a party member with a critical mind, saying skeptical things about the system, and asking probing questions. Another family member of the older generation remained loyal to the system, and I noticed people were cautious while speak in front of her—loving toward her as a person but avoiding politics, as she remained a true believer of the Party. On my 2017 trip to Moscow, I learned that some cousins were not told of the visit by my father and myself in 1966 when they were children, as it was dangerous to have foreign relatives. And nearly all of them had changed their names from Gourevitch to some other relative's name, less evidently Jewish. The only Gourevitchs descending from the Rabbi, Nachum Gourevitch, my great-grandfather, all live in the United States.

After they returned to the US from the 1963 trip, my parents tried to persuade Lyalya to come to live with them in Syracuse. There are some documents in my mother's papers that show their efforts to do this: letters to the State Department asking for a visa and some overtures to Eleanor Roosevelt toward the end of the First Lady's life. Lyalya decided to stay in Russia, thinking it too hard to cut all her ties, where she still had family, and to go where she knew few people and did not speak the language. My dad, Shura, died suddenly Feb 9, 1969, of heart failure, the likely consequence of cortisone shots, which he had taken for many years to combat emphysema, itself a likely consequence of the allergies provoked by the poor nutrition in the early years of his childhood. My mother had to write the news to his mother. Lyalya herself died a natural death not so many years later. My brother Sergei and I maintained some contact with the Russian relatives through trips we took for professional reasons over the next years until Sergei died early in 1999 at age 58. I have taken a few more, the last in 2017.

With the war in Ukraine, I am not inclined to visit Russia in the near future.

Endnotes

1 Nenarokov, op cit. The case of Ber Gourevitch.
2 Memorial webpage, http://www.scherbina.net/ukazatel_b.htm, accessed 17 Aug 2014).

Chapter 11

Peter's Parents In the US

When I asked my parents to describe their feelings upon arriving in New York Harbor in October of 1940, I sensed mostly relief. They were finally politically safe from the immediate dangers of Europe, the Nazis and Bolsheviks both. At the same time, they were very poor. Their possessions consisted of a knapsack each—a "knapsack on their backs"—to borrow the words of an old hiking song I learned at summer camp. They were found an apartment by the Joint Committee, thus a Jewish organization that also helped with food. My Dad got a job as a chemist working for Allied Chemical, with a long commute to New Jersey. My mother did fancy knitting, high-level piece work, for expensive clothing stores. That was intellectually surely a blow to someone nearing a Ph.D. in France in the field of chemistry, but it helped feed the family, four people with grandparents, five with my brother born in February 41, and six when I arrived in June of 1943.

After a number of years, my Dad was able to struggle back onto a Ph.D. track. With the efforts of the emigré network, Dad was able to get a fellowship at Syracuse University. This came from one of the superstars of the group, a quasi-genius mathematician, Lipman Bers, who got jobs upon arrival in the US teaching at Brown, then an assistant Professorship at Syracuse University, then NYU and Columbia. The Syracuse connection worked for Dad in finding a graduate opening and fellowship.

Why not Mom? Why was she not able to resume her chemistry studies? Another one of those paired questions I find myself confronting throughout this book: why him and not her? In part, I imagine the answer comes from Dad being more advanced in his doctoral studies while in France than Mom; he was already someone so far more advanced one could construct an application file around him. I don't think Mom's graduate credentials were that far along as she had come to   the study of chemistry later, after starting in different directions. So it was likely harder to make a case for her. Nonetheless, I always wondered why she was not able to return to science studies. Immigration cost her the career she wanted.

It was also perhaps timing. Those were not yet the years universities were starting to burst open with programmatic growth and dynamic expansion to accommodate not only returning veterans but the baby boom. Mother's job opportunities did open up in those years, but it was for her language skills— French, German, Russian—for which she had native-level, higher-education fluency and innate skills and could teach at the level of a university course, as well as the literature required at even higher levels. Demand for these materials was rising faster than supply because of the influx of veterans. And yet, Mom did not wish to be a language teacher, though she turned out to be very good at it. This was not surprising for a very smart woman. Yet it was not her vocation, something she would note when reflecting on her life trajectory, which was not that often but happened I think, when people complimented her on her language teaching achievements. Mother formed an attachment to science, not quite the same way as my Dad, but she had it, and it was a lifetime disappointment that she was not able to continue it—her personal greatest career loss from being a refugee, I think.

Mother suffered the shocks of gender. Money could be found for a bright man back then, though just barely. Dad lost eight years before going back to the Ph.D. track. But no money for a bright woman; again, to defend the system, which I don't particularly wish to do, she had not proven the science skills to merit it. A dozen years later, that might not have been the case. But in those years, her gender was exploited. She told me that in 1969 after my father died at a prematurely young age of 52 when she was 53, she started to pay attention to the facts of her financial arrangements at the university. She inquired about her retirement portfolio. In a discussion with the department secretary of the languages program, she noted that something did not add up properly between years of employment and years of contribution to retirement. Then she heard a voice float from the Department chair's office. "Yes, that's correct." He had used his discretionary authority to shift money from her retirement into the departmental account for other uses; since she was married, the Department chair decided Mom's need was lower, as she had a working spouse—a classic attitude and maneuver in those days. I talked to her about suing. By then, as she neared retirement, the atmosphere had changed, and women's rights came into existence. Nonetheless, Mom did not wish to sue. She still worked there and did not wish to sue her employer. I was shocked as I learned more about university administrative structures and how loose the rules were in those days. I had thought my employer, the University of California, to be bureaucratic, but I learned the private institutions made faculty much more vulnerable to abuse of this kind, leaving financial judgments to the discretion of departmental chairs rather than to the formal rules that the public institutions did. My observation was that rules protected people, especially the vulnerable, which was the point! What happened to Mom could not have happened in the very bureaucratic procedures on my campus, which gave less discretion to individuals in positions of authority and more insistence that they follow procedure. My sympathy for rules went up.

And yet, before I jump down the figurative throat of her employer, Syracuse University, it must be said that the fluidity of the situation in those years worked to her advantage as well. Mother had no degrees in language or literature nor a Ph.D. in anything. The modern bureaucratic rules would have blocked her entirely from a university career. She was made a member of Syracuse University's French Literature department, even to the point of voting power. She was, I am told, highly respected, and her opinion was sought by bright colleagues and advanced students. She was highly regarded as a language teacher, innovative in her methods and teaching guides. She was regularly invited when prominent people visited campus to sit with them at dinners and lectures, knowing she would make stimulating comments and ask insightful questions. Well, then they cheated her on the money. But it gave her a lot of other things they should not have. She got a job without a Ph.D. She got promoted to higher ranks. As she grew older, she managed to get a special parking spot to reduce the consequences of the bitter cold on her heath, which was substantial.

In the 1980s, when grandchildren arrived in California, she was long a widow, so she left upstate New York. Her friends, a few of them colleagues at the University, were genuine in their sadness. She had been a leader in their social life: she enjoyed putting on large parties at New Year's Eve or Summer Barbecue for some excuse or another. She loved inviting people to dinner and having stimulating conversations. She kept notes on what she served at each of these to avoid duplication with the same guests. The division of labor was classic American: my Dad barbecued and served drinks. Mom cooked and did everything else. The children helped out setting and clearing the table. I enjoyed gossiping about who said what, who said sharp things, and who did not. I took it for granted they let the children participate: we read *The New York Times* on Sunday also, so why not? She sustained much of these social customs even as a widow. My parents often commented how hard it would have been in Europe to construct such a wide network of friends, as people were siloed into narrower columns of family and blood ties and lineages.

My father's career was more intense. The years at Allied Chemical allowed him to earn a living to sustain a wife, two children and his in-laws. But it was below the level of his intellectual skills, and so he was pleased to return to graduate school to get the Ph.D. He was interested in microbiology. This was relatively new in university circles, so the program he entered was joint between biology and chemistry. One consequence of this I recall is that at summer picnics, when the graduate students would play baseball, Dad was always asked to umpire the inter-departmental games. Being in both programs guaranteed his neutrality, according to American principles, which derived fairness from the structure. In addition, he did not really know the game and could not really play any position, calling balls and strikes fit just right. That he had bad eyesight was perhaps not well registered. Dad was fair-minded and good-natured. He was perfect for this task.

I recall as well going to the lab with him at odd hours of the evening and on weekends to make adjustments to the equipment. During one period, this consisted of beakers containing microbes in liquids under special heat and light conditions placed on trays that shook as the lab searched for organisms that had special medicinal properties—penicillin, after all, had been discovered when Fleming noticed mold from bread-killing bacteria on some lab plates.

Another memory comes from childhood foraging: driving in the car on holiday or weekend trips, I recall we would stop, hop out of the car, and my brother and I would each be equipped with a small aluminum dish having a screwtop lid. We would open it, scoop up some dirt, attach the lid, then put it into a mail bag addressed to the lab in Syracuse, where it would be received to be processed in the relentless search for useful microbes, thus continuing Fleming's search for productive material growing wild.

Upon completing his Ph.D, Dad got an appointment at Syracuse University, and he published some papers solo and co-authored on drugs they were developing. He soon decided he would rather go to a lab for drug development as a career, not the university. I inferred the commitment to the applied in some way derived from the influence of his father, the socialist, seeking to make a better world for everyone. Twenty or thirty years later, university careers changed: large numbers of people doing drug development were able to do so within the structure of the university. They could get the labs, the capital, and some of the patents to benefit from their achievement. This followed the genetics revolution, which had not happened in my Dad's day. I recall Dad being paid $1 to sign off the rights to his discovery. He also got promotions, but unlike folks today, he was not able to found companies and share the profits. And would he have wanted to, had the opportunity been there? I don't know. I think he did not miss that opportunity. He cared about his lab and inventions, not the big money strike.

Dad's progressive attitudes were evident in his views on costs and the distribution of profits. He saw that profits were needed to pay for labs and the development of new products. But he also believed in the wide distribution of medicines vital to health. Standardized medicines should be broadly available at low prices. He was not a great fan of the "Big Pharma" system.

In graduate school, I met and became very close friends with a student, Suzanne Berger, who shared my strong interests in France and French politics. Imagine our mutual astonishment to discover our respective fathers had known each other for many years as they had comparable jobs—Director of Research—at rival companies and had discovered synthetic penicillin at about the same time. The two companies sued each other over patent rights on that drug. The two fathers sat next to each other at the trial, discussing professional themes, testified when called to do so, and then resumed their friendship. The companies cared deeply about the outcome, more deeply than the scientists given the way the payment system worked.

Dad moved rapidly up the hierarchy of Bristol. His advisor and boss left the firm to start a consultancy of his own. Dad became the Director of Research. He was, I believe, greatly admired for a kind of leadership based on knowledge, fairness, and balance. He had the capacity to lead from quiet strength. He listened well, thought clearly, sorted out the issues, and acted decisively and with meaningful purpose.

Dad's untimely death at age 52 was a great shock to everyone. It cut his career potential so short. After finally getting the Ph.D., he had so few years to use it. He had but a limited time to enjoy the mature years of his career. With children out of the house, he and my mother started to travel: Greece, Mexico, and France. His death hit hard: The loss to his children of not having a grandpa for their children, fewer people to share stories and experiences. The loss to my mother was losing her life's companion. How could she find anyone who had shared to much—from language, and refugee experiences? She never remarried.

Dad and Mom fit the America they arrived into, or more precisely, they found parts of America to fit into. I am sure there were worries. The McCarthy period was surely menacing. I don't know of people from their group who were attacked. McCarthy went after domestic leftists, it appears, not the refugees, perhaps as these were not active in US politics, had little influence, and the point was to weaken your political enemies. Nonetheless, It must surely have been chilling to them to watch this oppressive movement as it launched an attack on ideas they took seriously and on the right to free expression. It made it difficult, to this day, to convey that socialists could be democratic, having nothing to do with Stalin and the bad Bolshevik bugaboo. But that vulnerability had many sources, of which Joe McCarthy was but one. Those dangers came from many arrows. The US was, for my parents, a place of relative safety.

The song that comes to mind is Woody Guthrie's "This Land Is

Your Land, this Land Is My Land," written about the time they arrived in America. Did it convey what they thought, or is it the view of their children, the image of America their children had, the kind of folk song popular in the sixties protest movements for Civil Rights and against the Vietnam War? My parents joined us in supporting those movements. We, the native-born children and they the immigrants had very different experiences, with much to learn from each other.

The most powerful positive image of this country for my parents was the cultural openness in contrast to the closed hierarchical character of the Europe they had experienced, where life was built around family, lineage, and wealth. Oh, that exists in the US, but you could and can lead a good life without it—if you were fortunate enough to arrive as they did with substantial cultural capital and have the very important cultural and financial help of some established friends and social institutions, like universities which gave scholarships and rewarded merit.

The dark shadows from Europe were also often there in their self consciousness. Once, in the early 1990s, I took Mother to a major league baseball game in San Diego with my children. Midway through, I asked her what she thought. "Fantastic," was her reply. "There are no police." The forces of order and control were not visible to her. I pointed out who I thought were the non-uniformed equivalents patrolling the crowd, but it amazed her there were so few in uniform. Another time, I took her to an afternoon "fair" in our suburb for the local public grade school with games of various kinds, requiring tickets to raise money for the school. Again, she commented, "All this money and no police." Indeed, she continued to find uniformed police rather scary and their relative absence in American life worthy of note. She was not alive during the current controversies over abusive police behavior toward minorities, which would not have surprised her and which she would have deplored, while at the same time pointing out that the poor and oppressed also need and desire effective and accountable police protection.

I certainly benefited from being native-born, going to college here, and experiencing political security. Ethnic identity arrived into my consciousness in grade school. "Why," asked a student in class, " does Peter not go to church school with the rest of us?" as they trooped off to the weekly Catholic school; in this public school, 99% of the students were of Irish or Italian descent. "Because," explained the teacher, "he goes to a different religious school, as he is not Catholic." Well, that is partly true—I was not Catholic, but I did not go to Jewish school either. My parents did keep us home on Yom Kippur to make it clear we were not pretending to "pass" as non-Jewish, but we did not belong to a synagogue or attend services. The school was kept open for us and for a boy whose father was an atheist and would not let him attend Catholic classes. I recall being embarrassed by the attention being paid to me. After my father's Ph.D. and a new job, we were able to move to a neighborhood in a stronger school district, and there the classes were 1/3 each Catholic, Protestant and Jewish. I was promptly grouped among the latter and hung out with those kids though there was some mixing across religions. I joined the Jewish fraternity the school had, something my more non-conformist older brother refused to do. The point of my narration is that the awareness was cultural around me. I picked Oberlin College in part because it had no fraternities and sororities, and I was pleased to find a number of classmates when I got there who had picked it for the same reason. The first week in college, at Sunday lunch, I recall my wonder at hearing for the first time the Doxology ("Praise God from whom all blessings flow.") How little did I know of some aspects of America! Oberlin had religious origins like most colleges in America, though very tempered by the time I got there. It was very progressive in its religiosity. (As I like to sing, I soon learned it the way I learned Christmas carols in grade school).

Oberlin taught me a lot about this country. It helped me understand some of what made my parents comfortable. As I came to learn the history of the College and the values that formed it, for which it remains proud, I came to grasp how similar these values were to the values of my grandparents. One might imagine a vast gap: secular, anti-clerical, socialist, social democratic grandparents, Jewish in background, far removed from the missionary protestant culture that formed the core of Oberlin. Oberlin was founded in 1833 by liberal Protestants from New England. It was the first college in the US to admit African Americans, in 1835; and the first to admit women, in 1837; a stop on the underground railway, a hotbed of abolitionist views, known for its broad-minded political openness combined with a crusading zeal for reform. Indeed, there was much in the political culture of my grandparents that resonated with that, even with or without the not-so-minor presence or absence of God and Jesus. As I got older and studied Protestant and Jewish ideas, I came to see more of the Jewish origins of my grandparents' Socialism, the overlaps of Jewish and some Protestant sects. It stopped startling me that many Protestants from the Reformation identified with the "people of the book." It was the antisemites that did not fit their own theology.

The notion of the priest and the rabbi, furthermore, at least in some sects of each branch, struck me as similar: a learned leader among equals, not an anointed commander of the faithful, an intermediary to God. Many Jews and Protestants who came to America believed in a community of spiritual partners but not subordination. They subscribed to knowledge and questioning. Oberlin taught that. It was the belief system of my grandparents. An older Jewish colleague startled me a few years back by suggesting that by becoming a professor, I had picked a very rabbinical pathway.

So the cultural overlap between my grandparents and Oberlin seems less surprising than one might imagine. But the social openness was also very noticeable at Oberlin; it was a College of the Whole.

The student body council was elected at large from a voting system of rank-ordered weighted voting system, now being adopted in various places around the US. At Oberlin, it meant the constituency was the student body at large, a number of like-minded who found each other but did not necessarily live together. It being the pre-computer age, the ballots had to be counted by hand, a long and tedious process. I volunteered to be one of the counters. I loved it. Was I surprised when my younger son turned out to love numbers, voting, and polling and became a polling expert and an executive for a well-known polling company while my older son became a professor of political philosophy? I am the Venn diagram of my children, as I enjoy both the numbers and the political philosophy !

Dad did the things which helped his family and children, though he was not particularly used to them. For example, he took my older son on a boy scout canoe and camping trip with other fathers, though this may have been risky for his health. But he did it cheerfully as a commitment to his boy. I recall the encouragement he gave me on science projects: feeding mice different diets and growing seeds with different amounts of light and water. Another time he helped me make Fort Ticonderoga from plaster. He tried unsuccessfully to make me a lab type. I admired his discipline as a tutor of his child: he never did my homework. If I had a math question, he would make up new questions like one I brought to him until I got the concept, then do the assignment myself. As a child, I was the nut who wanted to stop at every historical road sign to read it. They indulged up to a reasonable limit. As we often drove past Gettysburg on the way to see the Woytinskys in Washington, I was the one who insisted we visit it, and eventually, they indulged me in that one, a memorable experience for me as I was early on fascinated by the Civil War.

For sure, there were many features of the US society my parents criticized. Segregation in the South and North enraged them. Our first important family vacation by car to Florida in 1953 shocked all of us as we entered the Jim Crow South and saw the Whites and Colored Only signs. My father signed a petition in Syracuse to promote public housing, and I recall a high school classmate yelling at me about his signature, saying that he did not want people like that living nearby. We went to hear a speech at Syracuse University by Martin Luther King, Jr., and as Dad stood in line to shake his hand, I saw strong emotion on his face as he expressed admiration for King for his activities. MLK was helping "his people." I imagine my Dad saw something of his own father there. My parents were active in politics at all levels, making sure they voted down to county representatives on the Democratic Party boards. My parents were more progressive than the US at the time, but they accepted the need to be pragmatic and to compromise. New York state allowed candidates to run on more than one party ticket, so the Liberal Party, moderately more left-wing than the Democrats, often had the same candidates, but voting on their ticket indicated support for that point of view. Where possible, Dad picked the Liberals.

When I meet immigrants of later periods, they, at times, reflect on their choice. They often miss their country of origin, reflect on the cultural gaps, and the loss of personal friendships, family and contact. It matters if they think they have a choice. My parents did not. I did not hear regret in the sense of options available. Uncle George provided the only written material I have expressing sadness by a family member, missing friendships he had made each time. Yet, he never thought there was an option and had an excellent career in the US as a researcher at the New York Federal Reserve. It was possible to return to Europe, but almost none of the Menshevik refugees did so. My parents did not regret it.

Nor do I have written material on what they thought of the Holocaust specifically or their lives as refugees and how these were related. I understood early on their escape was touch and go. The stories they narrated to us evoked that. They were young adults, expecting children, running for their lives. In the other danger point, Russia in 1919-23, they were little children, not conscious decision-makers, experiences not directly shared between them, whose danger was not so clear at the moment.

The shock of it was strong. Mother did not wish ever to return to Germany. She said this while at the same time being very critical of broadside national character interpretations of the Nazis, like "the Germans are all like this." She strongly disliked Eric Goldhagen's book, *Hitler's Willing Executioners,* for its rather broad brush assignment of blame to "many" if not " most" Germans. Indeed her dislike of the book which I shared was Goldhagen's lack of care in making just that distinction among "some," "many," " most," and "all." Having come to adulthood in those years, Mother had vivid memories of positive relationships with many Germans who did not care about her Jewishness. She also had negative experiences as well. But she saw the systematic persecution as institutionally led by the Nazis, drawing for sure on some cultural roots of antisemitism, but these were not, in her view, the structural causes of the Holocaust.

So Mom would not return to Germany but did not object to my going or buying a Volkswagen as my first car. In fact, she liked the rejection of stereotyping this involved, but she would not do it herself out of homage to her beloved Uncle. This made me reflect even more on how she would have responded to the Ukrainian crisis of today. I think she would have accepted the efforts of contemporary Ukrainians to rework their cultural framework to be more inclusive heterogenous, and liberal in its values.

From my Dad, I recall a deep distaste for racial interpretations. "There was more variation within each race than between them," he said, a phrase I heard from him often. A strong comment in our era, and one articulated through his science, fueled no doubt by his

Jewish identity and experiences in Europe fleeing Hitler's rise and the antisemitism he encountered in Russia. He didn't express much about his feelings on this or other topics. Dad's quietness was a powerful element of his personality. For a period of my life, this feature bothered me. I sought more from him. I imagined this attribute came from the isolation he had experienced, a defense he had built up to handle his own lack of contact. In my twenties, I saw a psychotherapist, not for this but for other reasons. I did talk about my wish that he, Dad, talked more. I decided in the fall of 1968 that the agency was not exclusively his. If I wanted more talk between us, I could take the initiative. So that December, while home for the Christmas holidays, I walked into my parents' bedroom where Dad was sitting on his "Barcalounger" and said to him, "So Dad, what are you doing these days." He seemed startled, looked at me and started to talk. I think he talked about his lab and the work he did there. I kept asking questions; he kept answering. This went on for a while, a couple of hours. I don't recall anything emotionally deep in the conversation, but I do recall finding it direct and expressive. It was between us. Dad seemed very pleased at the end and said something like, "We should do this again." It was clear to me he understood I had initiated a direct interaction with him, and he appreciated it a great deal. After returning to Cambridge, I called them and urged them to take a holiday in a warm climate. Six weeks later, on February 9, Dad died on a Sunday morning. The natural pacemaker of his heart stopped. He had gone out in the cold where Mother was operating the snow blower.

Why did the heart stop? The doctors guessed it was the consequences of cortisone shots taken for so many years to deal with acute asthma provoked by the allergies generated by the terrible exposures from early childhood onward and poor health care much of his life, perhaps exacerbated by emotional stress. Had he been near emergency medical experts or equipment, they could conceivably have restarted his heart. It moved me very, much that I had had this conversation with him. Only the one, but it was clear a contact had been made, and that the initiative from me, in this case, made a difference to our communication.

An interesting contrast between my parents had to do with language. They both spoke the same four fluently. My Dad knew some Yiddish from his experience with his grandparents, but my mother did not. My mother could switch from one language to another on a dime; she could do simultaneous translation. Famously, my dad often mixed them up. The standard farewell joke on a trip was "Shreib otkritke please," which equals "Write" (in German), "postcards" (in Russian), and "please" (in English). At the same time, Dad could give you any word from any of his four languages, whereas Mom got stuck in whatever language she had learned it in, so she counted in Russian, did basic science in German, Philosophy and Literature in French, and daily life in American English. Neither one could understand Cockney or British English, so Sergei and I had to explain "Beyond the Fringe" to them, as well as the Beatles. I took Dad to see *The Yellow Submarine*, and he loved it, just why I am not sure— the sheer fun of it. I remember him chuckling all the way through.

A distinctive feature of my Dad and the Russian language was his love of its proverbs. Dad thought you could not really be fluent unless you knew these sayings and could bring them out in conversation. He did this frequently, even while speaking English; he would translate them. I recall a few examples. "At the Rabinovichs, they have gone to bed already." Or a better version: "At the Rabinovichs, they've been asleep for some time already", said while looking out the window to convey that the guests had overstayed their welcome.

My older brother Sergei adored my father. He spoke of him in reverential terms, the only person in the world whom he ever referred to in that way. "He was a giant," said Sergei when Dad died. My brother majored in physics in college, got a Ph.D. in that field, became a research scientist, and was one of the inventors of geo-positioning satellite (GPS) technology. I visited him in his MIT lab, and he proudly said, "You are the first person outside this lab to see this photo: it shows the surface of Venus. Normally covered with clouds, our technology bounces a signal off the surface, allowing us to specify altitude, thus project a surface." From his work on this, he was hired by private industry to help generate GPS. He was not richly rewarded for it in monetary terms, nor in the history of the technology. Sadly, he too died young: Sergei at 59 in 1999, our Dad at 52 in 1969.

In family dynamics, Sergei had deep tensions with my mother until his twin girls were born. Then he saw how much she adored them, and as he did the same, they shared this bond very deeply. To some degree, Sergei did hold Dad accountable for our Mother's domineering quality, which bothered him. Could Dad have contained it? Or was Dad accepting of it out of his own shared experiences of stress? There are many possible interpretations here. I tend toward the accommodating and accepting. They, our parents, went through a lot and did a great deal for their family.

There is a lot of loss in our family: my Dad lived much of his life without his parents. I felt very protected and loved by my parents, but I did not have lots of extended family, which I observed others have enjoyed, such as my second wife, whose family did not have lots of cultural capital but many uncles and aunts and cousins from whom she felt much love. My dad felt the nurturance of the Menshevik network in Berlin and Paris and in the early New York years, but he did not talk about it much. I lost Dad when I was 26; he was only 52. Painful to me, to my mother and brother, and to our children. A great cultural, psychological, and historical loss. What does it tell us? I draw away from too much emphasis on it. People differ so much. Resilience can be powerful. Maybe it gives some insight into Dad. But I am cautious to overproject. It allows us to reflect and to compare.

Chapter 12

Conclusion

Go or Stay – Live or Die: Who Decides

"There is no private life that has not been determined by a wider public life."

George Eliot, *Felix Holt, the Radical*

Many of the family stories go through my mind as "might-have-beens" or "what-ifs." I just can't stop trying to reenact history, like rewriting a movie or novel. I know the difference. Fiction can be rewritten, but history cannot. Perhaps in my desire to meet these absent relatives, I am driven to do it anyway.

I wonder what decisions cost them their lives, what would have saved Grandpa Boris or Uncle Buka, and what decisions saved the relatives who made it to the US? I try to imagine dramatic scenes, to reconstruct them as scenarios, as movie scenes. One of the most amazing to me is Grandma at the Spanish border in September of 1940. How did that interaction with the border guard go?:

French Border Official, speaking to Uncle George: "Monsieur, where is your exit permit? And you are of fighting age; why are you not in the Army? You may not cross."

Grandma, shouting loudly: "If he doesn't go, I am not going and will stay here, do you hear me?"

Border Official: "Madame, shut up. Either cross by yourself or go back and stop causing trouble."

Grandma: "I will not be quiet. I will not go back. My son was in the Army and was demobilized; he has shown you those papers. We have visas and tickets to America."

Family, other people in line: "Let them cross; what is wrong with you? We are all waiting in line. What's the problem?"

Border Official: "They don't have the proper documents."

Grandma: "I will stay here all day and night."

People in crowd: "So what with your bureaucratic nonsense. They have all the exit and entrance stamps. Let them go." (general noise and loud mumors of agreement with Grandma.)

Border Official: "Ça alors. Go, go, and fast. Get out of here!"

Surely, the real scene had more vitality to it, more emotion, more color, and more drama than I have evoked here. How did everyone in the family feel in those moments? I reflect on it—my pregnant mother, my agitated grandparents, Uncle George, the center of attention. My father—why no controversy about him as he was also of combat age? And what if the guard had refused? Would they have gone back to Banyuls and tried the mountain route as did the Etkin family with a sick grandmother who had trouble breathing, and who I remember well when we children all played together in New Jersey, with both grandmas happily watching.

This is a case of a "what if" that I can specify in detail: a particular border guard in a specific spot in France. I wonder about other specific people in given moments being allowed to leave or forbidden: the border guard in Switzerland who said to Boris and Olga Fichman, "You may not enter" ; the Soviet KGB official who processed Boris **Ber**'s request to leave and decided "No, this would be a mistake"; the Soviet KGB official who, while reading the request for my father to leave for Berlin, said, "Yes, this boy may go."

Many important decisions are made at a far more general level. The granting of emergency visas to enter the US was done in Washington by the State Department under the command of Breckinridge Long and Cordell Hull with regard to several thousand people. The implementation of some of those visas was done by Hiram Bingham,

IV. My family had no personal connection to any of these individuals, but it was connected to the network in which Minkoff was constructing lists. The decision to exterminate Jews was made at the Wannsee meeting in January 1942 without designating specific individuals; the Fichmans were among the millions who were unnamed victims of that decision. The many decisions to imprison Boris Ber-Gourevitch derive from a larger set of decisions reaching back to Lenin and the people around him not to tolerate dissent. The decision to broaden that decision to widespread murder during the purges of 1936-1938 can be attributed to Stalin.

When I tell people my family story, very often, I am asked how did they realize they had to "get out." Very understandable that question, one which frames the family in contrast to the millions who did not. In the search for answers, I frequently turn to the very famous phrase "canary in the coal mines." What was the canary for them? But when I looked up this phrase, I realized it is not quite the right metaphor. Miners working underground brought in canaries because if the air turned foul, such as too much CO_2, the canaries would fall over, and the miners knew there was danger, and it was time to leave. I wanted a metaphor that was more like a noise: what altered the family members to danger afoot and to shout "Fire"!

What I see from working through the family story is the complexity of things, the multiple causalities, the relevance of context, and the need to sift through many factors. I appreciate the importance of political awareness and of networking, but I have to situate those factors in context.

My four grandparents, struggling against the Tsarist system, were so full of hope when the Tsar abdicated in February of 1917, then found their political project destroyed by the Bolshevik coup of October/November of that year. Two of them, the Bronstein-Garvys, became refugees outside their country like many of their brethren. Two of them became prisoners in their own country, the Ber-Gourevitch, like many of their political brethren, and one died as a victim of the regime in power, Grandfather Boris. My grandparents' lives intersected with monumental events of the 20th century, and so there is much drama with straightforward telling. Narrating the arc of their lives has yielded quite a range of stories, and it is very rewarding simply to lay these out. It is this that allows us to isolate the decision points.

Grandma Sophie arguing with Lenin in Switzerland, all of them participating with the noted players in the high drama of 1917-22 Russian Revolution, Great Grandma Styssia writing to Trotsky in 1925 on behalf of her son, Shura leaving his father to live in Berlin in 1931, the fall of the Weimar Republic and the Rise of Hitler in 1933, the escape from Nazi Berlin and the Gestapo in 1933, Grandpa Boris summoned by the Politburo leadership to send the Kazan telegram in 1934, the French Popular Front of 1936, the Spanish Civil War and the disappearance of Mark Rein in '36-'38, the flight from Paris in 1940 on the last train going south, the arrival of the Visas in Marseilles in summer of 1940, the escape to the US via Lisbon in September-October 1940 on a boat which was torpedoed at its next transatlantic crossing—plenty of epochal material. It is astonishing to me that any of them survived to reach the US.

Yet the stories themselves, dramatic as they are, compel questions and probing, and that means considering frames for those questions. One major frame that has guided the narrating has been the voice of the "Sleuth"--hunting for information that would place stories, what I have called Family Legends, in a context.

Having been mesmerized by hearing my family narrate their experiences, it has been fascinating to probe these stories, to interrogate them. On which could I find evidence, and which not? How exciting it can be to read of archaeological digs that find material on the Pilgrims arriving at Plymouth or items about the first settlements of Jerusalem at the time of King David, establishing that there really was such a person in that place. So I felt when I saw my uncle George's emergency entrance visa to the United States of 1940, with the signature of Hiram Bingham IV, and all the stamps from border guards tracing their progress from France to Lisbon; or the shock of seeing the names of Great Uncle Buka and his wife Teuta Olya on the train list from Drancy to Auschwitz 1943 and to see in the Carnets de Drancy the receipt of money taken from Great Uncle Buka; or how moved I was to see the photo of Grandpa Boris from Vladimir Prison of 1937, in the FSB files, and the letter, in his own handwriting, he wrote in 1923 demanding to know where was the visa he had been promised, and why had it been given to Peter Garvy, but not to him?

The greatest new fact I learned from the recent research in probing the Soviet sources was that Grandpa Boris had, in fact, applied to leave in 1922 at about the same time as Grandpa Peter. This over-turned the idea that the decision to leave or stay was based on ideo-logical differences between the two Grandfathers. The archives show they both wanted to leave and an additional surprise at the same time. The timing of those requests adds to the force of understanding who made the final decision— the agency, or the initiative and the power, lay with the OGPU, not with the Grandfathers. They decided to let one Grandpa and his family go, but not the other.

Were my parents wrong in their understanding about Boris' stay-ing in Russia, that it was his decision? Did they know he wanted to leave? Did I misunderstand the legend—so that this is Peter Goure-vitch's Legend, not the Family Legend? I think not completely, as other relatives have had the same understanding. I never heard of an alternative version. But possibly, there is some truth nonetheless in the Family Legend. Can I make the archives' documents fit the Fam-ily Legend?

These ideological differences shaped political consciousness among the members of the different factions within the exile community in-tensely. These differences were projected onto the two grandfathers, not falsely, and used as an explanatory mechanism of what happened to them. It is here the disagreements emerge: descriptions of disagree-ment, yes; explanations of what happened to them, no. So there was a kind of truth, one that mattered to them—the political position of the grandparents—which shaped their interpretation, not a literal truth about Boris having self-aware explicit reasons for not wanting to leave at a particular moment.

This distinction—literal truth, metaphoric truth, philosophical truth--- matters to me as I reflect on the past and present. I used to sit quietly and watch my mother and older brother quarrel and think, "Ah, she has just changed the subject somewhat. How many seconds before he gets angry over it?" And then I came to see these differenc-es mattered to me in my work—what sort of truth are we after? On certain topics, it mattered a lot; on others, not so much. And in my human relationships, on some issues, you stand aside rather than lose a friendship or love. On the question of the grandfathers, possibly the ideological interpretation has some truth, especially in the ear-ly 1920s: Boris was more reluctant to leave than other Mensheviks who left earlier, and delayed requesting permission till it was too late.

Might a request posed earlier have been successful? It seems clear that by 1922, Boris wanted to leave. The timing of his request seems no different from Peter Garvy's, but it should have been if ideology is the explanation alone. So the ideological interpretation contributes something to our understanding, if not a literal truth, but by itself, it is insufficient.

Or is this a son's or grandson's desire to integrate disparate strands of evidence into a harmonious story? The hard fact is the OGPU refused to allow Boris and his family to leave, while it allowed Peter and his family to depart. And we know the hard facts of the consequences, however much the uncertainty over just how to interpret these hard facts.

The fate of Dadia Buka and his wife Olga had no uncertainty attached to it. It is thus a good contrast for the Boris Ber (they are both named Boris; Buka is the family used diminutive for maternal Grandma's brother Buka Fichman, so here Boris refers to Boris Ber Gourevitch, my father's father) story—it sharpens our understanding of how to think about both of them. With Boris, there is some uncertainty; with Buka, there is not. In Buka's case, the sleuthing had to do with finding documentation of what the family had known for some time.

I had been doing this for a number of years, long before I thought of writing this memoir. The first evidence came from visiting the Holocaust Museum in the US in 1993 when I discovered the train lists in Klarsfeld's books. Seeing those lists moved me and my mother quite deeply. I found other documents in Paris. Thanks to the biography of Charlotte Salomon, I learned about the *Carnets de Drancy* and made the startling discovery that they took money from him and made a receipt! As a symbolic gesture of formally recording a public crime against Buka and Olya, I requested compensation from the French government for money taken from him and received a small amount. And I overcame my aversion to visiting the camps to go to Auschwitz Birkenau, where he and his wife died, and there I recited the Kaddish in their honor.

So several of the Family Legends stand the test of evidence to enter the honorable chamber of Verifiable Facts. Some Family Legends cannot be tested—phone calls, for example, from the Gestapo to the Garvys in 1933, or scenes at the French–Spanish border in 1940, or

Grandma Sophie Garvy talking to Lenin while he was sitting on her bed. These stories provide some vitality to the events . There could be some details that were different, but their minor accuracy does not matter much. Nothing different would have occurred. Some other little stories mean more: my grandmother getting medicine from the Kremlin pharmacy through a Bolshevik friend when my mother was sick. It shows she was indeed well-networked.

These stories frame the narrative of how my parents experienced these events. It was an escape from danger to save their lives. I think they told it as a factual narrative: escaping the evil of Hitler and of Stalin. They did not speculate much on options, choices, or judgments. Survival or death, those were how they thought about it. That they made it to the US seemed miraculous to me,so great were the many dangers. In my youth, I asked lots of factual questions and a few interpretative ones. The narrative arc of survival, reaching a land of opportunity, and having a stable, happy life here—is a classic American story. As I reflect on the narrative of the sleuthing operation, it is impossible not to probe for more interpretation. What options and choices did they have? One wonders what might have been and what decisions made by whom could have led to a different result, the life of one family member, the death of another.

At the same time, there are other ways of thinking about that narrative, asking questions about it. If "sleuthing" is one approach to checking out the Family Legend, "Explaining Why" and "Lessons Learned" are others. How do we explain why did the various family members experience their fates? Why did my parents make it to the US, whereas Grandpa Boris died in a Soviet prison and Great Uncle Boris at Auschwitz? There are lots of questions behind that enormous one: who made the critical choices, where did the power reside to decide? People had some ability to shape their fates, but in several circumstances, they did not.

I began this project quite focused on choices, on decisions made by each person. Now I think that misstates the issues. People were in situations, and the factors that determined their fates were multiple, some out of their hands entirely. This has a bearing on the "lessons" element of the "explaining why" question. People are compelled to ask not only why some survived, and others did not but what the lessons of this journey are, especially the life and death questions. Are there lessons to be drawn, and if so, which ones?

From this nest of interrelated questions, let me start with "choice." Why was this road taken, not that one, as the famous Robert Frost poem explores ?—"two roads diverged in a yellow wood." How many people remember he chose the one less taken, which is really the point of the poem? The poem sings of history as two paths that seem the same; why pick one and not the other? For most of my professional life, I have felt compelled to study choices, generally at the national level, comparing countries. Why, in one of history's most stunning contrasts, did the Nazis come to power in Germany, in January 1933, with substantial backing from rural voters, when exactly at the same time, on the same day, Denmark selected Social Democratic governments backed by the Agrarian Party, and Sweden did so a few months earlier. Similarly, in the US, the electorate, including many farmers in large numbers, opted for Roosevelt and the Democratic Party. Those national choices had a big effect on conditions that shaped individual choices. Life and death, war and the Holocaust turned on that difference between the selections made at the same time in these different countries.

These national choices shaped the context in which my family members had to make their individual choices to ensure survival. So, in the chapters on my family members, I have focused on choices at the individual level, not the national ones. What choices did family members have over their own destinies, and how did they make them? Indeed, life and death were at stake.

What did my family members have as substitute canaries? To what did they pay attention which alerted them of danger? Clearly, my grandparents and their friends were deeply engaged in politics through which they understood the world around them. Politics is what got them in danger, and politics is what saved some of them. By this, I mean they were more engaged in politics than most people. We are all affected by politics—taxes, war, highways, etc.—but many, if not most, people avoid involvement or even paying attention. In my family, politics was like air, essential to life. The grandparents chose it as a vocation, a profession, a way of life, a kind of secular religion. It permeated their existence and that of their children. My Uncle George, when emerging from the anesthetic after surgery while in his seventies, which took place during some tense time in Portuguese politics, said as his first comment upon awakening, "Et, le Portugal, what's happening?"

They chose politics, and in particular socialism—not Zionism, medicine, or business of some kind. This got them into trouble time after time: in Russia, with the Tsarist police before 1917; then the Bolshevik OGPU to 1922; in Germany with the Nazis in 1933; then again in France, the Nazis again in 1940. That political engagement was the fainting canary for them: it made them aware of the dangerous moment politics could bring. For them, not just any politics, but more specifically, the type of political commitment mattered greatly: they were socialists, on the side of labor, in Russia on the side of revolutionary change, and that made them especially vulnerable.

Just what did politics bring to them? Not superior analytic skills, or not that alone. It certainly helped to be well-educated and knowledgeable, but many such people did not leave at the right time. More significant was experience and the cues gotten from their network of people similar to them in the same boat. They learned by watching: Who was being seized, tortured, killed; what organizations were being closed down? Unions, party organizations, mayors and city councilors, church activists, essentially the political opposition—from that, they quickly saw life was dangerous to them. This happened to them first in Russia, then in Germany, and they knew it would be the same in France.

For the Garvys, my mother's family, Germany in the winter of 1933 was a dangerous place. The canary was flat on its back in its cage. They left early, in March of 1933—how did they know what was coming? That question is often asked from the perspective of German Jews. That group is not the right comparison frame for my family.

German Jews were well-rooted in their society, culture, and jobs. They had gone to school in Germany and served in the Armed Forces during the recent WWI (from which some had received decorations) had extended families, and in some cases, considerable economic assets. German society was more open toward Jews than Russia had been, and they were able to advance in professions and economically. They were thus strongly established in German society with much to lose from leaving and many reasons to think the Nazis were an aberrant minority that would not last.

The Menshevik refugees' situation was quite different. They were recent arrivals, not well-rooted in German society, with less to lose if they departed. They were well-networked in the Labor movement. Under Weimar, this gave them position and meaning and some access to resources, but it was just that group that was the primary object of attack by the Nazis who sought to eliminate a political rival. Mensheviks saw danger not from superior theoretical analysis about the nature of Nazis or Hitler but from observing who was being attacked and from being well connected to hear about it. The Reichstag fire in late February of 1933 was another turning point, after which the crackdown became swiftly worse. Talking to others was the key. The Mensheviks heard the terrible stories. Our refugee group knew it was in danger for multiple reasons: they were stateless, socialist, from the USSR, and Jewish. They left.

Once in Paris, that pattern repeated in 1940 as the German army approached. By now, the ruthless danger of the Nazis was very evident. Kristallnacht of November 9, 1938, brutal camps like Dachau, and the destruction of the Labor movement in Germany—this was all known by the time the Blitzkrieg of spring 1940 began and the peril approached. Some people did not fully grasp everyone was vulnerable: the German Social Democratic leaders Hilferding and Breitscheid are famous examples; in their case, people who thought their fame would protect them, but they were caught in Marseilles and died in concentration camps. Dadia Buka, who did understand the danger, perhaps hoped he was relatively safe under Vichy and Italian control in Nice, and that was true for a few years. Perhaps not being a labor leader, he felt less exposed and less vulnerable, and perhaps the Vichy structure also made him feel safer.

We have some sense of the warning signals for my family and other labor leaders in the 1930s. Can we construct "lessons" from the indicators their canaries signaled?

People repeatedly ask when discussing massive events, such as the Holocaust or the World Wars or the Great Economic Depression of 1929 or the banking collapse of 2008, what are the lessons learned? They want to know if the event in question, with all its massive cost, could have been avoided. Can we learn something from the past that insulates us for the future, that provides protection somehow from reoccurrence? Are there early warning signals?

A well-known book, *This Time It's Different*,[1] by economists Re-

Grave of Martov and Etkin in Berlin

inhard and Rogoff, suggests a gloomy answer. In the run-up to each financial crisis, people claimed we had learned from the past. Each time, it was claimed that the situation was actually different, so we would avoid the disasters of previous events because our greater understanding allowed us to plan for new occurrences. In finance, regulations are loosened, and the protections passed to stop repetition are diminished because we presumably know how to avoid the disaster. Then it turns out we have not escaped all of the past, and it happens again—disaster strikes.

In the academic world, the "what-ifs" are known as the "counterfactuals"—which facts would have had to change to produce different results. When I run the counterfactual sequence in my mind—what would have saved the lives of Buka and his wife Olya—I often focus on the swiftness of the French defeat in 1940, the collapse of its armies and the unwillingness of the French leadership to continue the fight from its colonies in North Africa. A more vigorous, imaginative military leadership, listening more carefully to the ideas of De Gaulle on tank strategy or more deeply patriotic to French ideals, might have kept a stronger, longer resistance. And a more courageous, less politically compliant government or less pro-fascist military leaders could have taken the French navy from Toulon across the Mediterranean to its ports in Algeria and continued the fight. This would have given Hitler a more serious opposition on the Western Front, possibly delaying or canceling the attack on Russia. And that might have had implications for the launching of the Holocaust—which in retrospect seems to seize a moment when Germany seemed very dominant: a prostate France, USSR in great disarray, with German tanks racing for the oil fields of Baku and about to envelope the granary of the black earth region centered in Ukraine. As the army swept through the shtetls and ghettos of Eastern Europe, the SS got to work, and the killing erupted.

Then I stop the counterfactual mind game and focus on the grim historical reality. The point of the counterfactuals is to deepen the lessons question: the lessons imply a sense of cause and effect; if only you, we, us, they had done this, or that, terrible things would not have happened.

This is difficult to do. Social causality is complex. There are many factors at work, and many aspects of history don't allow experiments: only one world war in 1914, for example, one Russian Revolution, so no controlled experiments. Counterfactual debates about history provoke intense disagreements. They reveal the outlook of those who try and those who are or are not convinced. But we must try our hand because these debates lie at the heart of important interpretations, understandings, and disagreements.

We can sort the discussion into two big bundles, perhaps poles on a continuum. On one side are the individually specific detailed events about individuals—my grandparents, for example, or major historical figures like FDR or Stalin. Here we are dealing with choices made by a specific, identifiable person at a specific moment in time. Examples from my family include decisions to leave Russia, Germany, and France, decisions by Hiram Bingham to sign the exit visas, or the border guard to let my grandmother and her family pass without the proper papers at the French–Spanish border in 1940. With this group of decisions, we can identify the person making them; we can limit the funnel of causality to   fewer people and thereby focus more easily on the facts and forces that led to them.

On the other end of the continuum, we have the big historical events, the mega-events, such as the outbreak of the World Wars, the

Russian Revolution, and the economic depression of 1929. There may be a specific person who made a decision, such as a declaration of war, but generally, there are huge numbers of people involved in these sorts of events.

The counterfactuals give tension, hope, despair: could it have been otherwise, could some relatives have survived? What chances gave the survivors their lives, and thus mine? We can go from the individual to the general. For my grandparents, the fateful choices begin with their engagement in politics and their commitment to the democratic socialist non-Bolshevik camp. Had they become professionals such as doctors, they might have stayed where they lived, and been killed when the SS arrived with the German Army in 1941. There is not much left of the city of Orsha from which my great-grandfather came, as it is right on the path of the advance from German-occupied Poland to Moscow. Or had they been Zionists, and among the few who escaped to Palestine, they may have had successful lives there, or their children may have been killed fighting in the various wars or terrorist bombs. Or they may have stayed in USSR and gone east with the various evacuations, as happened to the younger brothers of Boris, who survived both the Nazi invasion and Stalin.

But the grandparents did enter politics and on the socialist side.

For a time, they chose to stay in Russia. They did not join the Bolsheviks. Had they done so, they might have survived, at least for a time, though Boris had a Bolshevik younger brother who was killed in the purges in about 1940. So that would not have been a guarantee. The 20th century was a dangerous time in this part of the world. Whatever your choices, danger lurked.Let's keep them as the Mensheviks they were: could Boris have left, as did Peter? As noted, this turned out not to be their choice, but that of the OGPU. Had Boris been more passive, quieter, the OGPU might not have cared and let him leave. But he wasn't quiet; he was an activist. He did want to leave and the OGPU did not allow him to do so. And later, they killed him.

Just why Peter was allowed to go and Boris not, we have seen, could be interpreted in more than one way. A pragmatic, utilitarian version stresses the instrumental concerns of the Bolsheviks in preserving power in what were still dangerous times for them. They thought, according to this argument, that Boris was too threatening, or more so than Peter, with Boris having links both inside and outside Russia, his vigor and vitality, his ability to energize the refugee foreign delegation were he to go to Berlin; and at the same time, they found it useful have him inside the USSR to watch his political activity and watch who tried to contact him. Grandpa Peter was seen as less dangerous, with weaker networks, weaker attraction to the internal opposition, and less effective, as he was less energetic and less skilled. Perhaps they also sensed he was more divisive among the Menshevik Foreign Delegation and would cause argument and dissension.

This interpretation seems plausible to me, who thinks of organizations as quite important. And yet, we know organizations can make foolish or varied decisions and that other factors can have an impact on any given outcome.

The person who processed Grandpa Peter's file appears to have had some personal familiarity with him and, thus, more sympathy for his case. How sick was he, after all, as he lived another 21 years without good health care, despite fleeing twice as a refugee? Boris was just as sick, according to his file, though how can we compare the degrees of illness?   The first treatment of Boris' file in the fall of 1922 giving permission to leave was processed perhaps by someone more sympathetic—on humanitarian grounds or political ones—than the later reader who said the decision to let him go was a "mistake." Or was this a matter of hierarchy? The second reader might have been higher-up and less inclined to a personalist approach, more inclined to the party line, or was it that the party line was shifting, becoming more severe?

While I am inclined to the party instrumentalist explanation for blocking Boris' departure, I have trouble using it to make sense of a very big event in the family story: the exit of my father, Shura, from the USSR in 1931. What an incredible event! They refuse Boris, but they allow him to send his son! Why? Boris had no political influence at that time, nor certainly did Shura at age 15. That made it perhaps easier to let him go. But Stalin did strike at the children of his enemies, such as Mark Rein, the son of Raphael Abramovich, who was seized in Spain. Shura was saved in a sense by his father's imprisonment. Boris was the hostage; no need to strike at Shura.

On this event, I am inclined to the personalist explanation, here coinciding with the Family Legend: When Boris requested permission for Shura to leave, his application was processed by a Bolshevik friend, as I heard it said in my family. Why did the family think this?

Did they have evidence? I think not. I heard this Legend before the family visits to Moscow in the 1960s. I think the story was based on inference: how else could it have happened if not through the agency of a friend? They might even have known who. Finding the letter from 1928 requesting the visa for my Dad was something of a major revelation here—that it was granted at that time likely prepared the ground for re-granting three years later. So, a personalist interpretation makes sense to explain Shura's departure. Some links of the old pre-Revolutionary bonds among the members of the Russian Social Democratic Labor Party still existed and saved my father, Shura.

There are several individualist elements in the Garvy flight from France in 1940. Put a different US assistant consul general at Marseilles in 1940, someone other than Hiram Bingham IV, and it seems likely many people would not have gotten their emergency entrance visas from Marseilles in 1940-42. It would have taken an intervention from Washington to push a recalcitrant consul in the field, and the State Department was not pushing on behalf of refugees, particularly leftist Jewish ones. Bingham's story is a fascinating one; he lost his career because of efforts to save these people.

Other individuals mattered perhaps less overtly. A different guard at the French border in September 1940 and the family may have had to hike over the mountains, as did many of their friends. But they seem likely to have made it.

We are aware of Schindler's list. The person who actually prepared that one was the staffer/accountant. For these emergency entrance visas in France in 1940, the list for emergency entrance visas was constructed by Minkoff with input from Abramovich and other labor leaders in Paris among the Menshevik Foreign Delegation. The list included labor leaders from other European countries. How did they decide who to leave off? Was there discussion, or disagreement? What criteria? This was a kind of elite—the elite of the opposition to the traditional European elites, the labor opposition to the grand bourgeoisie, for once, in this situation, a privileged group. Lesser leaders, and people farther down in the organization did not receive visas. The list-makers were able to do their work because of key decisions made by US Secretary Cordell Hull and Breckinridge Long, who, at that moment, could have instead kept the door closed or closed it again, as they would a few months later.

In the USSR, what was the historical point of no return for Grandpa Boris? At what point would a different historical development have made a difference to his fate? Moving backward from 1938, when he died in prison, I would imagine it to be Stalin's launching of this last great wave of purges in 1937. Without that, he may have stayed under house arrest in Vladimir or elsewhere in the Gulag and possibly survived until Stalin's death in 1953, when the prisons were emptied.

What, then, could have prevented the purges, other than Stalin's death at an earlier date or a change of mind on his part? Most historians attribute the Great Purges of the 1930s to Stalin's decisions, not to something inherent in the Soviet system.[2]

The harsh repression of dissent by the regime, the collectivization drive of the 1930s, the forced industrialization, the end of the NEP economy, centralized planning—these are debated, but more likely the product of collective leadership and likely to have been undertaken by any of the top leaders of the Politburo, as it had emerged in the late-1920s.

The turn to authoritarianism, imprisonment and execution happens early in the Bolshevik regime even before the purges. The coup of October/November 1917 was challenged immediately, and civil war developed quickly. To establish control, the Bolsheviks organized force. Trotsky created the Red Army, using officers from the Tsarist army very effectively but causing tension for him with Bolshevik members. The OGPU was formed as a repressive apparatus. Opposition forces, especially the SR party leaders, were locked up and often killed. Foreign troops invaded and were beaten back. The Bolsheviks established control with a repressive regime that provided no space for disagreement, dissent and participation of other views. Levitsky and Way[3] argue that the character of the regime came with its founding. Repression begins even while Lenin is alive. Thousands die, are imprisoned, and flee. Some of the Menshevik top leadership are relatively lucky in being allowed to transfer their sentences out of the country.

Boris was still alive at the end of the Civil War in 1922/23. His loss of freedom turned on the Bolshevik victory. As Stalin won the struggles among the top Bolshevik leadership, Boris' ultimate fate lay in Stalin's hands.

Was another outcome possible in 1917? Several possibilities have been debated. Many people have wondered what would have happened had Martov as leader of the Mensheviks, not walked out of the fateful meeting on October 26, 1917, in Petrograd, which debated whether to seize power. Martov was against the Bolshevik coup, wanted a Constituent Assembly, and led a group of Mensheviks to leave the meeting. Trotsky shouted the famous line that Martov and friends were passing into the "dustbin of history." Had they stayed, some suggest, the Bolsheviks would have been part of a coalition, a kind of popular front, as it was called in the 1930s, and would have had to accept a less extreme course.[4]

This counterfactual fascinates me, as I wonder if it poses the political alternatives faced by my grandparents. I am not sure if they were at this meeting, but I expect they would have been on opposite sides of the debate: Peter, for sure, joining the walkout of the auditorium, and Boris wanting to remain in order to hold the alliance together. Hating Stalin, I have tended to side with what I know of Grandpa Peter's views, but in that situation, I am not so sure, and less so the more I probe the "counterfactual alternatives" whether the alternatives would have evolved quite as Peter hoped!

The Kerensky government was quite unstable and weak. The attempt by General Kornilov to overthrow Kerensky that summer of 1917 had been put down. Kerensky saved the provisional government but, at the same time, had no troops to defend him from the Bolshevik coup.

What was the alternative to the Bolsheviks at this moment? It was not likely to be a stable republic, even under a stronger leader than Kerensky, or an effective Constituent Assembly, which is what most non-Bolsheviks seem to have wanted. Such an Assembly would have been very heterogenous and without vigorous leadership. A counter-coup was in the air, led by a military group, a warlord, the sort of thing that happened all over the world in those years, from Europe to Latin America, China, and other parts of Asia. Instability leads to an authoritarian response from traditional social groups or a new, more mobilized authoritarianism, such as Franco in Spain in the 1930s. This would have repressed the socialist coalition, or the bourgeois coalition of the provisional government. The sort of stable parliamentary government for which Peter Garvy yearned, like Sweden or the UK, seems unlikely.

Mensheviks were very torn by this debate. Even in exile, as refugees from the Bolsheviks, many defended the Bolshevik regime against criticisms, on the grounds it was the only way to get some kind of substantial social change and the alternatives were reactionary governments of the old order.

This disagreement continued for decades, until Hitler's attack on the USSR in 1941, when all the Mensheviks rallied to defend the USSR against Hitler, forging an alliance of "Papa Joe (Stalin)" with the US and the UK.

It seems unlikely that had Martov not walked out, a successful co-alition of all socialists would have formed that could sustain a consti-tutional democracy in Russia. Everything we know of Lenin and his closest allies suggests he and they had a strong desire to seize power and rule in a particular way, not to share power. Had the disagreement not broken out that evening day in October at this famous meeting, it would soon have appeared at a different moment, days or weeks later, perhaps overrepressing the opposition and who belongs in the social-ist coalition and who should be tossed out.

Going back a few months in time from October/November 1917, suppose the German general staff had not shipped Lenin to Russia in a sealed railway car—at the suggestion, we recall, of my grandmother's one-time lover, Parvus—thus no arrival at the famous Finland station on 16 April 1917, and no Bolshevik coup in October of that year. It does seem likely that without Lenin, the Bolsheviks would not have tried the coup or perhaps not succeed. Here again, I have a pessimis-tic view of the scenario: not, as I have noted, a successful bourgeois republic, with Russia becoming a reformist version of some kind of Scandinavian quasi-democratic model. Rather, Petrograd would have seen some conservative authoritarianism, as I suggested above, as we saw in many parts of Europe (Admiral Horthy in Hungary, Pilsud-ski in Poland, Franco in Spain, and Mussolini in Italy)—all of these post-Bolshevik-era leaders, but even before, in Latin America for example, Porfirio Diaz in Mexico, and many other cases around the world.

Counterfactual speculation, alas, can go to extremes. Loosening the restraints of the facts, and there become too many conjectures and speculations, too many options, everything becomes possible—no killing of the Archduke in 1914, no World War I, thus no Russian Revolution, no Hitler, no Holocaust. In this scenario, my parents do not meet each other, I am never born, and we are not reading this book. So, the counterfactual exercise can go wildly askew. Less extreme examples are more plausible: Stalin dying earlier saves my grandfather; the French are more successful against Hitler in 1940, or Stalin less resistant to the intelligence he was is getting on the immediacy of the German attack, thus more effective against the invasion of 1941. The Holocaust was in part the result of wild success militarily by Germany on the Western and Eastern front, so earlier setbacks there to the German advances on either front might have saved Great Uncle Boris and Teutia Olya.

The point of this speculation in counterfactuals has been to clarify "lessons." Lessons imply that we are able to figure out what could have been done. By reading the past, we extract practices and procedures which, if put in place, prevent the repetition of terrible things from the past. What might some of these be?

Lessons: Labor, Networks, Politics, Institutions;

In my travels, I have often visited museums of the Holocaust, of Tolerance, or of WWII. I look at the way they memorialize the dead, at how they evoke Jewish culture—do they express it for themselves, or only show Jews as victims: I also pay special attention to what such museums say about the Nazi seizure of power, the development of the totalitarian state, the hegemony of the SS in the killing machine. How did the Nazis come to power? Explaining anti-semitism is important but insufficient. Democratic political institutions are needed, and as part of that, the autonomy of social institutions.

Building on the experience of my family, I stress labor. As a political science specialist, I would broaden that to include other groups like the press, churches, social clubs of various kinds, and professional associations. In the battle against fascism, a free labor movement matters a lot. The attack on labor by the Nazis was a warning signal, a canary dying in the coal mine of freedom. The Nazi terror against Jews, Gypsies, Slavs, and LGBTQ people, continues to shock the world and will properly do so for time immemorial. It will be the defining feature of the horror of Nazis. To understand how that horror developed, it is vital to grasp how the Nazis came to power and set about carrying out this terrible project. To explain that their racial hatred is insufficient as an account. When they campaigned for power in the Weimar

Republic and sought to persuade Hindenburg to make Hitler Chancellor, there was no project "Auschwitz" in their minds. To repeat, the Wannsee conference was in January 1942. There was, however, very much in mind of the Nazis and those who helped them take power, the project to control and destroy the autonomous labor movement, democracy and constitutional government.

Until fairly recently ,and perhaps in some approaches still, this is under-appreciated in the study of the Nazis and the Holocaust.
Labor was an early target and an early ringer of the alarm bells of Nazi dangers. Class politics is a neglected part of this story: many people don't want to talk about the labor movement much. Collomp's book on the American Labor Movement raises the importance of labor in saving lives and raising alarms. This is a general point, not specific to my family story. My family story is an example of it, a case that bears the message.

The Bolsheviks gave no freedom to labor either. They repressed independent labor early on. We see the awareness of this in the letter from the AFL to the Roosevelt administration requesting emergency entrance visas for the labor people in France but also labor refugees from Eastern Europe. It was part of the labor struggles in the inter-war years: the anti-communist wing was suspicious of the Bolsheviks because they saw the loss of freedom by the labor movement. It is an important component of Grandpa Peter's dislike of the Bolshevik approach.

Treatment of labor unions can be seen as an early indicator of danger. Systems or political movements that repress labor are headed down a path of repression that suggests trouble. Indeed the status of civil society organizations generally—churches, charities, social groups, the professions, business groups, and voluntary associations in general—are the indicators of freedom. The collapse of institutions that sustain these freedoms, that provide autonomy to social groups, sends bad signals. That is the point of view arising from a dislike of the authoritarianism of the 20th century and, indeed, those of the 21st- Those are grander themes of lessons from counterfactuals about the big processes.

Thinking about these grand counterfactual themes helps me build a relationship with my grandparents and the political situations they faced. It has helped me locate them in debates about history and political choices: about compromise and principles, when to push hard, when not, how to work for justice, change, and equality, what kinds of trade-offs among process, preserving constitutional procedures and autonomous civil society, and insisting on equality and greater access.

Mostly, I've thought of myself most of my life as a compromiser: looking for coalitions, pragmatism, and what works on behalf of progressive causes. I think of that as the Menshevik position, of Martov's position, and thus I've generally inclined toward the politics of Grandpa Peter. But in reading more about the situation of 1917 Russia, I see the context in which I would have sided possibly with Grandpa Boris: the Kazan telegram certainly, as in 1934, a Popular Front coalition to oppose Hitler was welcome despite the negatives toward Stalin and Bolsheviks. And I can see the strong desire for a socialist coalition in 1917 and a fear that the alternative was a right-wing counter-revolution that would have restored the old monarchy and aristocratic elite and destroyed democracy, constitutional government, and any kind of socialism at all. So again, I pause in wondering about Grandpa Boris' views at that moment and what happens when one faces supremely difficult political choices. I continue to be a pragmatist and coalition-builder in outlook, but in 1917, I think Grandpa Boris had a strong argument.

Between the great historical forces at work and the fatefulness of individual choices, some other factors played an important role in what happened to my family. Foremost among them is the role of networks.

My grandparents arrived in America with no money. They lived with the support of their children. I am used to thinking of them as disadvantaged in economic terms. They lived in Berlin, Paris and New York with very little money. They were nonetheless rich with education and what is called human capital: education, interpersonal skills, culture, experience, networks, and contacts—all of which helped my parents and family a great deal.

In America, I discovered an elite, a kind of non-titled aristocracy, of people who had been here for generations, owned houses, country places, children with trust funds, and elite networks. It operates in a variety of ways: private schools and universities, clubs and neighborhoods and towns, summer residences, firms and businesses, churches, intermarriage and friendship networks. However it operates, my family was not part of it. They arrived with a knapsack and what they wore on their backs. My older brother was born in a charity ward a few months after they arrived.

I am not used to thinking of my family as part of an aristocracy or an elite. Yet as I studied their story, I came to see that they did belong to a kind of elite network, not one with a high standing in our bourgeois capitalist economy, but one which gave them special benefits at key moments in their lives: the network of social democrats mostly in Europe from the 1900s to 1950s.

This network helped them in vital ways. First, it got the Garvys out of the USSR in 1922. Some members of the Menshevik leadership had already left the USSR, and it is likely they helped some numbers of other people were able to leave as well. In the chaos of the early years, the Bolsheviks were not so well organized to control the vast borders and border checkpoints. So, large numbers of people of all political persuasions left at this time. Berlin and Paris were filled with Russian speakers of many conflicting political points of view: aristocrats driving taxi cabs, working as cooks, doormen, seamstresses—as happened later in the century with Iranians fleeing different at different moments in that country's political development, or Chinese.

In Russia, the network of relationships aided those departures: they sent information to each other. The Mensheviks had some special standing among the Bolsheviks. In this, friendship, the bonds of having fought together, overcame ideological differences, at least for a while: some lives were spared, and people were released because of it.

In 1922, my grandmother used her contacts to get medicine from the Kremlin pharmacy for my mother's rheumatic fever. The archival material on Peter Garvy suggests the person processing his application leave had known him in a Tsarist prison camp. These are hints. The same set of relationships did not yield release for Boris. It did produce a visa for my father, Shura.

Networks mattered for the escape from the Nazis: It provided rapid information among the refugees in Berlin as to how dangerous the Nazis were and the same later in Paris. To the labor people, it was not only as Jews they saw the danger, but as labor leaders and stateless Russians. And in getting visas to the US, the labor network was critical: labor friends helped lobby the US State Department to get visas, and the labor network helped identify which labor leaders in France were in danger; it helped people cross the Spanish border, it helped get them across the ocean, and it helped them when they arrived in the US. So in this sense, too, they were part of an aristocracy, a labor aristocracy. Being involved in this political work got them into trouble and made them targets of the police and their political enemies. In other moments it linked them together in mutual assistance.

Being Jewish was a source of danger in both Germany and Russia/ USSR. At times it also provided invaluable assistance. The JOINT helped my family with boat tickets to the US, an apartment in NY, medical help, and living costs. The work for getting the visas was started by Jewish organizers and organizations, such as Minkoff and Dubinsky and the Jewish Labor Committee, who pushed on Green at the AFL, Hull at State and FDR to approve them. The network of Abramovich among the Mensheviks in Germany, then France, to Minkoff to Dubinsky had strong Jewish ties.

Studying individuals, especially one's family, perhaps, as opposed to macro-social processes, puts one directly up to chance and contingency. So many things could have been different. One can describe, analyze, question, and probe. Yet, much remains uncertain, from the huge to the small, all of them affecting my family and its destiny.

It makes one cautious and should make one cautious about judgment. It is not hard to be judgmental of the evils of the 20th century: Hitler, Stalin, the Holocaust, the famines, the purges, the Terror. It is much harder to be clear in judgment about individual decisions in uncertain conditions. So much of the literature assumes the virtuous are those who leave, and there is something wrong with those who stay, get caught and are killed. Yet so many contingencies confound that judgment. People stay for so many reasons, and some of them are virtuous: family, idealism, and local attachments. Great Uncle Buka and Grandpa Boris had reasons to stay. They were not less virtuous than those who left. And millions of people had no choice. Suddenly armies and police were upon them. They were trapped through no decision of their own.

Those who did escape made lives in the US. My parents were happy in the US. They said they had thought of leaving Europe upon finishing their studies, even without the war. Being refugees in Western Europe made them feel socially excluded. They spoke warmly about the relative openness of American society to newcomers and refugees and to the substantial educational and career opportunities the US provided. They were politically aware and acutely appreciative of the injustices in the US. We took a family holiday through the South in 1953, driving all the way to Florida from Syracuse, and were all shocked at "colored only" signs. We railed against the trap that was voting Democratic for Congress because they were more liberal than the local Republicans, nonetheless, putting Southern racists into committee chairships given the seniority system then at work. But overall, my parents felt little prejudice expressed toward them as Jews and as immigrants and welcomed the opportunity. I think almost all the Menshevik refugees felt this way. Only one family among the group returned to France after the war.

My parents retained a keen sense of political engagement their whole lives. Did they suffer from their parents' involvement, which made them refugees? In some ways, yes, but perhaps that engagement also saved them. It certainly helped form my parents' culture, their

Ph.D. Ceremony of Shura with family from Syracuse University, 1962. Top left: Sergei, Shura, Sylvia, Peter. Top Right: Sylvia and Shura. Bottom: Family relaxing: Shura, Sylvia, Peter, Sergei.

identity. It helped give them meaning and community.

My maternal grandparents led more or less isolated lives in the US. Grandpa Peter died not long after arriving in New York. Grandma Sophia continued to be active in refugee circles, now smaller and smaller. As a child, I used to receive birthday cards with dollar bills from the surviving widows, most of whose husbands, I think, had been in political disagreement with Grandpa Peter, conflicts the widows deemed irrelevant in comparison to the bonds of grandchildren! As the grandchildren grew and dispersed, the bonds weakened.

When I visited Russia and the contemporary US met some of the relatives, by now cousins three steps removed from the common great-great-grandfather, I felt the distance as well. There are blood ties and a few common stories to share, but not too many. And the political gap between Putin's Russia and the contemporary US has placed a great barrier before any shared understanding of the world as we experience it. One of the great novels of emigration—Wilhelm Moberg's series has as its last volume, *Last Letters Home*, where the families are increasingly finding it hard to write as they are losing their language ability (in those books, Swedish and English) as well as an ability to say much to each other). With the Russian Revolution now 100 years old, Putin's regime does not celebrate it so as not to remind people of protest. In Europe, Social Democracy is experiencing quite difficult times at the ballot box, weakened by several forces, among them ethnic diversity: nationalism and war fractured worker solidarity many times over the past two centuries, especially in 1914, and again with WWII and now again with the refugee crises in Europe. In the US, there has been something of a revival of discussion about socialism, social democracy, the meaning of Marxism, inequality, capitalism, the meaning of the Russian Revolution, the American Revolution, slavery, the American Civil War, the refashioning of the US constitution, and more. But there remain many points of contention: moderate Democrats blame radicals for loss of votes in down-ballot voting on too much talk of "socialism," while at the same time, glaring inequality is a rallying cry for the very same people who say they are repelled by socialist talk also vote for a raise in the compulsory minimum wage.

So these debates have come back, always in new forms and new meanings. It reminds us that rethinking history is a continuous process. As I write this history, I realize it would be different each time I worked through it. As the world changes going forward, so does my understanding of the past looking backward. Like reading historical novels and history books, writing history is richly rewarding. The Russian attack on Ukraine will be felt by everyone for decades. It certainly recasts the context of my family origins. So far, the Russian attack is forcing many of the residents of Ukraine to rethink the components of their nationalism, perhaps into a form it did not have, which is multi-cultural, pro-democratic, Western, and inclusive of Jews, Muslims and non-Christian minorities. This is not the culture my parents were born into, under Russian control. Whether it survives and in what form remains open, perhaps a hope, an illusion. So the storyline remains open, perhaps inspiring some future generation to add updates. History thus needs to be written as open and fluid chapters. Portions of my family have gone from there to here. This is how it all came about.

Endnotes

1 Carmen M. Reinhard and Kenneth S. Rogoff, This Time it is Different: Eight Centuries of Financial Policy. Princeton University Press, 2009.

2 In the huge literature on Stalin and purges, one can note some interesting Russian and Soviet era ones: Oleg Khlevniuk Stalin New Biography of a Dictator. translated by Nora Favorov, Yale University Press , 2017; Dimitri Volkogonov, Stalin : Triumph and Tragedy. Trans, Harold Shukman London : Weidenfeld and Nicolson, 1991.

3 Levitsky, Steven and Lucan Way , Revolution and Dictatorship: The Violent Origins of Durable Authoritarianism (Princeton University Press, 2022).
   The inability to resist the fall of the system into severe authoritarianism comes early with the repression of dissent and the destruction of constitutional processes of government. Levitsky S, Lachapelle J, Way LA, Casey A. "Social Revolution and Authoritarian Durability." World Politics . 2020;71 (4) :557-600.

4 A vivid reconstruction of this scene making this counterfactual point is in China Miéville's well-written account, October, The Story of the Russian Revolution.(London: Verso, 2017)

Acknowledgements

While writing this book, I came to realize I have spent my whole life getting ready to do it. To tell the story of my grandparents, I wind up exploring the various sources that influenced my own life. I began wanting to honor those of my ancestors who were blocked by political defeat from their efforts to make a better world, and I dedicate this book to them: My paternal grandfather Boris Naumovich Ber-Gourevitch, Lydia Evseevna Abramovich-Gourevitch, my father's very devoted stepmother—both blocked from leading professional lives at the height of their productive capacities. My maternal grandfather and grandmother, Peter Bronstein Garvy and Sophia Fichman Garvy, being able to leave the USSR, had much more freedom to live and act but were also deprived of the ability to be citizen participants in their native country. Sadly, I have personal memories in childhood only of Baba Sonia and then in adulthood a rich week in Moscow meeting Grandma Lyalya.

Other relatives had their lives shaped by the juggernaut of the great conflicts of those years: my grandmother's brother and sister-in-law, Boris (Buka) and Olga Fichman, very devoted to my grandmother and her family, killed in Auschwitz in October 1943; my father's half-sister, Galina Gourevitch, killed while fighting the Nazi invasion of the USSR in 1943; my father's uncle, Asrail (Asrunia) Gourevitch, killed by Hitler in 1942; another uncle of my father's, Meyer Gourevitch, died of illness and malnutrition in Siberia shortly after release from imprisonment there as a Bolshevik in Stalin's purges, 1943.

My parents enabled these interests of mine. They told me stories when asked, never pushing me to specialize in being the narrator of the family legacy, always encouraging my own interests, and always willing to share with me when asked to do so. Their lives were also damaged by these experiences. My mother was never able to return to science studies as there was no money for graduate training for her then; she supported the family as a language and literature teacher, but that was not her first choice. My father lost a decade of research from having to suspend his Ph.D. training because of the need to flee Paris in 1940; and then lost another 20 years of productive work, dying at age 52 surely as the result of health effects from living through the hunger period of the Russian civil war. My parents and their lives were the vital reference points to me for this book.

I also thank a large number of people who helped me at various points along the way. Among my relatives: Great Aunt Anna (Anja) Gourevitch, who, with her husband, great Uncle Asrail, took my Dad in to their small Berlin apartment when he arrived from Russia in 1931 and protected the letters sent by Grandfather Boris through all the turmoil, was always willing to talk to me and share her experiences and interpretations; and Anja's descendants: her older son Victor and daughter-in-law Jacqueline, for many extensive talks and meals about the family and its history and his special memory of my father; her younger son Harry and his wife Susie for many conversations as well. On my mother's side, I commemorate my Uncle George, his wife Juliette Blanc Garvy, and their daughter Helen Garvy—George's ability to hold on to documents, Helen's ability to hang to them after him, and George's transcripts of thoughts are all key to this book; my older brother Sergei, who sadly died long before I began the project of writing this project but shared many of the memories and story-tellings; Sergei's daughters Becca and Sasha Gourevitch did hear some talk as did their mother, Susan Boiko, and Becca helped me analyze George's Emergency Entrance Visa; my sons Alex and Nick heard many of these stories and met some of the people; they gave great feedback during the writing and applauded every step along the way.   print. Their mother, Lisa Hirschman, heard some of the pieces through her own family experiences and some of our shared stories. Natasha and Jan Etkin I count as relatives, though technically they are only distant ones by marriage, which none of us knew while growing up; Irene

"Inni" Etkin Goldman helped me with her much superior Russian language and her personal skills when we went to Moscow together in January of 2017; and fond memories of talk with her now-deceased sisters, Masha, Nora and Nina. In the Russia of today, I have a number of relatives who have been friendly and helpful when I have visited over several decades and shared some memories of visits. None of them bear the same last name as I do any longer, as over time, various people changed the name for partisan reasons (party name) or to avoid prejudice against Jews.

Without the encouragement of a number of friends and colleagues, I would not have been able to see my way forward: People who read the whole manuscript and gave specific comments along with encouragement: childhood friend Bob Sable who knew some of these people, including my parents and grandmother; Oberlin College friends, most especially and deeply, Steve Thomas, who kept pushing me to keep going; Raye Farr, who helped with bibliographical contacts, and at certain key moments with ideas about how to use the Holocaust Museum materials and to access materials; Ginny Swisher, who heard a lot of it way back when we were so close in college and who met my parents. At UCSD, Frank Biess, Eric Van Young, Judy Hughes, and Deborah Hertz, professors in the UCSD History Department, were early draft readers who insisted I needed to publish this story.

Deborah Hertz got me going by organizing a talk at the UCSD Holocaust series, one of the first times I presented the story in a non-family setting and tried to think of it in a coherent and systematic way. Other UCSD presentations followed: each one with feedback for which I am thankful: to the History Department, Political Science Department, the School of Global Policy and Strategy (GPS), Friends of the UCSD Library, and the Krushok Russian Studies group led at the time by Amelia Glaser, and including Martha Lampton and Bob Edelman, who all read some chapters early on during the process and encouraged me to continue.

Members of these departments and programs answered specific questions and gave encouragement: In History, Pamela Radciff, Bob Edelman; in Political Science, Phil Roeder, Lawrence Broz; in GPS, special thanks to Miles Kahler. Sheila Cole gave great comments. I am particularly grateful to David Lake, a wonderful colleague and collaborator in various projects over many years, for his help in this more personal project. I gave this talk also at the Watson Institute at Brown University in 2016 and received feedback from Rick Locke and Peter Swenson. My book club in San Diego graciously agreed to read the manuscript when it was still in draft and gave generous feedback, exciting encouragement to keep going, and in some cases, detailed editing advice; special thanks to them: Harry Carter, the late Jim Forbes, Faye Gersh, , the late Gordon Gill and Trish Gill, Cherie Halladay, Nigella Hillgarth, Dyanne Hoffman, Nora Jaffe, Juli Larson, and Molli Wagner.

At Harvard's Center for European Studies, I owe a massive debt to the late Stanley Hoffmann, my thesis advisor and mentor, and to numerous friends and colleagues connected to that Center who helped shape my ideas: Suzanne Berger, with whom I share a strong interest in France, and, it turned, having a father in the same profession who had been good friends for many years, as they were both leading researchers for rival pharmaceutical companies and had invented the same drug; Patrice Higonnet helped not only with ideas and encouragement but in dealing with the French judicial process concerning reparations involving my great Uncle Buka Fichman; and at Harvard, Mark Kramer, who helped me understand how to access Russian archives. At the University of Toronto, I have a special debt to Lucan Way, who read various pieces and gave me considerable encouragement and insight connected to his specialties and his personal connections; and a debt to Janice Stein, former director of the Munk School, who invited me to teach in Toronto and benefit from discussion with her and colleagues and continue conversations begun with her and her late husband Michael Stein when we first met at McGill in the 1970s.

In France, a number of friends and colleagues were always generous and warm to me on many visits, both they and their families, in Paris and at their various country abodes. I note especially Martha Zuber and her late husband Willy, Catherine and Pierre Gremion; I had valuable conversations with "emigration cousins," Daniel and Martin Andler, whose grandfather was Raphael Rein-Abramovich and uncle was Mark Rein in this story. I owe a deep debt to Catherine Collomp for her invaluable book on the American labor movement efforts.

To my French family, I owe a special piece of gratitude: Katia Hirschman Salomon, sister of my first wife, the late Lisa Hirschman, Katia's husband Alain, and their children Lara and Gregoire have always been warm in my visits to them over many years. The Hirschman story has several intersections with that of my family, as will be explained in the book here, but it is distinctly separate and different. The life and career of Albert Hirschman are very well told by Jeremy Edelman in his book, *The Worldly Philosopher*. Hirschman's involvement with the Varian Fry rescue operation of 1940 is important as a story, told in several books, but is again different from the operation that rescued my family.

In Russia, I am very moved by the work of people at Memorial. Their work uncovered the key pieces in the archive, which enables the partial telling of what happened to my grandparents. I feel toward them the deepest gratitude; I met wonderful people in their offices in Moscow and St. Petersburg. I thank the late A.P. Nenarokov and Alla Morozova for their research work, especially Nenarokov for knowing more about my grandfathers than anyone, Natalie Volodina for her very high-quality assistance in the archives, and Robin Lewis for inviting me to Moscow, and making contacts and arrangements.

Many friends and colleagues encouraged me along the way: Professors Peter and Mary Katzenstein, who helped prod me along and make contacts; Professor Joan Scott, with whom I had some long conversations on history writing, encouraged a more direct approach to writing such as the Casablanca story; Michael Walzer helped me with keen probing on how to think about the connections among Jewish and Labor linkages; and Andy Marcovits, who encouraged the writing of family history by someone used to a different kind of work. Friends who read with fine comments include Estrella Joselovich from Buenos Aires. An especially fine response was given by an old friend and fine writer, Laura Nathanson, widow of one of my dearest San Diego friends.

In San Diego, tremendous help from: Olga Lazitsky, research and translation, and smart, shrewd interpretive thinking; Emily Goldenberg, then an undergraduate research assistant, who, with the help of her grandmother, translated Boris Ber-Gourevitch's letter; I thanked the grandmother by making my mother's version of "eggplant caviar" , and who deemed it "authentic", which I took as high praise; Marie-Pierre Murry, who helped me with many logistics in dealing with MSW, Acrobat, printing, and countless other details of preparation and encouragement; and Lilly Dunn who helped me with manuscript preparation at the very end of the process.

In the last year of my work, I got superb advice and insights from David Groff, who helped me hugely with organizing the material, integrating the many strands of exploration, personalizing the presentation, and improving the chapter titles. Working with him was a rewarding lesson all its own!

Some of the deepest conversations about the meaning of this enterprise have been with my wife, Celia Jaes Falicov, herself, the child of immigrants to Argentina from a neighboring part of the Russian Empire, but with very different experiences. Celia helped me reflect on the value of networks in helping them leave as well as manage the exile; on the issues of migration and immigration, emotional, political, philosophical and intellectual ones; on the value of social capital and on the interaction of their Jewishness and their socialism. As she has constructed her own family history, we have had wonderful discussions on the meaning of doing such a project at our age, with what contribution, for whom, and with what meaning. I thank her for putting up with hearing the same story over and over again and for being so helpful with it—one of the many, many benefits of marriage.

People in the Manuscript

Abramovich, Lydia (Lyalya) Evseevna. 29 March 1894 Russian Empire –1972 USSR. Second wife of Boris Ber Gourevitch, m. 1920, Shura's stepmother, Mother of Galina, "Galka," my father's half-sister. Menshevik activist.Numerous arrests and imprisonments or internal exiles in Soviet period. Sent to Siberia in Stalin years. Found Shura and our family in 1962.

Abramovitch-Rein, Rafael. b. 1880 Russian Empire, d. 1963 New York. Leading Menshevik figure and Bundist. Key figure in the network between Mensheviks and American labor leaders. Father of Mark and Lia Rein.

Axelrod, Pavel. 1850–1928 (Berlin). Leading Russian Marxist theorist, Menshevik leader.

Ber Gourevitch, Boris, see also Gourevitch Ber. b. 1889 Orsha, Mogilev district Belo-Russia (Russian Empire), d. 30 March 1938, Vladimir Prison (USSR). Paternal Grandfather. Father of Alexander (Shura) Gourevitch. An important leader of Menshevik group.

Bingham, Hiram IV. 1903–1988.US Vice- Consul-General in Marseilles 1940. Saved thousands of refugees, Jewish, labor, intellectuals with visas to the US. Pushed out of State Department career because of these actions.

Bronstein, Peter Garvy – see Garvy, Peter.

Dan, Fyodor. 1871–1947. Important leader of Menshevik group in Russia, exiled from Russia in 1921, led Foreign Delegation in Berlin and Paris from early 1920s to 1940. Died in New York.

Dan, Lydia. 1878–1963. sister of Martov and wife of Fyodor Dan, Menshevik activist in Russia and during their refugee period in Germany, France and the US. Maintained social relationships among the faction-torn Menshevik group. Died in New York.

 Etkin, Jacob. (Jan, Janni) b. 10 June 1914, Berditchev, Russia (Ukraine) d. 30 July 2003, Boston) and Natalie (Natasha) (b. 30 April 1915, née, Emanuel, St. Petersburg, d. Boston 16 May 2005). Emigrated to Berlin with his Menshevik father in 1922–23. Married Natasha in Paris in mid-1930s and emigrated to US with Gourevitch-Garvy Menshevik group in 1940. Parents of Maria (Masha), Irene (Inni) , Nora and Nini.

Etkin, Irene, See Goldman, Irene.

Falicov, Celia Jaes. b. 1940. Buenos Aires. Ph.D. in Human Development, University of Chicago, leader of work on family therapy and immigration. First marriage to Dr. Raul Falicov, died 1987. Second marriage to Peter Gourevitch, 2016.

Fichman, Samuel. b. about 1850, Odessa Russian Empire – d. Odessa, USSR. Grain Merchant, my great-grandfather, father of Sophia and Boris Fichman.

Fichman, Boris (Buka). b. about 1885 in Orgev, Bessarabia, Russian Empire –d.1943, Auschwitz. Brother of Grandma Sophia Garvy. Favorite uncle of my Mother Sylvia and my uncle George Garvy.

Fichman, Olga. b. Olga Kauschansky, about 1885 – d.1943, Auschwitz. Wife of Boris Fichman.

Fichman, Sophia. See Garvy, Sophia. Name used before her marriage to Garvy.

Garvy, Peter Bronstein. b. 1881 Odessa, Russian Empire – d. 1944 New York. Maternal Grandfather. Early member of Menshevik group, trade union activist and writer for union papers and on union activities. Known among historians for writing on Russian trade unions.

Garvy, Sophia Fichman Bronstein "Baba Sonia". b. 1881 Orgev, Bessarabia, Russian Empire (Moldava) –d. 1958 New York. My maternal grandmother. Menshevik activist in youth. Relationship with Parvus in 1905 in Europe. Married Peter Garvy in 1910.

Garvy, George. b. 1913 Riga (Latvia, Russia Empire)– d. 1987, Manhasset, N.Y.,son of Peter and Sophia Garvy brother of Sylvia Garvy Gourevitch. Ph.D. in Economics from Columbia University. Senior Advisor, Federal Reserve Bank of New York. Father of Helen Garvy.

Garvy, Juliette Blanc, wife of George. b. 1910 Maubec France – d. 1996, Santa Cruz, Ca. Came to US in 1941 via relationship to George.

Garvy, Helen, daughter of George and Juliette, my first cousin. b. 1942. New York. Graduated Radcliffe, 1964. Active in SDS and other reform political movements in the US.

Goldman, Irene (Inni) Etkin. b. 1943. Daughter of Jan and Natasha Etkin, close childhood friend, and distant cousin. Went with me on a 2017 visit to Moscow to visit Nenarokov. Sisters Masha, Nina, and Nora.

Gourevitch, Sylvia Garvy. b. Odessa, Russia (Ukraine) 1915 – d. Solana Beach Ca. 1994. Daughter of Peter and Sophia Garvy, wife of Alexander Gourevitch, my mother. Studied chemistry in France. Taught French and Russian Language at Syracuse University from the late 1940s to early 1980s.

Gourevitch, Alexander (Shura). b. 1916 Ekaterinoslav, Russia (Dnipro, Ukraine) – d. 1969 De Witt (Syracuse). N.Y. son of Boris Ber Gourevitch. My father, and father of Sergei Alexander Gourevitch. Married Sylvia Garvy in 1938 (Paris). Studied chemistry at Curie Institute in Paris. Ph.D. in Microbiology at Syracuse University, 1953. Director of Research, Bristol Laboratories in Syracuse, New York.

Gourevitch, Boris Naumovich Ber. See also Ber, Boris Gourevitch. b.1889 Orsha, Mogilev, Russian Empire (Belorussia) – d. 1938, Vladimir Prison, Russia. My paternal grandfather, father of Shura. Ber is name he used as Party activist. Important leader of the left Menshevik anti-Bolshevik faction among Russian Social Democratic Workers Party. Died while being questioned in Vladimir Prison.

Gourevitch, Lydia (Lyalya) Evseevna Abramovich – see Abramovich, Lydia.

Gourevitch, Anna Moisevna , b. 1897, Russian Empire – d. 1991, New York. Wife of Azriel. Received and kept letters from Boris Ber. Housed Shura in Berlin upon his arrival in 1931. In US, practicing lay analyst in NY. Parents with Azriel of Victor and Harry.

Gourevitch, Azriel. (b. 1895, Ekaterinoslav, Russian Empire – d. 1943 Paris), one of several younger brothers of Boris. The uncle with whom Shura went to live in Berlin 1931. Most of Boris's letters written to him and his wife Anna. Shot by Nazis as hostage in reprisal for actions by French resistance.

Gourevitch, Bacia. b. 1900, Ekaterinoslav, Russian Empire – d. 1947, New York) sister of Boris, left USSR in early 1920s, and lived in France. Migrated to New York in 1940.

Gourevitch, Geza. (b. 1898 Ekaterinoslav, Russian Empire – d. 1976 USSR) brother of Boris.

Gourevitch, Meyer (b.1891 Russian Empire– d. 1943, USSR). Brother of Boris. USSR, Bolshevik, sent to Siberia during Stalin's purges in 1937, died of illness and malnutrition shortly after release.

Gourevitch, Mosei (b 1894 Russian Empire – d1968, USSR). brother of Boris. Shura lived with him while going to school in Moscow about 1929–30. I met him in the summer of 1966 and some of his descendants in later visits.

Gourevitch, Nahum (b. 1857 Russian Empire – d. 1930 USSR), my great grandfather, father of Boris Ber Gourevitch. Rabbi, in region today, started in Belorussia then moved to the larger city of Ekaterinoslav, today Dnipro, Ukraine.

Gourevitch, Peter Alexis. b. 1943, N.Y. B.A., Oberlin College; Ph.D. in Political Science, Harvard University, 1969. Professor at Harvard 1969–74, McGill 1974–79, UC San Diego, 1979–2012. Married Lisa Hirschman 1976–1999. Married Celia Falicov 2016. Father of Alexander and Nicholas. Uncle of Sergei's children Sasha and Becca. d

Gourevitch, Sergei Alexander. b.1941 New York – d, 1999 Palo Alto, Ca.). son of Alex and Sylvia, older brother of Peter. Physicist, Ph.d. Case Western. Researcher at MIT and private industry. Important contributor to the development of geo-positioning satellite technology. Married to Susan Boiko, father of Sasha and Becca Gourevitch.

Hilferding, Rudolf (b. Vienna, 1877—d. Paris, 1941). Famous writer on Marxist international political economy, noted author of *Finance Capital (1910),* stressed varieties of capitalist forms, inlucding concepts of "organized capitalism" as well as finance capital. Leader of Economics ministry of Social Democrats who rejected the unorthody of the WTB plan which was a forerunner of what became Keynesian economics and sectoral approaches.

Hirschman, Albert O. (1915 b. in Berlin – d. 2012, Ewing Township, N.J. Father of my first wife, Lisa Hirschman. Renowned economist. Close friend of Abramovich family and other Mensheviks in Berlin and Paris. Active with Varian Fry in Rescue operation of intellectuals in Marseilles. See biography of Hirschman by Jeremy Adelman, *The Worldly Philosopher.*

Hirschman, Lisa, (b. 1946, Washington, D.C., – d. 1999, Solana Beach Ca.) Psychologist, My first wife, mother of Alexander and Nicholas. Psychologist, author of some work on psychology.

Hirschman, Sarah, .(b. 1921, Lithuania –d. Princeton, 2012.),wife of Albert O Founder of People & Stories/Gente y Cuentos. With Albert , parents of Katia and Lisa.

Hirschman Salomon, Katia (Katherine), (b. 1944 Los Angeles --) sister of Lisa. Wife of Alain Salomon.

Hull, Cordell. (1871–1955). US Secretary of State from 1933–1944.

Kautsky, Karl (1854–1938), noted Austrian-German theorist of Marxism.

Klarsfeld, Serge. (b. 1935, Bucharest). Important documenter of Holocaust material, especially on French records showing complicity with Nazi deportations to concentration camps.

Long, Breckenridge, (1881–1958). Assistant Secretary of State from 1940–1944, in charge of visa office during critical period of 1940.

Martov, Julius, (b 1873 Constantinople – d. 1923 Schomberg, Germany, Major figure in the formation of the Russian Social Democratic Labor Party. Leader of Menshevik group in Russia and in Berlin, head of the Foreign Delegation in Berlin

Nenarokov, Albert Pavlovich.(b. 1935 USSR – d. 2020, Moscow, Russia.) Eminent historian of Russian Socialists party, especially its dissidents after Bolshevik coup. Important authority on Ber Gourevitch. I visited him in 2017 with Irene Etkin Goldman.

Nicholaevsky, Boris, (b. 1887, Bessarabia Russian Empire, (Moldava)– d.1966, New York.) Menshevik activist, noted archivist, collected primary documents of party member activities. Archives in his name in Moscow and in Stanford Libraries.

Parvus (Alexander Gelfand)(b. 1867 Belarus, Russian Empire– d. 1924 Berlin.) Russian revolutionary. Controversial figure. Active in revolutionary circles. Among his many affairs, he had a liason with my grandmother Sophia Fichman Garvy fin 1905. Thought to have conjured up and facilitated the German transfer of Lenin from Switzerland to Russia.

Rein, Mark. (b 1909 Russian Empire –d. 1937 ?)Oldest child of Raphael Abramovich disappeared in Spain in 1936, thought to have been killed by Communists in Barcelona or in USSR.

Rein, Lia. (b 1916 Russia – d. 2004 France) Sister of Mark, daughter of Raphael Abramovich, and friend of Sylvia Gourevitch in Berlin and Paris. Also friend of the Etkins andof Albert Hirschman.

Salomon, Katia Hirschman. (b.1944 Los Angeles) Older sister of Lisa Hirschman., daughter or Albert and Sarah. sd

Selman, Styssia, (b. 1865, Russian Empire-d. 1939 USSR). Wife of Nachum Gourevitch Grandmother of Alex (Shura) Gourevitch.

Woytinsky, Vladimir ("Wolik"). (b. 1885 St. Petersburg, d. 1960, Washington, D.C.) Important Menshevik leader, active in Revolution of 1917. Moved to Berlin in 1922, worked as chief economist for German trade union organization. Fled Hitler in 1933 for Switzerland. To the US in 1935, major technical advisor on US Social Security legislation in 1935–36. Close friend of Garvys in Europe and to my parents and Uncle George. Aided Garvys in visa process to the US in 1940.

Woytinsky, Emma Shadkhan (b. 1893 Russian Empire – d. 1968 Washington) wife of Vladimir, co-authored numerous books with him. Close friends with Garvy family.

Timeline

Historical Context of the Garvy and Gourevitch Saga

(**Boldface refers to my family;** regular type refers to events in the world)

1903: split in Russian Social democratic workers party into Bolshevik and Menshevik

1905: Revolutionary outbreaks In Russian Empire

1914–1918: WW I

1915: birth of Sylvia Bronstein (eventually Garvy Gourevitch) in Odesa

1916: birth of Alexander Gourevitch in Ekaterinoslav (today Dnipro

1917: Russian Revolution: February: fall of Tsar, formation of Kerensky government

1917: Garvys and Gourevitch return from various exiles outside or in remote Russia to St. Petersburg

1917: October/November, Bolshevik coup, seizure of power

1917–22: Russian Civil War 1922 Russia becomes USSR

1922: Boris and Peter request and receive permission to leave USSR

1923: Garvys leave USSR for Berlin, Boris Ber sent to prison and internal exile in USSR, Permission to leave withdrawn

1929: Great Depression gets underway; October 1929, stock market crash in NY.

1931: Shura (Alexander) Gourevitch leaves USSR for Berlin

1933: Hitler comes to power to Germany, Social Democrats in Sweden and Denmark, Roosevelt in the USA

1933: Garvys leave Berlin for Paris

1930s: Collectivization of agriculture in USSR; considerable famine there, especially in southern region Ukraine

1930s: Japan invasion of China

1933: Garvys leave Berlin for Paris, after Hitler's appointment as Chancellor and burning of the Reichstag

1934: Kazan telegram to Mensheviks near Paris at time of Popular Front discussions, signed by Boris Ber Gourevitch and others

1934: Shura leaves Berlin for Paris

1936: Spanish Civil War begins, Franco seeks to overthrow the Spanish Republic

1936: Popular Front government formed in France

1937: Mark Rein disappears in Spain

1936–38: Stalin's purge trials in USSR

1937: Last letters from Boris Ber in USSR to Gourevitch family

1938: July, marriage of Sylvia Garvy and Alexander Gourevitch Paris

1938: death of Boris Ber Gourevitch in Vladimir, USSR

1939–1945: WW II begins In European theater with German and Russian partition of Poland 1940: German invastion of Denmark and Norway in April, then in May German attack on France, Belgium and Netherlands

1940: Garvys flee Paris, as do various other family members, Socialists, and Jews and others in danger

1940, October: Garvys arrive in New York

1940:Arrest of Azrunia Gourevitch, in Paris, killed by Hitler

1941, June 22: German attack on USSR

1941 December 7: Pearl Harbor attack by Japan, US enters war

1943: Death in October of Buka and Olga Fichman in Auschwitz

1943: Death of Galia Gourevitch, half-sister of Shura, killed during war

1944 death of Peter Garvy from heart attack in New York

1945 May: End of WW II in Europe; September 1945: end of WWII in Asia

1953: Death of Stalin, release of prisoners from Gulag in USSR

1958: Death of Sophia Garvy in NY

1962: Letter arrives from Lyalya to Shura in Syracuse, NY

1963: Shura and family visit Lyalya and Gourevitch family in Moscow

1966: Shura and Peter visit Lyalya and Gourevitch family in Moscow

1969: Death of Alexander (Shura) Gourevitch, in De Witt (Syracuse, NY)

1972: Death of Lydia Abramovich-Ber Gourevitch in USSR

1981: Death of Anya Gourevitch, Shura's aunt, wife of Asrunia, in NY

1989: Fall of Berlin Wall

1991: Fall of USSR and Russian Communist Empire

1994: Death of Sylvia Garvy Gourevitch (my mother), in Solana Beach

1999 May 7: Death of Sergei Gourevitch May 11, 1999: Death of Lisa Hirschman

1999, May 11, death of Lisa Hirschman Gourevitch

Nov 17, 2016: Marriage of Peter Gourevitch and Celia Jaes Falicov

Printed in the USA
CPSIA information can be obtained
at www.ICGtesting.com
LVHW010930260224
772821LV00002B/119